THE
WESTMINSTER CONCISE
BIBLE
DICTIONARY

THE
WESTMINSTER CONCISE
BIBLE
DICTIONARY

by
Barbara Smith

THE WESTMINSTER PRESS
PHILADELPHIA

First published in a hardbound edition entitled
Young People's Bible Dictionary

Published by The Westminster Press®
Philadelphia, Pennsylvania
PRINTED IN THE UNITED STATES OF AMERICA

9 8 7 6 5 4 3 2

Library of Congress Cataloging in Publication Data

Smith, Barbara, 1922–
　　The Westminster concise Bible dictionary.

　　First published under title: Young people's Bible dictionary.
　　"Westminster historical maps of Bible lands, edited by G. Ernest Wright and Floyd V. Filson": p.
　　Bibliography: p.
　　Includes index.
　　SUMMARY: Defines terms and identifies persons, places, and objects mentioned in the Bible. Also includes references to Biblical passages, maps, and a time line.
　　1. Bible—Dictionaries. [1. Bible—Dictionaries] I. Wright, George Ernest, 1909–1974. Westminster historical maps of Bible lands. 1981. II. Title. III. Title: Concise Bible dictionary.
BS440.S59　1981　　　220.3′21　　　80-25771
ISBN 0-664-24363-0 (pbk.)

ILLUSTRATIONS

Illustrations on:

pp. 31, 65, 82, from *Everyday Life in Old Testament Times*, by E. W. Heaton (Charles Scribner's Sons, 1956).

pp. 39, 117, 134, from *Everyday Life in New Testament Times*, by A. C. Bouquet (Charles Scribner's Sons, 1953, 1954).

pp. 45, 52, 97, 144, 151, 155, from *The Westminster Dictionary of the Bible*, by John D. Davis; revised and rewritten by Henry Snyder Gehman (The Westminster Press, 1944).

pp. 36, 109, from *Men of Tomorrow*, by Ewald Mand (The Westminster Press, 1958).

pp. 90, 111, from The Oriental Institute of the University of Chicago.

p. 103, from *Gezer II*, used by permission of the Palestine Exploration Fund.

pp. 27, 43, 158, from the American Schools of Oriental Research.

Photographs:

opposite p. 66, (Top) from the National Aeronautics and Space Administration; (Bottom) from Ewing Galloway.

opposite p. 67, (Top) from the British Museum; (Bottom) from the American Schools of Oriental Research.

How to Use This Dictionary

Reading the Bible is sometimes difficult because of the unfamiliar words found in it. Some words only look difficult, like "Tiglath-pileser," a name you might read in the Old Testament. Sometimes you have no idea how to pronounce a word. Take, for example, "Caesarea Philippi," a town mentioned in the New Testament.

When you don't know what a word means, you tend to leave a blank space in your understanding, or you put in its place a familiar word that seems the same. Jesus' words, "Woe to you, scribes and Pharisees, hypocrites! for you tithe mint and dill and cummin," are likely to become ". . . for you _____ candy [?] and pickles [?] and [something]."

Other words are familiar but have special meaning in the Bible. For example, Paul's words, "The grace of our Lord Jesus Christ be with your spirit. Amen." (*Gal. 6:18*), may mean little or a great deal.

This book is planned to help you with the words of the Bible, so that you can read with understanding instead of confusion. No dictionary can help you understand everything. Some things in the Bible will make you use all your mind and even all your life to understand them. In addition, only some, not all, of the difficult words of the Bible are included in this dictionary. Most of the words that you will need are here. Once you have learned to use this dictionary, you will be ready to use more advanced and complete Bible dictionaries.

You will find the names of some, but not all, persons who are mentioned in the Bible, the names of some places, and the words for some objects and actions of life in Bible times. You will find information about the books of the Bible. You will be able to look up, also, words that are used in the Bible which you seldom come across in reading other books. You will find here some of the big words (though they are often small in size) that have special meanings in the Bible. Other words, those commonly used in books and other writings, that do not have a particular meaning in Scripture, you will need to look up in a standard dictionary.

The pronunciation is given in parentheses after personal and place names, and after a few other words. The key to the symbols used to show pronunciation is on page 13.

Each definition gives briefly the main information about a person, place, or thing. Except in a few cases, common definitions are not given. For example, it is assumed that you know what a cup is. The definition tells you what a cup looked like and what purposes it served in Bible times. Definitions also tell the general time in Bible history that a person or place was important. Sometimes objects are given a general date also.

Bible references show where you can read about persons or places, or where you can see examples of the way in which a word is used. Often these references fill out the information in the definition, and a few minutes of additional work in looking them up will help you understand the word better.

Other words or entries in the dictionary that can be looked up for help in understanding the word are printed in italics and are in a parenthetical sentence. The Time Line, on page 15, shows when people lived and the main eras of Bible history. The maps show Bible lands at different times in history. Drawings throughout the dictionary make clear what some things and actions were like. Certain definitions include related words for cross reference, which, when studied together, give a general view of a subject.

Abbreviations used are:

adj. (adjective)	N.T. (New Testament)
c. (*circa* — about)	O.T. (Old Testament)
i.e. (*id est* — that is)	pl. (plural)
fem. (feminine)	sing. (singular)
masc. (masculine)	v. (verb)
n. (noun)	

Abbreviations of the books of the Bible:

OLD TESTAMENT

Gen.	Genesis	*Deut.*	Deuteronomy	*1 Sam.*	1 Samuel
Ex.	Exodus	*Josh.*	Joshua	*2 Sam.*	2 Samuel
Lev.	Leviticus	*Judg.*	Judges	*1 Kings*	1 Kings
Num.	Numbers	*Ruth*	Ruth	*2 Kings*	2 Kings

1 Chron.	1 Chronicles	*S. of Sol.*	Song of Solomon	*Obad.*	Obadiah
2 Chron.	2 Chronicles	*Isa.*	Isaiah	*Jonah*	Jonah
Ezra	Ezra	*Jer.*	Jeremiah	*Micah*	Micah
Neh.	Nehemiah	*Lam.*	Lamentations	*Nahum*	Nahum
Esth.	Esther	*Ezek.*	Ezekiel	*Hab.*	Habakkuk
Job	Job	*Dan.*	Daniel	*Zeph.*	Zephaniah
Ps.	Psalms	*Hos.*	Hosea	*Hag.*	Haggai
Prov.	Proverbs	*Joel*	Joel	*Zech.*	Zechariah
Eccl.	Ecclesiastes	*Amos*	Amos	*Mal.*	Malachi

New Testament

Matt.	Matthew	*Eph.*	Ephesians	*James*	James
Mark	Mark	*Phil.*	Philippians	*1 Peter*	1 Peter
Luke	Luke	*Col.*	Colossians	*2 Peter*	2 Peter
John	John	*1 Thess.*	1 Thessalonians	*1 John*	1 John
Acts	Acts of the	*2 Thess.*	2 Thessalonians	*2 John*	2 John
	Apostles	*1 Tim.*	1 Timothy	*3 John*	3 John
Rom.	Romans	*2 Tim.*	2 Timothy	*Jude*	Jude
1 Cor.	1 Corinthians	*Titus*	Titus	*Rev.*	Revelation
2 Cor.	2 Corinthians	*Philemon*	Philemon		
Gal.	Galatians	*Heb.*	Hebrews		

An Experiment

Let us take two paragraphs from The Gospel According to Mark and see how this dictionary can be of help.

" And Jesus went on with his **disciples,** to the villages of **Caesarea Philippi;** and on the way he asked his disciples, ' Who do men say that I am? ' And they told him, **' John the Baptist;** and others say, **Elijah;** and others one of the **prophets.'** And he asked them, ' But who do you say that I am? ' **Peter** answered him, ' You are the **Christ.'** And he charged them to tell no one about him.

" And he began to teach them that the **Son of man** must suffer many things, and be rejected by the **elders** and the **chief priests** and the **scribes,** and be killed, and after three days rise again. And he said this plainly. And Peter took him, and began to rebuke him. But turning and seeing his disciples, he rebuked Peter, and said, ' Get behind me, **Satan!** For you are not on the side of God, but of men.' " (*Mark 8:27-33.*)

The words in boldface type are ones you can look up in this dictionary. " Disciple " is a familiar word, but it may be a good idea to check your understanding of it. " Caesarea Philippi " is the name of a place, as you can see from the fact that it is called a " village." The dictionary will help you know how to pronounce it and also how to locate it. " John the Baptist," " Elijah," and " prophets " are all obviously persons, since the names are given in answer to Jesus' question about himself. Looking them up will help you know why the disciples mentioned them. You will understand Peter's answer better if you will look up "Christ." It will remind you that Peter was saying something more than, "Of course I know you."

"Son of man" is another title for Jesus that has special meaning. "Elders," "chief priests," and "scribes" may already be familiar to you. The phrase "after three days rise again" refers to Christ's resurrection, an important but difficult thing to understand. To help yourself think about it, you might look up "resurrection." You will find an explanation of the word "Satan," also.

Some Special Helps

It helps to remember that the Bible covers a long span of time. Things changed over the centuries. Especially between the last recorded events of Old Testament times and the time of Jesus, there is a long gap. Some sources outside the Bible help us fill in events and developments of thought between the two times. The background of history and even of ideas in New Testament times is considerably different from that in Old Testament times. Other differences in the use of words occur because the two Testaments were written in two different languages. Many definitions give an Old Testament meaning and a New Testament meaning. When a word is not labeled O.T. or N.T., or does not give an indication of a change in meaning, it has the same meaning in both Testaments.

In reading the Old Testament, one must have in mind certain key events and people. A definition may refer to the Israelites' conquest of Canaan as a key to the times, for example. If you do not recall the order of events or the approximate time, refer to the Time Line, on page 15. After you have used it for a while, you will probably become familiar with the general outline of Old Testament times.

Names of persons can be stumbling blocks in reading the Bible. They are often used in many different ways. See the definition under "name" for help in these multiple uses. Sometimes there are several people of the same name. Just as in our time, parents of Bible times named their children for ancestors or for famous people. For example, there are several persons with the name Uzziah in the Old Testament. The important Uzziah, the one you are likely to read about, was a king of the Southern Kingdom, Judah, in the eighth century B.C. One way to distinguish people of the same name is to read enough of the surrounding verses (the context) to get some clues to the times and events being related. This dictionary takes up only the main persons of the Bible story. The word "Other" (or "Others") at the end of a definition means that there is another person (or other persons) of the same name who is not described in the dictionary.

Many words that are difficult at first sight become easier when something is known about Hebrew styles of writing. Especially in the poetical passages in the Old Testament, but in other places also, writers made use of balanced words. Such words may be synonyms (or nearly so) or opposites, and thus they may explain each other. For example, you may not recognize the word " extol," in *Ps. 117:1*, on first reading it, but you can tell what it means because it is balanced with " praise." In *Isa. 45:7*, " weal," an uncommon word, is balanced with its opposite, " woe." Another kind of balance occurs in *Ps. 17:2*: the second half of the verse is a statement that explains " vindication " in the first line. Synonyms are sometimes used merely to intensify the meaning. " Shield " and " buckler," often used together, have the same meaning.

In reading the Bible, you should always recall that everything was written many years after the events it relates. Nothing is equivalent to the eyewitness account you might read in the evening newspaper of something that happened in the morning. You may find it helpful to look up the word " Genesis " in this dictionary and study the account of the writing of the first five books of the Bible. The process described is typical of the forming of many Old Testament books. The books of the New Testament had a different kind of history and are, generally, closer in the time of composition to the events they relate.

Like artists who portray Jesus in the clothes and settings of their own times, the writers of the books of the Old Testament used details their readers would recognize. For example, Abraham travels west on camels, although many scholars believe that camels were not used until several centuries after the time of Abraham. The writer of Chronicles tells about coins in the time of David, whereas coins were not invented until the sixth century B.C. (That gives us a clue as to when the writer lived.) Most of the Old Testament books were written in the last five or six centuries B.C. The general picture of Bible life that we get fits that time, with here and there an authentic detail dating from earlier times. Archaeologists and scholars specializing in ancient languages have helped us with more details. Definitions of objects and actions are based on the results of the sciences that help us reconstruct what life was like among the people whose story the Bible tells.

The habit of looking up unfamiliar words will help you read the Bible with understanding. What really helps is thoughtfulness. Perhaps knowing the words will help you read the Bible thoughtfully.

KEY TO PRONUNCIATION

ă	act, bat	ou	out, loud
ā	able, cape	p	page, stop
â	air, dare	r	read, cry
ä	art, calm	s	see, miss
b	back, rub	sh	shoe, push
ch	chief, beach	t	ten, bit
d	do, bed	th	thin, path
ĕ	ebb, set	t͟h	that, other
ē	equal, bee	ŭ	up, love
f	fit, puff	ū	use, cute
g	give, beg	û	urge, burn
h	hit, hear	v	voice, live
ĭ	if, big	w	west, away
ī	ice, bite	y	yes, young
j	just, edge	z	zeal, lazy, those
k	kept, make	zh	vision, measure
l	low, all		
m	my, him	ə	occurs only in un-
n	now, on		accented syllables
ng	sing, England		and indicates the
ŏ	box, hot		sound of
ō	over, no		a *in* alone
ô	order, ball		e *in* system
oi	oil, joy		i *in* easily
o͝o	book, put		o *in* gallop
o͞o	ooze, rule		u *in* circus

TIME LINE

IN THE TIME OF	DATES	PERSONS AND EVENTS	OTHER NATIONS
the patriarchs	2000 B.C. 1700 B.C.	Sarah ———— Abraham ———— Hagar Isaac —— Rebekah · · · Ishmael Esau · · · Jacob (Israel) 12 sons Joseph brought Jacob's family to Egypt	Amorite kingdom in Mesopotamia Hammurabi Egypt in control of Canaan
Moses	1300 B.C.	Moses led Israelites out of slavery in Egypt, journey to Canaan, covenant at Sinai	rise of Assyrians in Mesopotamia
the conquest	1250 B.C.	Joshua led the taking of Canaanite cities	
the judges	1200 B.C.	Barak and Deborah ⎫ Gideon ⎬ and other war leaders against Canaanites, Jephthah ⎪ Midianites, Philistines Samson ⎭	Philistines settle in coastal areas
the one kingdom Israel	1020 B.C. 1000 B.C. 961 B.C.	Samuel chose, anointed, a king for Israel Saul, first king, fought Philistines David enlarged the kingdom Solomon levied taxes that led to division of the kingdom	Hiram of Tyre

the two kingdoms	922 B.C.
	 876 B.C.
	 869 B.C.
	
	 783 B.C.
	
	 737 B.C.
	 732 B.C.
	
	 721 B.C.
	 640 B.C.
	
	 609 B.C.
	
	 597 B.C.
	 587 B.C.
		ISRAEL **JUDAH**
		 Jeroboam Rehoboam
		 Omri (prophets)
		 Ahab Elijah
		   Elisha (prophets)
		   Amos Uzziah Isaiah
		   Hosea
		 Pekah Ahaz
		 Hoshea
		   Hezekiah Micah
		 Fall of Samaria
		   Josiah
		     Jeremiah
		   Jehoiakim Nahum
		     Zephaniah
		   Zedekiah
		   Fall of Jerusalem
			Syrian kingdoms
			
			 Assyrian empire
			
			 Tiglathpileser
			 Shalmaneser
			 Sargon
			 invasion by Neco, of Egypt
			 Chaldeans took Assyrian empire
			 Nebuchadnezzar

the exile		Judeans taken captive to Babylon Ezekiel	Persian empire
between O.T. and N.T. times	538 B.C. 458 B.C. 445 B.C. 333 B.C. 63 B.C.	return from exile Ezra Judah, a province of Nehemiah Persian empire Greek empire Romans took Greek empire	Cyrus Darius Artaxerxes Roman Empire
Jesus Christ	5 or 4 B.C. A.D. 30	birth John the Baptist Herod the king death 12 disciples	Augustus Tiberius
the early church	 A.D. 100	began in Jerusalem Peter Paul spread through the world Luke John Mark	Claudius

A

Aaron (âr'ən). Brother of Moses. Aaron sometimes helped Moses, as when he was Moses' spokesman in Egypt, and sometimes worked against him, as when he led the Israelites in making the golden calf. Stories in the books of Exodus, Leviticus, Numbers, Deuteronomy; *Acts 7:40; Heb. 5:4.*
sons of Aaron or **house of Aaron.** Members of the family descended from Aaron. Priests were of this family, inheriting their positions from Aaron, who was the first priest. *Ex. 28:1; Lev. 3:5; Ps. 115:10.*

Abaddon (ə băd'ən). O.T. word for place beneath the earth where it was believed the dead lived. *Job 26:6; Ps. 88:11.* (See *Sheol* for explanation of O.T. views of life after death and for words with same meaning.)

Abba (ăb'ə). An Aramaic word meaning "father," used by children in addressing a parent. *Mark 14:36; Rom. 8:15; Gal. 4:6.*

Abel (ā'bəl). Son of Adam. He was a shepherd, and was murdered by his brother Cain. *Gen. 4:1-16; Matt. 23:35; Heb. 11:4.* (See *Genesis* for general background.)

Abiathar (ə bī'ə thər). A priest when David was king. *1 Sam. 22:20-23; 23:6-14; 2 Sam. 15:24-29.*
In the story of Jesus' disciples eating grain on the sabbath, Abiathar is mentioned as the priest who gave David the bread of the Presence to eat. *Mark 2:23-28.* However, the account in *1 Sam. 21:1-6* names the priest Ahimelech, Abiathar's father.

Abimelech (ə bĭm'ə lĕk). Son of the judge Gideon, and king of the city of Shechem for three years during the time of the judges. *Judg., ch. 9.* Others.

Abner (ăb'nər). Commander of Saul's army, he introduced David to Saul. He supported Ishbosheth, Saul's son, as his successor on the throne, then changed his allegiance to David, but was shortly killed by Joab, David's commander in chief. *1 Sam. 14:50; 17:55-58; 2 Sam. 2:8-10; 3:6-30.*

abomination. Anything hateful or repulsive to man or to God. Eating with foreigners was an abomination to the Egyptians. *Gen. 43:32.* Worship of images was an abomination to God. *Deut. 7:25.* Sometimes the word was used of gods of other nations, as in *1 Kings 11:5.*

Abraham (ā'brə hăm), or **Abram** (ā'brəm), meaning "God is high." A man from the east (Mesopotamia) who migrated into the land of Canaan, probably around 2000 B.C. God promised to make him the founder of a great nation. *Gen. 11:26 to 25:11; Rom., ch. 4; Gal. 3:6-9; James 2:21-23.* (See Time Line; map Plate II.)

sons of Abraham, or **Abraham as our father.** In later Hebrew history, Abraham was thought of as the father of the Jews, as in *Luke 3:8; John 8:39; Gal. 3:7-9.*

Abraham's bosom. Jews in Jesus' time expected that they might be reunited after death with Abraham and other fathers of the faith. *Luke 16:22; Matt. 8:11.*

Absalom (ăb'sə ləm). A son of David who revolted against his father and tried to take the throne from him. *2 Sam., chs. 13 to 18.*

abyss. N.T. word meaning "the deep," or the place under the earth where it was believed the dead lived. In *Rom. 10:7* there is an explanation of this word. *Luke 8:31.* (See *Hades* for explanation of beliefs concerning life after death in N.T. times.)

according to. . . . A phrase in the titles of many of the psalms, probably meaning "to the tune of. . . ." For examples and names of some tunes, see *Ps. 22; 45; 56 to 59; 69; 80.*

Achaia (ə kā'yə). In N.T. times, a province of the Roman Empire, south of Macedonia, in what is now the country of Greece. The Roman governor had his headquarters in Corinth, the chief city, where Paul founded a church. *Acts 18:1-17; 2 Cor. 1:1.* (See *Gallio;* map Plate XV, D-3.)

acre. A measurement of land, the amount that a yoke of oxen could plow in a day. *1 Sam. 14:14; Isa. 5:10.*

Acts of the Apostles, The. N.T. book concerning the thirty years or so following Christ's death, considered to be a very accurate history of the beginnings of the church. The author was a Gentile Christian, Luke, who also wrote The Gospel According to Luke. *Acts 1:1.* The Acts was written sometime between A.D. 75 and 85.

Adam (ăd'əm), meaning "human being" or "mankind." In the stories of creation, the first man. Adam's story is meant to be the story of all persons. Man is made in the image of God. But he wants to be equal with God or to know as much as God, instead of being dependent. In this way he impairs his own abilities and his relationship with God. *Gen. 1:26 to 5:5* (in most of these stories called "the man"); *Rom. 5:12-17.* (See *Genesis.*)

Adonijah (ăd'ə nī'jə). A son of David who plotted to take over the throne when his father was dying. Abiathar, the priest, and Joab, the commander of the army, supported him. On becoming king, Solomon had Adonijah killed. *1 Kings 1:5 to 2:25.* Other.

Adullam (ə dŭl'əm). O.T. town in the territory of the tribe of Judah. It was an old Canaanite town before the Israelites moved into the area. In a cave near Adullam, David hid from Saul. Rehoboam, the first king of Judah, fortified the town. *Josh. 12:7, 15; 1 Sam. 22:1-2; 2 Chron. 11:5, 7.* (See map Plate IV, C-5.)

adultery. Sexual relationship between a married man and a woman not his wife, or vice versa. Forbidden in the ten commandments, *Deut. 5:18,* adultery was punished by death. *Lev. 20:10; John 8:3-7.* In the O.T., forsaking God and worshiping the gods is often called adultery, as in *Ezek. 23:37.*

Agrippa (ə grĭp'ə), Marcus Julius. A member of the Herod family of N.T. times, appointed by the Romans as king over a small territory north of Galilee, A.D. 50. Bernice, who visited Caesarea with him and listened to Paul's defense, was Agrippa's sister. *Acts, chs. 25 and 26.*

Ahab (ā'hăb). Seventh king of the Northern Kingdom, Israel, from about 870 to 850 B.C. To cement a political alliance, he married Jezebel, the daughter of the king of Sidon, who introduced the worship of Baal. The prophet Elijah opposed Ahab and Jezebel. Throughout his reign Ahab was at war with Ben-hadad, king of Damascus (or Syria), except when the Assyrians threatened both of them. A stone monument (called the Black Obelisk) on which are recorded the conquests of Shalmaneser III, of Assyria, is the source of our information about Ahab's fighting the Assyrians. *1 Kings 16:28 to 22:40.* (See *king;* Time Line.) Other.

Ahasuerus (ə hăzh'ŏŏ ĕr'əs). A king of the Persian empire, and husband of Esther in The Book of Esther. Some scholars think he is meant to be Xerxes, famous in history for his defeated expedition against the Greeks in the fifth century B.C. *Esth. 1:1.*

Ahaz (ā'hăz). King of the Southern Kingdom, Judah, beginning about 735 B.C. He set up a Syrian-type altar in the temple. During his reign, Jerusalem was besieged by Pekah, king of the Northern Kingdom, Israel, and Rezin, of Syria. Ahaz wanted to get help from Tiglath-pileser, king of Assyria. The prophet Isaiah advised against such an alliance. Nevertheless, Ahaz became a vassal of the Assyrian king. *2 Kings, ch. 16; 2 Chron., ch. 28; Isa. 7:1-6.* (See *king;* Time Line.) Other.

Ahijah (ə hī'jə). A prophet from the town of Shiloh who told Jeroboam that Solomon's kingdom would be divided. His announcement is an example of the way in which prophets sometimes dramatized their messages. *1 Kings 11:29-33.* Others.

Ahimelech (ə hĭm'ə lĕk). A priest of the sanctuary at Nob who gave the sword of Goliath and the bread of the Presence to David when he was fleeing from Saul. He and all the other priests were killed by Saul for helping David. Ahimelech's son, Abiathar, escaped and joined David's forces. *1 Sam. 21:1-9; 22:11-20.* In the story of Jesus' disciples' eating grain on the sabbath, *Mark 2:23-28,* the priest who helped David is called Abiathar. Others.

Ai (ī). A Canaanite city near Bethel in O.T. times. Accounts in *Josh., chs. 7 and 8,* say that the Israelites made an unsuccessful attack on it and reattacked, leaving the city in ruins. Archaeologists believe that this account tells of the capture of Bethel, because excavations show that Ai had been destroyed and was only ruins when the Israelites entered Canaan. (See *Joshua, The Book of;* map Plates III, G-2; IV, C-5.)

Alexandria (ăl'ĭg zăn'drĭ ə). A city on the north coast of Egypt, founded during the Greek empire (fourth century B.C.); second in importance to Rome in N.T. times. *Acts 27:6; 28:11.* Before the time of Christ, a colony of Jews lived in the northeast section of the city. Probably the translation of the Old Testament books into Greek (called the Septuagint) was begun here in the third century B.C. Alexandrian Jews were among those who argued with Stephen. *Acts 6:9.* There were Christians in Alexandria from early times. *Acts 18:24.* Later the city became famous for its schools for the instruction of new Christians. Today it is known as al-Iskandariyah. (See *Greece;* map Plate XV, E-5.)

allotment. In O.T. times, an amount of land assigned to a family or tribe by lot. The land of Canaan was thought of as the special gift of God to his people. It was shared out among the Israelites and, from time to time, reassigned. *Josh. 11:23; 14:1-2; 16:1; Ezek. 45:1; 48:10.* (See *inheritance; lot; portion* [three words with similar meanings]; also *cast lots.*)

alms. In the N.T., help given to the poor and needy. *Matt. 6:2-4; Luke 12:33; Acts 3:2-3.*

Although the word is not used in the O.T., the obligation of giving to those in need was taught, *Deut. 15:7-11,* and the practice was often identified with righteousness. *Job 29:12-17; Isa. 58:6-8.*

almug (ăl'mŭg); also **algum.** Wood imported in the time of Solomon, used in building and in making musical instruments; probably a kind of sandalwood. *1 Kings 10:11-12; 2 Chron. 2:8.*

aloes. Spice from the resin of a tree, imported from India; used for incense and perfume, and for anointing the bodies of the dead. *Ps. 45:8; Prov. 7:17; John 19:39.*

Alpha and Omega (ăl'fə, ō měg'ə). The first and last letters of the Greek alphabet. *Rev. 1:8; 22:13.*

altar. A mound of earth, a stone, or a platform built of stones on which an animal was burned as a sacrifice or offering to gods or to God. Incense was also burned, and sometimes worshipers placed food on the altar or poured wine over it. Many peoples of ancient times used altars and sacrifices of different kinds. Altars to God were at first built wherever a person felt that God had made himself known. *Gen. 26:23-25.* In *Ex. 17:8-16* we are told of Moses' building an altar because of victory in battle. Thus there were many altars throughout most of O.T. times. But sacrifice tended to center in the altars of the temple in Jerusalem, *2 Chron. 4:1, 19,* and was eventually restricted to them. Some Israelites worshiped also at altars of the gods, such as Baal, or built altars for them. For example, see 2 *Kings 16:10-14. Matt. 5:23-24; Acts 17:22-23.* (See, for additional information, *offering; priest; sacrifice.*)

Amalekites (ə măl'ə kīts). A nation of nomadic people in O.T. times, centering in the Negeb, originally around Kadesh-barnea, where they harassed the Israelites under Moses and opposed their entering Canaan. Amalekites were among the groups making raids against whom the judge Gideon fought. They were finally defeated by Saul. *Num. 13:29; 14:39-45; Deut. 25:17-19; Judg. 6:3-5; 1 Sam. 15:4-8.* (See map Plate III, F-3 — Kadesh-barnea.)

Amaziah (ăm'ə zī'ə). Priest at the sanctuary in Bethel who reported the preaching of Amos the prophet to Jeroboam II, king of the Northern Kingdom, Israel, and warned Amos not to prophesy at Bethel. *Amos 7:10-15.*
Also a king of the Southern Kingdom, Judah, in the eighth century B.C. *2 Kings 14:1-20.* (See *king.*) Others.

ambush. A type of warfare consisting of attack from a hiding place, often at dawn. Ambush was much used by the Israelites, especially in taking Canaan, because their troops and weapons were often inferior to those of the enemy. In *Josh. 8:1-17* there is a description of the use of ambush combined with a trick. *Judg. 9:34-41; 2 Chron. 13:13-14; Ps. 64:4; Jer. 9:8; Acts 25:2-3.*

Amen. A Hebrew word, an exclamation, meaning "Let it be so," or

"Surely." It was spoken by a person or a group of persons on hearing a statement made or a prayer given, and indicated that they affirmed what was said. For examples of different uses, see *1 Kings 1:36; 1 Chron. 16:36; Neh. 8:6; Jer. 28:6; Gal. 1:5; 6:18.*
In *Rev. 3:14* "the Amen" is used as a title for Christ.

Ammonites (ăm'ə nīts). A people of O.T. times living east of the Jordan River in what is now part of the Hashemite Kingdom of Jordan. They joined with the Moabites in opposing the Israelites. The judge Jephthah fought them, as did Saul later. Under David and Solomon the Ammonites were controlled by Israel. Their chief god was Milcom. *Deut. 23:3-4; Judg. 10:17 to 11:33; 1 Sam. 11:1-11; 2 Sam., chs. 10; 11:1; 12:26-31.* (See map Plates IV, E-5; V, D-5 — Ammon.)

Amorites (ăm'ə rīts). One of the nations of O.T. times that occupied Canaan before the Israelites conquered it. They lived chiefly in the hill country that was taken by the tribe of Judah, but they also controlled territory east of the Jordan, called Sihon. The few Amorites who remained in the land were put to forced labor by Solomon. *Ex. 3:8; Num. 13:29; Josh. 10:5-6; Judg. 3:5; 2 Chron. 8:7-8.* (See map Plate III, G-2 — Sihon.)
Much earlier in history, the Amorites had controlled the Babylonian empire. Their most famous king was Hammurabi, of the eighteenth century B.C., noted for his law codes. (See *Babylon;* Time Line; map Plate II, F-2 — Babylonia, the territory of the Amorites in the time of Abraham.)

Amos (ā'məs). A prophet from about 760 to 746 B.C. Amos lived in Tekoa, a town in the Southern Kingdom, Judah, working as a shepherd and a dresser of sycamore trees. He prophesied in a town in the Northern Kingdom called Bethel, where the royal sanctuary and palace were located. (See Time Line.) Other.

Amos, The Book of. O.T. book containing the teachings of the prophet Amos, many of which are in poetry. They were collected sometime after the prophet's death. Some passages illustrating the theme of his prophecies are: *Amos 2:6; 5:1-15, 21-24.*

Anakim (ăn'ə kĭm). An O.T. nation of very large people, a few of whom were in Canaan when the Israelites took it over. Perhaps Goliath was of the Anakim. *Num. 13:32-33* ("sons of Anak"); *Deut. 2:10-11; Josh. 11:21-22.* (See *giants.*)

Anathoth (ăn'ə thŏth). An O.T town in the Southern Kingdom, Judah, about two and one half miles northeast of Jerusalem. It was one of the cities allotted to the priests, and was the home of the prophet Jeremiah. *Josh. 21:18-19; Jer. 1:1.*

Andrew. One of the twelve disciples of Jesus, and a brother of Simon Peter. A native of Bethsaida, Andrew lived in Capernaum, where he worked as a fisherman. *Matt. 4:18-20; 10:2; Mark 1:29; John 1:44; Acts 1:12-14.* (See *disciple* for Bible references to lists of the twelve.)

angel. In the O.T., usually a messenger of God in human form. The word was used to avoid saying that God himself had appeared or spoken to a person. *Gen. 16:7; Ex. 3:1-2; Judg. 6:11;* also *Matt. 1:20; Luke 2:9.* Toward the end of O.T. times, under the influence of Persian ideas, there developed belief in angels as definite beings, and certain ones were identified by name or by function. This development is reflected in the mention in the N.T. of archangels, *Luke 1:19; 1 Thess. 4:16,* and in the idea of a guardian angel, indicated in *Matt. 18:10.*

Annas (ăn'əs). High priest at Jerusalem when John the Baptist began preaching; appointed by the Roman governor of Syria. By the time Jesus was tried, Annas' son-in-law, Caiaphas, was high priest, but Annas was still important and still called high priest. He was also at the trial of Peter and John. *Luke 3:2; John 18:13, 24; Acts 4:6.*

anoint. To put oil on the head or on another part of the body, or on an object to sanctify it. Anointing was used: as part of good grooming, *2 Sam. 12:20; Matt. 6:17;* for medicinal purposes, *Isa. 1:6; Mark 6:13; James 5:14;* as a gesture of hospitality, *Luke 7:44-46;* in preparation of a body for burial, *Mark 16:1.* In O.T. times, priests and kings were anointed in the way Saul was anointed by Samuel, *1 Sam. 10:1.*
the anointed. One chosen and dedicated to be a leader by the pouring on of oil. *1 Sam. 26:9; Ps. 105:15; Acts 10:38.* The word Christ means "the anointed one."

antichrist. A personification of opposition to or disbelief in Christ. *1 John 2:18, 22* (an explanation); *4:3; 2 John 7.*

Antioch (ăn'tĭ ŏk). In N.T. times, the capital of the Roman province of Syria. It was the third largest city, after Rome and Alexandria, in the Roman Empire. Although some miles inland from the Mediterranean Sea, Antioch was on a navigable river and had a harbor. Several overland highways ended there also. Christians forced to flee Jerusalem after the death of Stephen went to Antioch, and the word "Christian" was first used there. *Acts 11:19-26; 13:1; 14:24-28; 15:1-35* (about a dispute that arose at Antioch). (See map Plate XV, G-3.)

Antioch of Pisidia (pĭ sĭd'ĭ ə). In N.T. times, a town in Phrygia visited by Paul. There were sixteen Antiochs in the world of that time, all built by the same Greek ruler and all named for his father. *Acts 13:14-52; 14:19-21; 2 Tim. 3:11.* (See map Plate XV, F-3.)

Apollos (ə pŏl'əs). A Jew from Alexandria who became a worker in the early church. One of the factions in the church at Corinth centered about Apollos, and was perhaps made up of persons he had taught. Paul considered him a faithful fellow worker. *Acts 18:24; 19:1; 1 Cor., chs. 1; 3; 4; 16:12; Titus 3:13.*

apostle, meaning "messenger" or "ambassador." In the Gospels, the twelve disciples of Jesus. *Mark 6:30; Luke 6:13.* In The Acts, often used for the twelve, with Matthias taking the place of Judas. *Acts 1:23-26; 4:33.* The term also includes other persons, such as Paul and Barnabas, and others. *Acts 14:4; 1 Cor. 15:5-9; 2 Tim. 1:11.*

apple of the eye. The pupil of the eye, thus something valuable and precious. *Deut. 32:10; Ps. 17:8; Zech. 2:8.*

apron. A girdle worn around the outer garment. *Acts 19:12.* (See *girdle.*)

Aquila and Priscilla (ăk'wə lə, prĭ-sĭl'ə), also Prisca (prĭs'kə). A Jewish-Christian couple, originally from Pontus, who lived for a time at Rome but were forced to leave there when the emperor sent away all Jews. Paul met them at Corinth and stayed with them. Like Paul, they were tentmakers. They became influential leaders in the early church. *Acts 18:1-4, 18, 24-26; Rom. 16:3-4; 1 Cor. 16:19; 2 Tim. 4:19.*

Arabah (ăr'ə bə), meaning "desert." The area south of what is now called the Dead Sea, to the Gulf of 'Aqaba (modern name). The Arabah is a continuation of the great north-south trench containing the Sea of Galilee, the Jordan River, and the Dead Sea. From the Dead Sea, which is over twelve hundred feet below sea level, the Arabah rises to about three hundred feet, then drops again to sea level. In O.T. times there were mines in the area. The seaport, Ezion-geber, important in Solomon's time, was at the southern end, on the gulf. *Deut. 1:1; 2:8; Ezek. 47:8.*
Sea of the Arabah, as in *2 Kings 14:25,*

was the Dead Sea, usually called in Bible times the Salt Sea. *Deut. 3:17.* (See *Canaan* for description of main geographical areas; map Plates I, C-8; III, G-3.)

Arabia (ə rā'bĭ ə). The word means " desert." Arabia was a large peninsula between Egypt and Asia and the area east of the Jordan River. Today most of it is the country of Saudi Arabia. The Israelites traveled into Arabia on their way from Egypt to Canaan. The peoples who lived there in O.T. times were always wanderers and tent dwellers. Some of them were: Ishmaelites, Midianites, Amalekites, Edomites, Sabeans (people of Sheba). *2 Chron. 9:13-14; 17:10-11; 21:16-17; Isa. 13:20; 21:13-14; Acts 2:11; Gal. 1:17.* (See map Plate II, F-3 — Arabian Desert.)

Aram (âr'əm). In O.T. times, a region in the upper valleys of the Tigris and Euphrates Rivers, also known as Syria. The people who lived there, the **Arameans,** were sometimes acknowledged as relatives of the Israelites and sometimes considered enemies. Haran, where Abraham stayed for a time, was in Aram (also called Paddanaram), and some of his relatives stayed there. *Gen. 25:19-20.* In *Deut. 26:5,* the Aramean referred to is Abraham. There were strong states in Aram, such as Damascus and Zobah, that were often at war with the kingdom of Israel, and later, with the Northern Kingdom, Israel, and the Southern Kingdom, Judah. *2 Sam. 8:5-6.* (See *Syria;* map Plates II, F-2 — Paddan-aram; VI, D-3 — Aram, Syria.)

Aramaic (ăr'ə mā'ĭk). In O.T. times, the language of the Arameans, closely related to the Hebrew language. In the time of Isaiah, Aramaic was an international language. *2 Kings 18:26.* Later, it was the official language of the Persian empire. *Ezra 4:7.* In N.T. times it was the everyday language of the Jews, Hebrew being used only in the synagogues and the schools. Thus Jesus and his disciples spoke Aramaic. There are some phrases in Aramaic in the Gospels, such as *Talitha cumi,* in *Mark 5:41,* and Jesus' cry from the cross in *Matt. 27:46.* (See *Hebrew* [language].)

archangel. *1 Thess. 4:16; Jude 9.* (See *angel.*)

archers. In O.T. times, troops equipped with bows and arrows were a regular part of the armies of Israel and of the Northern Kingdom, Israel, and the Southern Kingdom, Judah, as well as of the armies of other nations. Archers were both foot soldiers and charioteers. They were also used for defense on city walls. *1 Sam. 31:3; 2 Chron. 35:23; Jer. 51:3.* (See *army.* See, for equipment, *arrow; bow; quiver; sheath.*)

Areopagus (ăr'ĭ ŏp'ə gəs). Part of the Acropolis, or civic center, of Athens in N.T. times. Also a court that met there. Paul may have had to appear before the court for permission to make speeches in Athens, or it may be that he spoke to a group of philosophers gathered for discussion. *Acts 17:19, 22.* (See *city,* in N.T. times.)

Aristarchus (ăr'ĭs tär'kəs). A Gentile Christian in the early church, a Macedonian from the city of Thessalonica. He traveled and worked with Paul. *Acts 19:29; 20:1-5; 27:1-2; Col. 4:10; Philemon 23-24.*

ark. A ship or houseboat, as in the story of Noah. *Gen., chs. 6 to 9.* Usually in the O.T., the **ark of the covenant** or **ark of the testimony** or **ark of God.** A chest or box mounted on poles for carrying. Other ancient peoples had similar portable shrines to carry idols of gods, especially into battle. The Israelites seem to have had a similar feeling for the ark. The box contained the stone tablets inscribed with the law, not an idol. It was also considered a throne for God. Carried before the Israelites when they moved from place to place in the time of Moses, and with the soldiers into battle, it symbolized the presence of God, who was leading his people like a king. David had the ark moved to Jerusalem, and it was later placed in Solomon's temple. In *Num. 10:35-36* there is an indication of how the Israelites thought of the ark. The description in *Ex. 25:10-22* was written much later, and may or may not be what the ark looked like in the time of Moses. In *1 Sam. 4:1 to 7:2* there are some stories about the ark. *2 Sam. 6:12-19; 1 Kings 8:1-9.* (See *cherub; enthroned.*)

armlet. A band or bracelet, often made of copper, worn on the upper arm in O.T. times as jewelry or, in the case of a king, as a sign of authority. *Ex. 35:22; Num. 31:48-50; 2 Sam. 1:1-10; Isa. 3:18-23* (in a list of many kinds of jewelry and luxury items of the prophet's time).

armor. In O.T. times, armor consisted of shield, or buckler; helmet; breastplate, or coat of mail; perhaps some plate armor; and greaves. Probably officers and leaders only were fully equipped with armor. Metal armor was not used until the time of Solomon. *1 Sam. 17:38; Eph. 6:11.* (Paul probably had in mind the Roman soldier of his time). (See, for details, *breastplate; greaves; helmet; mail; shield.*)

armor-bearer. Attendant to an important warrior, same as shield-bearer. *Judg. 9:54; 1 Sam. 16:21; 1 Chron. 10:4-5.*

armory. Place for storage of weapons in O.T. times. *Neh. 3:19; Isa. 39:2; Jer. 50:25.*

army; also **armed men** and **men who drew the sword.** In early O.T. times each tribe supplied fighters from among able-bodied men over twenty years of age. *Num. 1:2-3; 31:3-4.* When needed, they were mustered by messengers or signals. *Judg. 6:34-35.* Saul was the first to organize a standing army, consisting of three thousand foot soldiers. *1 Sam. 13:2.* David enlarged the army, adding mercenary troops, *1 Chron. 27:1-15,* and Solomon added chariot troops and horses, *1 Kings 10:26.* The two kingdoms of later times also had armies. Little is known about the organization of the army. There were commanders such as Abner and Joab. Part of the army served as the king's guard. *Ex. 14:6; Josh. 5:13-15; Judg. 8:10; 1 Sam. 14:50.* (See, for types of troops, *archers; bodyguard; chariot; footmen; horse; mighty men; sling; spear.*)

Arnon (är'nən). River flowing into the east shore of the Dead Sea. At the time of the Israelites' conquest of Canaan, the river was the northern boundary of the Moabites, and the territory north of it was controlled by the Amorites. Both nations had fortifications along the river. Today it is known as the Wadi el-Mojib. *Num. 21:13; Josh. 13:15-16; Judg. 11:18;.Isa. 16:2.* (See map Plates III, G-2; IV, D-6.)

arrow. Shaft of wood or cane with a flat tip of bone, flint, iron, or copper. Flint tips were used for a long time after the use of metal became widespread. *2 Kings 19:32; 1 Chron. 12:2; Ps. 11:2; Hab. 3:9.* In siege warfare, arrows were sometimes set afire and shot into the besieged city. *Ps. 7:13.* (See, for use in warfare, *archers; bow.* See also *quiver.*)

Artaxerxes (är'tə zûrk'sēz). Persian king, starting to reign about 465 B.C., who permitted Ezra to return to Jerusalem from Babylon, taking a group of exiles. He later sent Nehemiah, his cupbearer, to Jerusalem to direct the rebuilding. *Ezra 7:1-28; Neh. 2:1-8.* (See Time Line.)

Artemis of the Ephesians (är'tə-məs). A goddess widely worshiped in Asia in N.T. times (not the same as the Artemis of Greek mythology). The temple at Ephesus was an important center of the worship of Artemis. The silversmiths there made small replicas of the temple to sell. *Acts 19:21-41.*

Ascents, A Song of. The title (some-times with the name of David or Solomon) of *Psalms 120 to 134.* These psalms were sung by processions going up (ascending) to the temple or by pilgrims going up to Jerusalem for a feast.

Ashdod (ăsh'dŏd). A Philistine city in O.T. times, one of a chain of five that fought against the Israelites in the time of the judges and later. The city was ruled by a lord or king; its god was Dagon. It was finally conquered by the Southern Kingdom, Judah, under King Uzziah, in the eighth century B.C. *Josh. 13:3; 1 Sam. 5:1-8; 2 Chron. 26:6.* (See map Plates IV, B-5; V, B-5.)

Azotus (ă zō'təs) in the N.T. is the same city. *Acts 8:40.* (See map Plate XIV, B-5.)

Asher (ăsh'ər). One of the twelve sons of Jacob; also the name of the tribe descended from him, or **sons of Asher,** and the area they occupied in the extreme northwest of Canaan bordering on Tyre. *Gen. 30:12; Josh. 19:24-31; Judg. 1:31-32; Luke 2:36.* (See map Plate IV, C-3.)

Asherah (ə shĭr'ə), sing.; pl., **Asherim,** (masc.), and **Asheroth** (fem.). At high places in O.T. times, the pillar or image that symbolized Asherah, a Canaanite goddess often associated with Baal. *Ex. 34:13-14; Judg. 3:7; 6:25; 1 Kings 14:23; 2 Kings 23:4-7* (the king was Josiah). (See *gods* for list of related words.)

ashes; often **sackcloth and ashes.** Putting ashes on the head was a part of mourning for the dead, or a sign of repentance. *Job. 42:6; Jer. 6:26; Luke 10:13.* (See *mourning* for list of other customs.)

Ashkelon (ăsh′kə lən). A Philistine city of O.T. times, located on the shore of the Mediterranean Sea. It was one of a chain of five cities that resisted the Israelites. It was captured, but held only briefly, by the Israelites during the time of the judges. The word "scallion," for a type of onion, comes from the name Ashkelon. *Josh. 13:3; Judg. 1:18; 2 Sam. 1:17-20; Jer. 25:20; Amos 1:8.* (See map Plates IV, B-5; V, B-5.)

Asia (ā′zhə). A Roman province in N.T. times in the western part of what is now the country of Turkey. Ephesus was the capital. The city of Colossae was also in Asia. *Acts 2:8-10; 19:10; Rev. 1:4.* (See map Plate XV, E-3.)

ass. The domesticated animal most widely used for riding, plowing, carrying burdens, drawing carts. *Gen. 22:3; Isa. 30:6; Matt. 21:2.* The prophet Zechariah felt that the future king of Israel (the Messiah) would ride on an ass rather than on a horse or in a chariot, as did most kings of ancient times. *Zech. 9:9; Matt. 21:1-7.*

assembly; holy assembly; solemn assembly; assembly of the Lord or **assembly of Israel.** In O.T. times, a gathering of the Israelites called to celebrate the sabbath or a feast. *Ex. 12:16; Lev. 23:36; 1 Kings 8:14; Neh. 5:13.* (See *convocation.*)
In the N.T. the word "assembly" has its usual meaning.

Assyria (ə sĭr′ĭ ə). An area of O.T. times east of the Tigris River, in what is now the country of Iraq. Different peoples ruled the area at various times,

Assyrian soldier

among them Sumerians (pre-Biblical), Babylonians, Assyrians, Chaldeans. *Gen. 25:18; Ps. 83:8; Micah 5:6.* (See map Plate II, F-2.)

Assyrians. People who ruled a widespread empire from about 1000 B.C. to 612 B.C. and often invaded the lands of the Israelites. They are known both in the Bible and in general history as a warlike people who frequently invaded neighboring nations and deported the populations. King Ahab, of the Northern Kingdom, Israel, was the first to fight the Assyrians, as we know from sources outside the Bible. Some of the Assyrian rulers who are mentioned in the O.T. are Tiglath-pileser III, Shalmaneser V, Sargon, and Sennacherib. Samaria, the capital of the Northern Kingdom, Israel, fell under siege by the Assyrians. They also attacked Jerusalem. The Assyrian empire was taken over by the Chaldeans. *2 Kings 15:29; 17:3, 6, 24; 18:9, 13-25; 19:35-37.* (See *nations;* Time Line; map Plate VIII.)

27

at his right hand. Guests were seated at the right of the host as a mark of honor. *1 Kings 2:19.* The right hand was considered the hand that wielded power. *Ps. 16:8.* The right hand of God is a symbol of his power. Pictures and statues of ancient times often show the king seated at the right hand of his god, meaning that his power came from the gods. *Ps. 110:1.* In the N.T. the figure of speech often describes the risen Christ. *Eph. 1:20; Col. 3:1; Heb. 12:2.*

Athens (ăth'ĭnz). A Greek city in the Roman province of Achaia in N.T. times, now the capital of Greece. In the ancient world, even after the Romans had taken over the Greek empire, Athens was the center of art, literature, and philosophy. *Acts 17:15-32; 1 Thess. 3:1.* (See *Greece;* map Plate XV, D-3.)

atonement. In the O.T., the taking away or covering of sin, chiefly by offerings and the sacrifice of animals, so that the relationship between God and man might be restored. *Ex. 29:33; Lev. 4:20; 2 Chron. 29:24; Neh. 10: 32-33.*
day of atonement. A yearly day of fasting and repentance, held in the autumn, on which the high priest offered special sacrifices on behalf of all the people in the most holy place. This was the only time that anyone entered the inner part of the temple. *Lev., chs. 16* (description); *23:28; 25:9.* It is the fast referred to in *Acts 27:9.*

augury. In O.T. times, a form of magic in which future events were foretold by signs in nature, such as the pattern of a flight of birds. See *Deut. 18:10* for a list of similar magic practices that were forbidden to the Israelites. *2 Chron. 33:6.* (See *magic* for list of related words.)

avenger. In early O.T. tribal laws, the nearest relative of a murdered person, who was obligated to pursue and kill the murderer. *Num. 35:9-21; Josh. 20:1-6; 2 Sam. 14:11; Ps. 99:8.* (See *refuge, cities of.*)

axe. In O.T. times, used on both wood and stone, and also as a weapon. Before the use of metal (about the time of David and Solomon) the axe head was made of flint or other stone. The metal blade of later times was flat, with a projection riveted into a wooden handle. In late O.T. times, pickaxes were much like those of today. *1 Sam. 13:19-21; 1 Kings 6:7; Jer. 10:3; 46:22.*

B

Baal (bā'əl), meaning " lord." The chief god of the Canaanites in O.T. times; also **Baals,** numerous local gods presiding over every area and believed responsible for the growth of crops and flocks. High places, Asherim, and pillars were associated with the worship of Baals. Jezebel, the wife of Ahab, king of the Northern Kingdom, Israel, worshiped Baal. That the Israelites were much tempted by Baal worship is shown by the number of place names and personal names that include " baal," such as Jerubbaal, another name for Gideon. *Num. 25:3; Judg. 2:11-13; 1 Kings 16:29-32; 18:17-40* (the prophet Elijah's contest with

28

the priests of Baal); *Jer. 19:4-6; Rom. 11:2-4.* (See *gods* for list of related words.) Also a personal name.

Babylon (băb'ə lən). An ancient Mesopotamian city on the lower Euphrates River. At the time of Abraham's migration to Canaan, Babylon was the capital of the Babylonian empire, of which Hammurabi, of about that time, was the most outstanding emperor. The area around Babylon is called Shinar in Genesis. Nebuchadnezzar, a Chaldean emperor of the sixth century B.C., rebuilt Babylon and made it his capital. When he captured Jerusalem, the Judeans were taken captive to Babylon and surrounding towns. *2 Kings, chs. 24 and 25; Matt. 1:11.* Cyrus took Babylon from the Chaldeans and founded the Persian empire, in which **Babylonia** was a province. *Ezra 7:16.*
Babylon in *1 Peter 5:13* and *Rev. 14:8* is a code word for Rome. (See *Chaldeans; exile;* map Plates II, F-3; IX, C-3.)

bag. Pouch made of skin or cloth for carrying weights (used as money in O.T. times) or food, as in the case of a shepherd or traveler. *Deut. 25:13; 2 Kings 5:23; Micah 6:11; Matt. 10:9-10; Luke 10:4.* (See *purse.*)

bake. Bread was baked daily by the women or the servants of a household in an oven or on heated stones or on a bowl turned upside down over the fire. In cities there were some commercial bakeries. *Gen. 19:3; Lev. 2:5; 1 Sam. 28:24; 1 Kings 19:6; Jer. 37:21.* (See *bread* for list of words related to bread-making.)

Balaam (bā'ləm). A seer of Aram in Moses' time. The king of Moab, knowing that the Israelites were approaching his territory, asked Balaam to place a curse on them, but the seer pronounced a blessing instead. Later, he seems to have led some of the Israelites astray, so that N.T. references to him are unfavorable. *Num., chs. 22 to 24; 31:15-16; 2 Peter 2:15; Jude 11.*

balances. Device for weighing, in which two pans were suspended from a balanced arm. Standard weights of stone or metal were put in one pan and the goods measured into the other. To pay for goods in O.T. times, the purchaser gave an amount of metal equal to a standard weight or he gave bars or rings of metal cast to the correct weight. These were also weighed before the transaction was completed. Same as scales. *Isa. 40:12; Ezek. 5:1; 45:10; Amos 8:5.* (See *money; weigh.*)

banker. In N.T. times, bankers sat at their tables in the market places, where they received deposits and made loans on which interest was charged. They also changed money from the currency of one nation to that of another. Checks and drafts were used for large payments or for transactions made in long-distance trade. *Matt. 25:27.* (See *money,* in N.T. times; *pound; talent,* in N.T. times.)

banner. In O.T. times, a pole on which was mounted a symbol; used to muster fighters or carried into battle. Probably each tribe, and later the army or divisions of it, had its own banner. The serpent on a pole that Moses made, *Num. 21:8,* may have been such a banner. Same as ensign and standard. *Ex. 17:15-16; Ps. 20:5; 60:4; Jer. 50:2.*

banquet. In *Amos 6:4-6* there is a description of a banquet such as might have been given by a king or a wealthy person of O.T. times. See also *Esth. 1:1-9.*
In N.T. times the banquet was a custom taken over from the Greeks. The guests were all men, usually nine in number. Servants were sent out several days beforehand to issue invitations, and again on the day of the banquet to remind the guests. Each guest was welcomed with a kiss and anointed by his host. The guests lay on couches, three persons to a couch, and ate from small low tables beside them. There were elaborate rules for the seating of guests. Such meals, usually held in the late afternoon or the evening, might last for hours and have many courses of food and some entertainment. *Mark 6:21; Luke 14:7-14, 16-24; 20:46.* (See *place of honor.*)

baptize. In the N.T., to wash with water, as done by John the Baptist to symbolize repentance and readiness for the Messiah. *Mark 1:4-8.* Elsewhere in the N.T., baptism is the symbol of confession of faith in Jesus Christ and of becoming a member of the church. *Matt. 28:19; Acts 2:38; 1 Cor. 1:14-16.*

Barak (bâr'ək). One of the leaders of the Israelites during the time of the judges. With Deborah he led in battle against the Canaanites. *Judg., chs. 4 and 5; Heb. 11:32.* (See Time Line.)

barbarian. In the N.T., a person who was neither a Jew nor a member of the Greek-Roman civilization of the time, such as an inhabitant of northern Europe or of lands east of the province of Syria. To the Greeks, the word meant a person who did not speak Greek, and who was, therefore, uncivilized. *Rom. 1:14; Col. 3:11.*

barley. A grain extensively grown for flour, less expensive than wheat, and therefore cultivated by the poor. It was sown in October. The barley harvest, beginning in March, marked the beginning of the Passover feast and the start of the seven weeks between it and the feast of Pentecost, or weeks. *Deut. 8:7-8; Hos. 3:2; John 6:8-9.* (See *wheat* for other grains and for words related to farming.)

Barnabas (bär'nə bəs). A Jew from Cyprus who became a follower of Jesus Christ in the early church. He traveled with Paul and with Mark. *Acts 4:36-37; 9:27; 11:22-30; chs. 14 and 15; 1 Cor. 9:6; Gal., ch. 2.*

barracks. Headquarters of the Roman cohort stationed in Jerusalem in the time of Paul. The barracks was in the Tower of Antonia, a fortress adjoining and overlooking the temple. *Acts 21:30 to 23:35.* (See *citadel; Claudius Lysias.* See *Rome* for list of words related to army. See map Plate XVI, D-4 — Tower of Antonia.)

Bartholomew (bär thŏl'ə mū). One of the twelve disciples of Jesus, prob-

30

ably the same as Nathanael in the Gospel of John (*1:45-51*). *Matt. 10:2-4; Luke 6:13-16; Acts 1:12-13.* (See *disciple* for Bible references to lists of the twelve.)

Baruch (bâr'ək). Assistant to the prophet Jeremiah of O.T. times. He was a scribe to whom the prophet dictated his teachings. Some of Baruch's transcriptions may be parts of The Book of Jeremiah. *Jer., chs. 36; 43:4-7.* Others.

Bashan (bā'shən). In O.T. times, a mountainous region east of the upper Jordan River, between the river and the Arabian Desert; occupied by the Amorites. The defeat of Og, king of Bashan, by Moses was a famous victory for the Israelites. *Deut. 3:1-11; Josh. 9:9-11; 1 Kings 4:19; 2 Kings 10:32-33; 1 Chron. 5:11.* The passages *Ps. 22:12* and *Amos 4:1* mention the cattle for which the area was noted. (See map Plate IV, D-3.)

basket. Common type of container used for foods, harvested grain and fruit, bricks, clay, and the like. Some, such as the kind in which Paul escaped from Damascus, were very large. *Acts 9:25.* Others were large enough to be carried on a pole between two men. Baskets were woven of various materials: palm fibers, reeds, rope. *Gen. 40:16-17; Judg. 6:19; Jer. 24:1-2; Luke 9:17.*

bath. In O.T. times, a measure for liquids. It was probably equal to about nine gallons in our system of measurement. Archaeologists have found jars labeled " royal bath," meaning the

king's measurement, which was often different from the standards commonly used in the market place. *1 Kings 7:38; 2 Chron. 2:10; Isa. 5:10* (of wine); *Ezek. 45:10-11* (gives some

Top of storage jar with inscription, "Royal Bath," c. 700 B.C.

equivalent measures of that time). (See *cor* for table of liquid measurements.)

Bathsheba (băth shē'bə). One of David's wives, the mother of Solomon. She was instrumental in having Solomon declared the next king. The way in which David secured Bathsheba as his wife led the prophet Nathan to accuse him. *2 Sam. 11:1 to 12:25; 1 Kings 1:11-31.*

battalion. A division of the Roman Army in N.T. times, also called a cohort. It was one tenth of a legion, or about six hundred men. Battalions were used, as in Jerusalem in Jesus' time, to keep order and to quell riots. As the guard for a prisoner, a battalion was present at an execution. *Matt. 27:27.* (See *Rome* for list of words related to army.)

battering ram. A machine used in O.T. siege warfare to attack city walls. From inside a wooden shelter on wheels, soldiers rocked a long

31

beam with an iron tip until enough force was generated to break part of the wall. The defenders tried to ward off the attack with chains and hooks. *2 Sam. 20:15; Ezek. 4:2; 21:22; 26:9.* (See *siege* for description and list of related words.)

bdellium (dĕl′ĭ əm). It is uncertain whether the substance was a mineral or the gum of a tree. *Gen. 2:12; Num. 11:7.*

beard. Men of O.T. times wore beards, which they cut off only as a sign of mourning. *Ezra 9:3; Isa. 15:2; Jer. 41:4-5.* The Egyptians shaved, but some Pharaohs, and also their queens, wore false beards. It was necessary for Joseph to shave before appearing in the Pharaoh's court. *Gen. 41:14.* Trimming the hair or beard in certain ways was forbidden, *Lev. 19:27,* because to do so would make an Israelite look like those who "cut the corners of their hair," that is, non-Israelites. *Jer. 9:26; 25:23; 49:32.* In N.T. times probably most men were clean-shaven. (See *shave.*)

beaten oil. Olive oil of a fine quality used in lamps in the sanctuaries in O.T. times and for certain offerings. It was not made in a press as was most olive oil, but was made of the drippings from olives that were crushed and beaten by hand. *Ex. 27:20; 29:40; 1 Kings 5:11.*

bed. For most people, a rug or a mat laid on the floor or on a low ledge along the wall of the house. Coverings consisted of the clothes worn during the daytime. Wealthy people had beds more like those of today, made of wood and sometimes with ivory inlays for decoration. *2 Kings 1:4; 4:10; Prov. 7:16-17; Amos 3:12; Matt. 9:2, 6; also Gen. 28:11; Ex. 22:26-27.* (See *couch; pallet.* See *house* for list of other household furnishings.)

Beelzebul (bē ĕl′zĭ bŭl). A name used by Jesus for Satan; also "prince of demons." *Matt. 10:25; Mark 3:22-23.*

Beer-sheba (bĭr shē′bə), meaning "well of seven" or "well of an oath." O.T. town in the Negeb wilderness, considered to be the southern limit of the kingdom of Israel or of the lands which God had given to the Israelites. The phrase **from Dan to Beer-sheba** means from the northernmost point to the southern boundary. *Gen. 21:14, 31; 28:10; 1 Sam. 8:2; 2 Sam. 24:7; 1 Kings 19:3; Amos 5:5; also Judg. 20:1; 1 Sam. 3:20.* (See *Dan* [the town]; map Plates II, E-3; III, F-2.)

Belial (bē′lĭ əl). A N.T. personification of worthlessness or ungodliness, equivalent to Satan. *2 Cor. 6:15.*

Benjamin (bĕn′jə mən). Youngest of the twelve sons of Jacob, who were the fathers of the tribes. Also the tribe descended from Benjamin, called **Benjaminites,** and the territory they occupied to the northwest of the Salt Sea, including the towns of Gibeah, Gilgal, and Michmash. *Gen. 35:16-18; Josh. 18:11-28; 1 Sam. 9:16, 21.* (See map Plate IV, C-5.) Others.

besiege. To lay siege, to attack a

city by surrounding it and cutting off supplies until the people surrender. Frequently used war strategy in O.T. times, especially during the time of the two kingdoms. *Deut. 20:10-14; 2 Kings 6:24; 24:10-17; 2 Chron. 32:9.* (See *siege* for description and list of related words.)

Bethany (bĕth'ə nĭ). A N.T. town just outside Jerusalem, one and five eighths miles east, on the road to Jericho. *Matt. 26:6-13; Mark 11:1; Luke 24:50; John 11:1.* (See map Plate XIV, C-5.)

The **Bethany beyond the Jordan** mentioned in the Gospel of John as the place where John the Baptist worked was another town, the location of which is unknown. *John 1:28.*

Bethel (bĕth'əl), meaning "house of God." A city of O.T. times, twelve miles north of Jerusalem, a Canaanite city until taken by the Israelites. After it was rebuilt, it sometimes belonged to the Benjaminites, in whose territory it was located, and sometimes to the Canaanites. When Jeroboam set up the Northern Kingdom, Israel, he made Bethel the chief sanctuary. *Gen. 12:8-9; 28:18-19; Josh. 12:7-9; 1 Sam. 7:15-16; 1 Kings 12:25-29; Amos 3:14.* (See *Ai;* map Plates IV, C-5; VI, C-5.)

Beth-horon (bĕth hôr'ən). Two O.T. towns in the territory of Ephraim. Situated on a mountain pass between the coastal plain and the hill country, they were the scene of many battles and were fortified by Solomon. *Josh. 16:5; 21:5, 22; 2 Chron. 8:3-5.* (See map Plate IV, C-5 — Beth-horon Lower.)

Bethlehem (bĕth'lĭ hĕm), meaning "house of bread." A small town five miles south of Jerusalem in the hill country of Judah. In the O.T. it is also called Ephrath and Ephrathah. It was the home of David's family and the birthplace of Jesus. *Gen. 35:19; Judg. 17:7; Ruth 1:1, 19; 1 Sam. 16:1; Micah 5:2; Luke 2:4; 11* (city of David). (See map Plates IV, C-5; XIV, C-5.)

Bethsaida (bĕth sā'ə də), meaning "house of fishing." A city of N.T. times on the Sea of Galilee east of where the Jordan River enters on the north. It was the center of a well-developed fishing industry in Jesus' time. *Matt. 11:20-21; Mark 6:45; John 1:44; 12:21.* (See map Plate XIV, D-3 — Bethsaida Julias.)

betroth. The betrothal of a man to the woman chosen for him by his father was of greater importance than the marriage ceremony. At the time of betrothal the groom gave his gifts, or marriage payment, to the bride's family and to the bride. The betrothed girl continued to live at her father's house for a year before the marriage. *2 Sam. 3:14; Matt. 1:18; 2 Cor. 11:2.*

birthright. In the O.T., special privileges of the first-born, or eldest, son in a family. On his father's death he became head of the family. Also, he inherited more of his father's wealth than his brothers did. *Gen. 25:29-34; 43:33; 1 Chron. 5:1.*

bishop. In the N.T., a person who had certain (unknown) responsibilities in a church; probably the same as elder. *Phil. 1:1; 1 Tim. 3:1-7* (qualifications); *Titus 1:7.* (See *church* for list of other officers.)

bitumen. Pitch, i.e., petroleum that has been semihardened by exposure to the air. *Gen. 11:3; 14:10; Ex. 2:3.*

blaspheme. To speak or act in a way that dishonors God. In O.T. laws, blasphemy was punishable by stoning. *Lev. 24:16; Acts 6:11-15; 7:54-60.* Blasphemy was the chief charge brought against Jesus at his trial. *Matt. 9:2-3; Mark 14:61-64.* (See *tore his robes.*)

bless. To wish good things for someone, as in a father's blessing on his sons. Such a blessing was highly regarded and not considered to be mere words, because words were believed to have power. *Gen. 27:1-4.*
Also, to give good things to someone. **Blessings** from God in O.T. times were usually thought of as long life and prosperity. *2 Sam. 6:11.* God's goodness is acknowledged and returned in blessing him. *Ps. 103; 2 Cor. 1:3.* See also *Luke 6:20-26,* where "Blessed are you" is used as the opposite of "Woe to you."

blind. Blind people usually had hard and poor lives because they could not work. Often they became beggars. The O.T. laws required kindness to the blind. *Lev. 19:14; Deut. 27:18.* The blind were one of the groups that Jesus mentioned in announcing the work he was sent to do, *Luke 4:18-19,* and he healed many blind persons. *John, ch. 9.*

bloodguilt. Responsibility for the death of another person. A murderer, or even an animal that killed a person, was to be killed, according to O.T. customs. Unlike other kinds of guilt, bloodguilt could not be atoned for in any offering or sacrifice. In early times the murdered person's nearest relative took the responsibility of avenging the death. Later, punishment became a community responsibility. *Ex. 22:2* (see also *21:28*); *1 Sam. 25:26; Ps. 51:14.* (See *avenger; refuge, cities of.*)

boat. In the N.T., small craft used for fishing on the Sea of Galilee or for ferrying across the lake or the Jordan River. It was propelled by oars or a single sail, or both. *Matt. 4:21-22; Mark 3:9; Luke 5:1-3; John 6:22-24.*

Boaz (bō'ăz). In The Book of Ruth, the man who married the heroine of the story. He was the great-grandfather of David. *Ruth; Matt. 1:5.*

bodyguard. Group of soldiers who attended a king or were runners in front of the king's chariot. *1 Sam. 22:14; 2 Sam. 23:22-23; 2 Kings 25:8; Jer. 32:2.* (See *mighty men.*)

bondage; house of bondage; bondage in Egypt. O.T. expressions for the time during which the Israelites worked as slaves in Egypt. *Ex. 2:23; 13:14; Josh. 24:16-17; Neh. 9:16-17; Micah 6:4.*

book. In N.T. times, a scroll. *Luke 4:17.*

Several books, similar to those in the O.T. and probably used in the writing of them, are mentioned in the O.T. For example, see *Josh. 10:13; 1 Kings 11:41; 2 Chron. 27:7.* (See *scroll.*)

booth. A temporary shelter, usually made of branches, in fields or vineyards for watchmen during the harvest, and for the feast of booths. *Gen. 33:17; Neh. 8:13-18; Job 27:18; Isa. 1:8; Matt. 17:4.*

booths, feast of; also called **feast of tabernacles** and **feast of ingathering.** A festival at harvest time during which families built booths and lived in them seven days to commemorate the tent life of the Israelites on their journey from Egypt to Canaan. *Deut. 16:13; Neh. 8:14-18.* (See *feast.*)

booty. Spoil, or things taken from conquered peoples by the victors in O.T. warfare. Anything of value was taken, including people, who were made slaves. Among the Israelites, booty, or a part of it, was supposed to be devoted. What was left over, and sometimes all of it, was divided among the soldiers, probably as their only pay. *Num. 31:9, 26-54* (description of typical booty); *Josh. 11:14; 2 Chron. 14:13.* (See *devote; spoil.*)

bow. One of the most widely used weapons of war in O.T. times; also used by hunters. The bow was made of wood or bone, with a string of hide or gut. Besides the archers, foot soldiers and chariot troops also carried bow and arrow. *Gen. 27:3; Josh.*

24:12; 2 Kings 6:22; 1 Chron. 5:18; 12:2; 2 Chron. 14:8; Ps. 11:2. (See *archers; sheath.*)

bread. The most important item of food; the word often means food in general. The women or servants of the household did the work of making bread, starting with the grinding of grain early in the morning. Bread was baked in flat, round cakes of wheat or barley flour. Most people ate barley bread; wheat flour was almost a luxury. The flat pieces of bread were often used to scoop up food, in place of forks and spoons, which were not used. *Gen. 18:4-6; 1 Sam. 16:20; 2 Sam. 16:1; Luke 11:3; 22:19; John 6:35; 1 Cor. 11:23-26.* (See, for other details of bread-making, *bake; grind; kneading bowl; leaven; loaf; meal; mill; oven.* See, for other foods, *curds; fig; goat; grape; lamb; oil; olive; palm; sheep; wine.*)

bread of the Presence; also **holy bread** and **showbread.** Twelve loaves of bread displayed on a table in the temple and in other sanctuaries as an offering to God. They were changed each week, and the old loaves were eaten by the priests. *Ex. 25:30; 1 Sam. 21:4-6; Luke 6:1-5.* (See *temple* for location. See also *unleavened bread.*)

break bread. In the N.T., to take part in the supper commemorating Jesus' last supper with his disciples. *Acts 2:42; 20:7; 1 Cor. 10:16.* (See *Lord's supper.*)

breastpiece. A garment worn over the ephod by a priest when carrying out his official duties. A pocket contained the Urim and Thummim. *Ex. 28:15-30* (description).

breastplate. Armor to protect the breast, back, and shoulders. In O.T. times, before the use of metal, it was made of leather or quilted cloth. Later, the coat of mail was used. *1 Kings 22:34; Isa. 59:17.* (See *armor*.)
The breastplate of the Roman soldier of N.T. times (to which Paul probably refers in *Eph. 6:14* and *1 Thess. 5:8*) was made of padded leather or of two sheets of metal.

brick. The most common type of building material in ancient lands, especially where stone was scarce. Clay was mixed with water, sometimes reinforced with straw or stubble, kneaded by foot, poured into wooden molds, and dried in a kiln or under the sun. Many of the bricks that have been found in ruins and excavations bear names stamped on them, names of the buildings they were intended for or the name of the king under whose direction the building was being done. The work of brickmaking was often assigned to forced labor. *Ex.*

Brickmaking, from an Egyptian wall painting

breeches. An apronlike garment worn by priests; not trousers. *Ex. 28:42; 39:28; Lev. 16:4; Ezek. 44:18.*

brethren. In the O.T., brothers or fellow members of a tribe, or fellow Israelites. *Deut. 24:14; Judg. 20:13; 2 Chron. 11:4.*
In the N.T., a form of address for members of the church. *Acts 1:15-16; Rom. 1:13; 1 Cor. 15:58; Phil. 4:1; Heb. 3:1.* (See *Christians* for other names for members of the church.)

1:13-14; ch. 5; 2 Sam. 12:31; Nahum 3:14. (See *mason* for list of words related to brick and stone work.)

bronze. An alloy of tin and copper, widely used in O.T. times especially for cast items, before the use of iron was developed. For uses of bronze see: *Ex. 38:8; Judg. 16:21; 1 Sam. 17:5-6; 2 Sam. 8:8; 22:35; 1 Kings 7:14-16; 2 Kings 16:14-17; Job 20:24; Ps. 107:16; Jer. 52:17; Mark 7:4.* (See *furnace* for list of related words.)

brook. A small stream that flows only during the rainy seasons and dries up in summer, today called a wadi. *2 Sam. 15:22-23; John 18:1; 1 Kings 17:3; 18:40.*

Brook of Egypt. A boundary line between Canaan and Egypt in O.T. times. *Num. 34:2-5; Josh. 15:1, 4; 1 Kings 8:65; 2 Kings 24:7.* (See map Plate III, F-3 — River of Egypt.)

buckler. A shield. The two words, often used together, do not represent different kinds of shields, although two different types were used in O.T. times. *2 Chron. 14:8; Ps. 91:4.* (See *shield* for description; *armor.*)

bulwark. Wall for protection and defense. *Ps. 8:2; Isa. 26:1; Jer. 50:15; 51:32; 1 Tim. 3:15.* (See *fortified city* and *wall* for general description.)

bushel. In the N.T., a container used to measure dry substances, equal to about three tenths of the modern bushel. *Matt. 5:15.*

C

Caesar (sē'zər). In N.T. times, a title given to the Roman emperor; used with names, as Caesar Augustus, or as a symbol of the Roman Government. *Luke 2:1; Matt. 22:15-22.* The title was the family name of Julius Caesar, the forerunner of the emperors. After him, all emperors added Caesar to their own names. Caesars who appear in the N.T. are: Caesar Augustus, Tiberius Caesar, Claudius. (See *Rome* for list of words related to government.)

appeal to Caesar. Roman citizenship, which Paul possessed, included the right to ask for a trial in Rome. *Acts 25:10-12, 21, 25.*

Caesar's household. People employed as servants of the emperor in Rome. *Phil. 4:22.*

Caesar Augustus (sē'sər ə gŭs'təs). Roman emperor at the time of Jesus' birth. His rule began in 31 B.C. He was the first emperor; the Romans had formerly had a republican form of government. *Luke 2:1.* (See *Caesar; Rome;* Time Line.)

Caesarea (sĕs'ə rē'ə). A city in N.T. times on the east coast of the Mediterranean Sea. It was built by the first " Herod the king " in typical Greek style, and named for Caesar Augustus. The Roman governors, such as Pontius Pilate, had their headquarters there, and a cohort of the Roman Army was stationed in the garrison. *Acts 8:40; chs. 10; 23:23-24.* (See *city,* in N.T. times; map Plate XV, F-4.)

Caesarea Philippi (sĕs'ə rē'ə fĭ'ə-pī). N.T. city north of the Sea of Galilee near Mt. Hermon, a center for worship of the Roman god Pan. The tetrarch of the area, Philip, rebuilt the city and renamed it for Tiberius Caesar and for himself. *Matt. 16:13.* (See map Plate XIV, D-2.)

Caiaphas (kā'ə fəs), Joseph. N.T. high priest appointed by the Roman governor in A.D. 18 to replace Annas. *Matt. 26:3; Luke 3:2; John 11:47-50; 18:13-14; Acts 4:6.*

Cain (kān). Son of Adam. Cain,

who was a farmer, murdered his brother and was sent into exile. *Gen. 4:1-16; 1 John 3:11-12; Jude 11.* (See *Genesis* for general background.) Others.

camel. Animal used as a means of travel, and as a beast of burden in merchant caravans. Its milk was used; and cloth was woven from its hair, chiefly for tents, sometimes for clothing. *Gen. 30:43; 32:13-15* (it is uncertain whether camels were used as early as the time of Abraham); *Judg. 6:5; 1 Kings 10:1-2; 2 Kings 8:9; Isa. 30:6; Mark 1:6.*

camp. The temporary community set up by the Israelites on their journey from Egypt to Canaan, or the dwelling place of an army in the field. The Israelites under Moses probably set up their tents in a circle for protection. An ideal arrangement is described in *Num., ch. 2.* See also *1 Sam. 4:3; 2 Kings 7:7.*

Cana (kā'nə). A village in N.T. times in the division of Galilee, about eight miles north of Nazareth. The disciple Nathanael was from Cana. *John 2:1-11; 4:46-54; 21:2.* (See map Plate XIV, C-3.)

Canaan (kā'nən). In O.T. times, the area bounded by the Mediterranean Sea on the west and the Jordan River on the east, and by the nations of Egypt to the south and Syria to the north. Often called Palestine, the area today includes the countries of Israel and Lebanon, and part of Jordan. In the time of Abraham, Canaan was under the control of Egypt. When the Israelites conquered it, there were **Canaanites** and numerous other peoples living there, organized into city-states, each city with its own king. The chief Canaanite god was Baal, and the lesser gods were known as Baals. After the Israelites conquered Canaan, some Canaanites remained; some were put to forced labor. Many of them migrated to the area called Phoenicia to mingle eventually with the people there. *Gen. 12:5; Num. 13:17-20, 25-29; Josh. 14:1; Judg. 1:28-29; Matt. 15:22.* (See map Plate III, G-2.)

Canaan can be divided into three areas running north and south, widely different from each other in geography and climate. On the west, bordering the Mediterranean Sea, are the plains of the coast, fertile, low-lying lands; on the eastern border of the coastal plains is the Shephelah, foothills country. The second north-south area is the hill country, rocky mountains rising to heights of three thousand feet above sea level. This area was the main theater of events in both the Old and New Testaments. To the east, the third strip is the Jordan River valley, starting at the Sea of Galilee to the north and ending in the Dead Sea to the south. Much of this area lies below sea level and consists of lowlands along the meandering river. The area east of the Jordan River, a region of high plains bordering on the desert, was largely occupied by other peoples in O.T. times, although parts of it belonged to the Israelites from time to time. To the south of Canaan are two desert (wilderness) areas: the Negeb to the west, and the Arabah, a continuation of the Jordan River valley, to the south. (See map Plate I – Palestine. See, for further information, *Arabah; coast; Galilee, Sea of; hill country; Jordan; Negeb; Salt Sea; Shephelah.*)

Capernaum (kə pûr'nĭ əm). N.T. town on the Sea of Galilee. There was a Roman military post there, and a tax collector was stationed on the important east-west highway that passed through the town. It was the home of the disciples Andrew and Peter. Jesus made Capernaum his headquarters. *Matt. 4:12-13; 8:5-13; Mark 2:1, 14; John 6:24.* (See map Plate XIV, D-3.)

Cappadocia (kăp'ə dō'shə). In N.T. times, a province of the Roman Empire, east of Galatia, in what is now the country of Turkey. *Acts 2:9; 1 Peter 1:1.* (See map Plate XV, G-3.)

captain of the temple. In the N.T., a priest in charge of the temple guards who served as watchmen and as a police force. *Luke 22:3-6; Acts 4:1; 5:24.*

captivity. Usually, in the O.T., the exile of the Judeans in Babylon in the sixth century B.C. *2 Kings 24:15; Ezra 3:8; Neh. 8:17.* Also with its usual meaning. (See, for description, *deportation; exile.*)

caravan. A group of people traveling together, especially traders with pack animals — asses or camels — transporting goods from one area to another. They traveled over caravan routes that crisscrossed the ancient world. The cargo was often spices. Some towns, such as Haran, were caravan stops offering rough shelter and markets. In some cases, local merchants supplied accommodations. *Gen. 37:25; Judg. 5:6; 8:11; Job 6:18-19; Isa. 21:13.* (See *highway; inn; merchant; spices; trade.*)

carbuncle. A gem in O.T. times, the nature of which is uncertain; perhaps an emerald or a ruby. *Ex. 28:17; Isa. 54:12; Ezek. 28:13.*

Carmel, Mount (kär'məl). A ridge or range of hills about fifteen miles in length that juts into the eastern Mediterranean Sea, dividing the coastal plain of Canaan into two parts. In O.T. times it was a fertile, cultivated area. On this mountain the prophet Elijah held a contest with the priests of Baal. *1 Sam. 15:12; 1 Kings 18:17-46; Isa. 35:2; Amos 1:2.* (See map Plate I, B-3.)

carpenter. Builder of farm tools,

Palestinian carpenter

such as plows, yokes, threshing sledges; of furniture, such as beds and benches; of parts of houses; and of boats. Some carpenter tools are listed in *Isa. 10:15* and *44:13*, in the latter case used in making idols. Tools of early Bible times, such as axes and hammers, were made of stone, later of metal. The tools of a carpenter in N.T. times would have been similar to those used today. *2 Sam. 5:11; Matt. 13:53-56; Mark 6:3.*

cart. Usually a box mounted on two wheels; sometimes the wheels were solid wood. Used to carry persons, goods, army supplies, grain to the threshing floor, and the like. Oxen and asses, sometimes men, were used to draw carts. Same as wagon. *1 Sam. 6:7-14; 2 Sam. 6:3; Isa. 5:18; Amos 2:13.*

cassia. Sweet-smelling bark of a tree, somewhat like cinnamon; used as a spice. *Ex. 30:23-25; Ps. 45:8; Ezek. 27:18-19.*

cast lots. Frequently used way of making decisions. The allotments of land for the tribes taking over Canaan were made by casting lots. *Josh. 14:1-2; 18:6.* The lot was cast to find a guilty person, *1 Sam. 14:41-42; Jonah 1:7;* to settle an argument, *Prov. 18:18;* to choose attendants in the temple, *1 Chron. 24:5;* and, in the N.T., it was cast to choose someone to replace Judas, *Acts 1:15-26.* An explanation of what was believed about the casting of lots is given in *Prov. 16:33.* (See *inquire of God; lot; Urim and Thummim.*)

cattle. In the O.T., domesticated animals in general, including sheep, goats, oxen, asses, cows, camels. *Gen. 1:24* (animals in general); *2:20; 13:2; 31:17-18; Ps. 50:10; John 4:12.*

census. In O.T. times, a counting or numbering of the Israelites for taxing or for military service. Only men over twenty years of age were listed, by their tribes and families. *Ex. 30:12-14; Num. 1:2-3; 2 Chron. 2:17* (another kind of census). In *Ezra, ch. 2,* there is an example of a census, typical of many lists of names and families given in the O.T. (See *enrollment,* including information about census-taking in N.T. times. See also *genealogy; register.*)

centurion (sĕn tyŏŏr'ĭ ən). In the N.T., a Roman Army officer in charge of a division of one hundred men, part of a battalion, or cohort. His duties included guarding prisoners and overseeing executions. *Matt. 8:5; Mark 15:39; Acts 10:1; 21:32; 27:1.* (See *Rome* for list of words related to army.)

Cephas (sē'fəs). A name given to the disciple Simon Peter by Jesus. Cephas was an Aramaic name; Peter was a Greek name. Both mean "rock." *John 1:42; 1 Cor. 1:12; 9:5; Gal. 2:11.* (See *Peter.*)

chaff. The husks of grain separated in threshing and blown away in the process of winnowing. *Ps. 1:4; Zeph. 2:2; Matt. 3:12.* (See *harvest* for list of words related to harvesting processes.)

Chaldeans (kăl dē'ənz). One of the O.T. peoples of the area between the Tigris and Euphrates Rivers. They overcame the Assyrians and took over their empire in the seventh century B.C. The Chaldeans made Babylon the capital of their empire. It was the Chaldeans (often referred to as the "king of Babylon") under Nebuchadnezzar who conquered Jerusalem and took the Judeans into exile. The Chaldeans founded the science of astronomy and from their observations figured the length of a solar year within thirty minutes of modern calculations. The Chaldean empire was taken over by the Persians. *Gen. 11:31; 2 Kings 24:1-2; 2 Chron. 36:17-21; Jer. 24:5; Acts 7:2-4.* (See *nations; Time Line;* map Plate IX — see legend: "Babylonian empire.")

chamberlain. An officer of a king's court in charge of the private rooms of a palace; similar to eunuch and steward. *2 Kings 23:11; Esth. 1:10; Acts 12:20.* (See *eunuch; steward.*)

champion. Occasionally in O.T. times, instead of carrying out full-scale war, each side appointed representatives to hold a contest. *1 Sam. 17:4-54;* also *2 Sam. 2:12-17.*

chariot. A two-wheeled horse-drawn vehicle used in war and by kings and royal officers. The body of the chariot was high in front and open at the back, and the wheels were placed toward the back. The occupants, a driver and a warrior, stood. The chariot allowed for rapid maneuvering and gave a great military advantage over troops on foot. David first equipped the Israelite army with chariots, but it was Solomon who made full use of them. He established a number of chariot cities, such as Megiddo, in which troops and horses were quartered. The armies of the later kingdoms of Judah and Israel used chariots for a time. *Gen. 41:41-43* (Egyptian records show that this means that Joseph was second in command to the Pharaoh); *Ex. 14:5-9; 2 Sam. 8:4* ("horsemen" means chariot troops); *1 Kings 10:26; 22:29-35.* (See *bow; horse.*)

cherub (chĕr'əb); **cherubim,** pl. A mythological being in the religion of the Canaanites and of other O.T. nations. The cherub had the body of a bull, the head of a man, and was winged. Such figures were placed at palace and temple doorways or used as supports for thrones. They were believed to speak to the gods on behalf of men. Cherubim were adapted by the Israelites as symbols of God's presence and of God as king over the people. For example, cherubim supported the ark, because it was considered to be God's throne. *Ex. 25:18-22; Num. 7:89; 1 Kings 6:29* (the house of God built by Solomon); *Heb. 9:1-5.* (See *enthroned.*)

chief priests. In N.T. times, the high priest currently in office and the former high priests, all of whom were appointed by the Roman rulers. *Matt. 2:4; 20:18.* (See *Annas; Caiaphas.*)

children of God. N.T. term for the people of God, similar to the usage of

" sons of God " in the O.T. See *Hos. 1:10.* " Son of God " in the N.T. is used for Jesus Christ; " children of God " is used for his followers, who were the new people of God, replacing Israel. *John 1:12; Rom. 8:15-16; Phil. 2:15; 1 John 5:2.*

Chorazin (kō rā′zĭn). A city of N.T. times two miles north of Capernaum, inland from the Sea of Galilee. One of the towns that did not respond to Jesus' work. *Matt. 11:20-24; Luke 10:13-15.* (See map Plate XIV, D-3.)

Christ, meaning "the anointed one" or " Messiah." A title given by Jews of N.T. times to the coming king, and applied to Jesus by his followers. It soon became linked with his given name and was used like a name. *Matt. 1:17-18; Mark 8:29; John 1:41; 10:24; Acts 2:36; Rom. 9:4-5; Col. 2:6.* (See *anoint; Messiah.*)

Christians, meaning "Christ's men." A name used by pagans for members of the early church, probably at first in derision. Christians called themselves brethren, disciples, saints, those who believed or believers, or (persons) of the Way. *Acts 11:26; 26:28; 1 Peter 4:16.*

Chronicles, The First and Second Books of the, meaning "events of the past." O.T. books written by the same author, originally one book. They continue the history of Israel told in the books from Genesis to Kings, relating events in the reigns of David and Solomon, and in the history of the Southern Kingdom, Judah. The au-thor, known as the Chronicler, compiled other books in the O.T. Events related in the Chronicles are also covered in 2 Samuel and in 1 and 2 Kings from a different point of view. The Chronicler wrote from a priestly point of view, which means that he stressed things having to do with worship. The books were probably compiled in the fourth century B.C. Other chronicles not included in the Bible are mentioned, such as the one in *2 Chron. 33:19.*

church. In the N.T., the community of persons committed to Jesus Christ. The Greek word used in the N.T. means " a gathering of people called together for a purpose." Sometimes used to mean a group in one place, as in *Acts 8:1; 1 Cor. 1:2;* also to mean a wider community made up of churches at several places, as in *Acts 9:31* or *Eph. 3:21.* (See Time Line.)
For some of the officers in the early churches, see the following (they were probably not officers in the modern sense, but leaders of different types; little is known definitely about their duties or positions in the churches): *apostle; bishop; deacon; elder* (church); *evangelist; minister,* in N.T. times; *pastor; Teacher.*
For worship and customs, see: *baptize; break bread; distribution; lay hands on,* in N.T. times; *Lord's supper; tongues; worship* (church).
For names used for members of the church, see list under *Christians.*

Cilicia (sĭ lĭsh′ə). In N.T. times a district in the southeastern part of what is now the country of Turkey. The main town was Tarsus. Goat's-hair cloth was one of the chief products of Cilicia. *Acts 6:8-9; 15:41; 22:3; Gal. 1:21.* (See map Plate XV, G-3.)

circumcise. To cut off the foreskin. Many ancient peoples practiced circumcision. Among the Israelites it was considered a symbol of covenant between God and his people. *Gen. 17:9-27; Lev. 12:3; Deut. 30:6; Jer. 4:4; Luke 2:21; Acts 15:1-35.*
The **circumcised** in the N.T. refers to Jews or Jewish Christians. *Acts 10:45; Gal. 2:7.* (See *uncircumcised.*)

cistern. In O.T. times, used to store rainwater from roofs or water from a nearby spring. The use of plaster, discovered about the time the Israelites conquered Canaan, made it possible for them to build cisterns and thus occupy the hill country in which the Canaanites had not settled. Cisterns were dug in earth or rock to a depth of twenty feet, and the insides plastered. Usually the opening was narrower than the bottom. *2 Kings 18:31; Isa. 30:14; Jer. 38:6.* (See *water* for list of related words.)

citadel. Fortress, usually within a

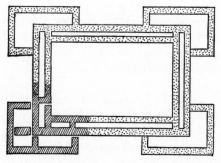

Citadel of Saul, excavated at Gibeah

city, often adjoining a palace in O.T. times. A citadel dating from the time of Saul has been excavated north of Jerusalem. The rectangular building was constructed with double walls made of stone, with a tower at each corner. It was probably also the king's home. The Tower of Antonia in Jerusalem, built in O.T. times, is an example of a citadel. *1 Kings 16:18; 2 Kings 15:25; Ps. 48:3, 13.* (See *barracks; garrison; stronghold* [three words with the same meaning]. See also *tower;* map Plate XVI, D-4 — Tower of Antonia.)

city. In the O.T., usually means a walled city in contrast to an unwalled village. ("Town" means either village or city.) Cities were built on hills to make possible defense from sudden attack. Most of the Israelite cities were ones that they had taken from the Canaanites. City streets were narrow and unpaved. The outer walls of houses adjoined the streets without sidewalks or lawns. Cities furnished markets, and in time of war, refuge, for the people in surrounding areas. Making provision for water, especially for sources that could be used in time of siege, was very important. *Num. 13:17-20; Deut. 3:5; Judg. 20:15; 1 Kings 16:23-24; 20:34.*
cities of the priests. Cities given to the Levites, who were not assigned portions of Canaan. They were also cities of refuge. *Num., ch. 35; 2 Chron. 31:15.*
royal cities. Capitals or cities where kings lived or had lived. *Josh. 10:2; 1 Sam. 27:5.* (See, for other special types of cities, *chariot; fortified city; refuge, cities of; store-cities.* For other

details, see, *citadel; gate; market place; square of the city; wall.*)

In N.T. times, Greek and Roman cities, such as Caesarea, were planned cities, with a broad street from gate to gate, a theater, and a central market place. Areas such as the Areopagus in Athens, *Acts 17:19,* and the theater at Ephesus, *Acts 19:28-29,* were typical.

city of David. O.T. name given to the Jebusite stronghold captured by David's men, also called Zion, which David made his residence. *2 Sam. 5:6-9; Neh. 3:15.* (See map Plate XVI, E-7.)
In the N.T., means Bethlehem. *Luke 2:11.*

Claudius (klô'dĭ əs). Roman emperor whose rule began in A.D. 41. He banished Jews from the city of Rome. *Acts 11:28; 17:6-7* (the Caesar referred to); *18:2.* (See *Caesar; Rome; Time Line.*)

Claudius Lysias (klô'dĭ əs lis'ĭ əs). Commander of the Roman soldiers stationed in the barracks at Jerusalem in the time of Paul. He is the tribune in *Acts 21:30 to 23:30.*

clean. In O.T. times some things were declared unclean; for example, certain animals were not to be eaten, and there was to be no contact with anything dead. Things not listed as unclean were clean. *Gen. 7:2; Lev. 10:10; 22:6-7.* Contact with unclean things meant that a person was defiled or unclean and must **cleanse** himself by washing or by special rituals of purification to be clean again.

In N.T. times the Pharisees had fanatical ideas about cleansing, of which Jesus was critical. *Mark 7:1-8, 14-23.*

cloak. An outer garment worn over the coat. Usually a large square of cloth falling to the knees, or longer, and having short sleeves. The ends were called skirts. For many people the cloak was also their only bedcover. *Deut. 22:12; 24:10-13; Jer. 43:12; Matt. 5:40; 1 Thess. 2:5.* (See *coat* for information about other clothing. See also *mantle* and *robe,* words with the same meaning.)

coast. One of the main geographical divisions of Canaan, the eastern coast of the Mediterranean Sea; considered in O.T. times the western boundary of the land given to the Israelites, but seldom possessed by them. The southern portion was occupied by the Philistines and, in later times, the Phoenicians commanded the northern area. Except in the north, at Tyre and Sidon, there were few seaports. Though narrow in width, the area was level and fertile, offering good land for agriculture. *Num. 34:6; Josh. 9:1; Judg. 5:17.* (See *Canaan* for description of main geographical areas; map Plate I.)

coastlands. Areas relatively distant from Canaan, the islands and shores of the Mediterranean Sea. *Ps. 97:1; Isa. 41:1; Jer. 31:10.*

coat. Long shirt or tunic worn under other clothing by both men and women. In early O.T. times the garment covered one shoulder and extended to the knees. Later it was more

Asiatic people migrating into Egypt, from an Egyptian wall painting, c. 1900 B.C., showing clothing of people in the time of the patriarchs

like a shirt with short sleeves. It was held in at the waist by a girdle. The coat was the basic garment, equivalent to underwear today, although often workers stripped off cloaks and worked in their coats. *Lev. 16:4; 2 Sam. 15:32; Matt. 5:40; Luke 3:11; Acts 9:39.* (See, for other pieces of clothing, *apron; cloak; festal garments; fringe; gird; girdle; mantle; robe; sandals; shoes; skirt; swaddling; tunic; veil; waistcloth.*)

The clothing of men and women was much alike except for the veil, worn only by women. The items described under the listed entries are more or less typical of all Bible times. Fashions in dress did change, but much more slowly than in modern times. They tended, rather, to stay the same.

cohort. A division of the Roman Army in N.T. times, also called battalion. Cohorts were usually stationed in outlying parts of the Empire to guard the frontiers. In Jerusalem the cohort's headquarters was the Tower of Antonia. The names of two cohorts are given in *Acts 10:1* and *27:1.* (See *barracks.* See *Rome* for list of words about the Roman Army.)

Colossae (kə lŏs'ĭ). N.T. city in the area of Phrygia, part of what is the country of Turkey today. Located on a trade route from Ephesus to the inland, Colossae was noted for wool products. *Col. 1:2.* Names of some of the members of the church there are given in *Col. 1:7; 4:9, 12, 17; Philemon 2.* (See map Plate XV, E-3.)

Colossians, The Letter of Paul to the (kə lŏsh'ənz). N.T. book, a letter written by Paul, probably when a prisoner in Rome around A.D. 62, to the church at Colossae (also to the church at Laodicea, *ch. 4:16*). It was de-

45

livered by Tychicus and Onesimus, possibly along with the letter to Philemon. False teachers had been misleading the Colossians, and Paul wrote to correct their ideas.

commandment. An order from someone in authority. *Gen. 26:5; Ex. 34:32; Deut. 4:13; 2 Chron. 29:25; Ps. 112:1.* Often used with " statutes " and " ordinances," as in *Deut. 7:11.*
In the N.T., the word refers to the ten commandments as the heart of God's commands to men. *Matt. 5:19; 15:3-4; Mark 10:17-19; 12:28-31; Rom. 13:9.* (See *law* for related words.)

common. In addition to the usual meanings, such as " shared " or " ordinary," the word was used for the opposite of " holy " or to mean unclean. *Lev. 10:10; 1 Sam. 21:4; Ezek. 22:26; Acts 10:14-15, 28.*

concubine. In O.T. times, when men married several wives, a female servant who also bore children by the master. A good example is Hagar, *Gen. 16:1-3.* See also *2 Sam. 5:13.* (See *family.*)

conduit. Underground tunnel, cut in rock, to carry water to a city. It was part of the arrangements for water supply, which was of great importance to cities in O.T. times. *2 Kings 18:17; Isa. 7:3.* Among archaeological finds in Jerusalem is the conduit from water sources outside the city to the pool of Siloam, made under the orders of Hezekiah, king of the Southern Kingdom, Judah. *2 Kings 20:20.* The pick marks of the diggers can still be seen on the walls of the tunnel. An inscription in the wall near the Siloam end, evidently made on completion of the work, tells how the workmen dug from both ends and met underground with only a slight discrepancy between the two diggings. Hezekiah ordered the tunnel dug as preparation for possible siege of the city. (See *water* for list of related words.)

confess. In the O.T., and also occasionally in the N.T., to acknowledge sin. *Ezra 10:11; Ps. 32:5; Mark 1:5; Acts 19:18.* Usually in the N.T., to declare or affirm that something is true. *John 9:22; Rom. 10:9; Phil. 2:11; Heb. 4:14; 1 John 2:23; 4:15.*

congregation. All the Israelites, especially referring to the time of Moses. *Ex. 12:3; 16:1-2; Lev. 4:13; Josh. 22:16; Acts 7:38.* Occasionally an assembly, as in *Ps. 22:22.*

consecrate. To set apart, or sanctify, for holy use, at times by means of a ritual such as anointing. *Ex. 29:36; Lev. 20:7; Deut. 15:19; 1 Sam. 16:5; 2 Chron. 7:7; John 17:19.*

convocation. In the O.T., usually a **holy convocation,** a gathering of the Israelites for worship on a sabbath or a feast day. Also called a solemn assembly. *Lev. 23:3-8; Num. 28:16-18, 26.*

copper. Widely used metal in O.T. times, especially before the use of iron became widespread. Used for utensils, weapons, and the like, often in the alloy bronze. Part of the commercial expansion of Solomon's time consisted of the development of copper mines and refineries in the Arabah. *Deut. 8:9; Job 28:2; Ezek. 24:11.* (See *furnace* for list of words related to production of metals.)

copper coin. Smallest coin of N.T. times, equal to about one eighth of a cent. It was probably a Jewish coin issued a century before the time of Christ. *Mark 12:42; Luke 12:59; 21:2.* (See *money*, in N.T. times.)

cor (kōr). An O.T. unit of measure for liquids, approximately sixty gallons in our measurements. The cor was equivalent to the dry measure called the homer. *1 Kings 5:11; Ezek. 45:14.* The following table shows the relationship between different liquid measures.

> 12 logs = 1 hin
> 6 hins = 1 bath
> 10 baths = 1 cor

coriander. An herb. Its small white seeds were used for seasoning foods, as we use caraway seeds today; used also for medicine. *Ex. 16:31; Num. 11:7.*

Corinth (kôr'ĭnth). A Greek city of N.T. times, capital of the Roman province of Achaia, now in the country of Greece. Corinth was an important commercial city. From its port, ships were hauled overland to the western shores of the isthmus, thus saving many sea miles. The city was noted for its nightclubs. The place where Paul was probably tried has been excavated. It was an open square with benches around it, located in the market place. *Acts 18:1-18; 1 Cor. 1:2; 2 Cor. 1:1.* (See map Plate XV, D-3.)

Corinthians, The First and Second Letters of Paul to the (kə rĭn'thĭ ənz). Two N.T. books made up of three or four letters from Paul to the church at Corinth. They were written probably around A.D. 57, when Paul was in Ephesus, and take up problems that faced a Gentile church, such as: what to do about contacts with pagans; how to conduct worship.

couch. In the O.T., a bed. *2 Sam. 11:2, 13; Job 17:13; Ps. 6:6; Amos 3:12.* (See *bed*.)

couched, *v.* Lying down, especially in concealment. *Gen. 4:7; Num. 24:9; Ezek. 19:2.*

council. In the N.T., the governing body of the Jews, the central council or senate in Jerusalem; also, local councils in other communities. The senate consisted of seventy members; the majority of them were Sadducees, but there were also Pharisees and scribes. The high priest presided. The council could decide on death for an accused person, but the execution had to be carried out by Roman authorities. *Matt. 26:59; Luke 22:66; John 11:47; Acts 5:21; 6:12; 22:30.* Local councils are mentioned in *Matt. 5:22* and *Mark 13:9.*

counselor. An officer in a king's court, an adviser; probably next in power to the king. *2 Sam. 15:12; 1 Chron. 27:32; Isa. 9:6; John 14:16.*

courier. Messenger for a king, traveling on foot or on horseback. Some ancient empires had well-developed courier systems, which were used only for royal edicts and letters.

2 Chron. 30:6, 10; Esth. 3:13.

covenant. An agreement between two persons (or more), or between God and man. For covenants between men, see *Gen. 21:27; Deut. 7:2; 1 Sam. 18:3; 1 Kings 20:34.* The covenant between God and his people, Israel, is the subject of the O.T. In *Jer. 7:23* there is an explanation of this covenant. See also *Gen. 17:1-7; Ex. 19:5; Deut. 5:2; Jer. 31:31-34; Matt. 26:27-28; 1 Cor. 11:25; Eph. 2:12.* The word " testament," as in Old or New Testament, means covenant. *2 Cor. 3:14.*

covet. To desire strongly or to fulfill one's desires in a way that disrupts relationships among men or the relationship with God. See *Eph. 5:5* for one explanation. *Ex. 20:17; Micah 2:2; Mark 7:21-22; Rom. 7:7.*

craftsman. A skilled worker such as a jeweler, dyer, potter, carpenter, wood or ivory carver, goldsmith or silversmith, worker in leather, basket maker, rug maker, or tentmaker. At least in early O.T. times, much work was done at home or in a street shop adjoining a house. In later times there is some evidence of guilds of workers, and streets or even towns in which several workers of one craft lived and worked. *1 Chron. 22:15; 2 Chron. 2:13-14; Jer. 29:2; Hos. 13:2; Acts 19:24.*

creation. God's act of calling the world and life into existence. *Gen. 2:3; Isa. 40:26, 28* (**created,** and **Creator** as a name for God). The word is used chiefly in the N.T., where it also means that which God created. *Mark 10:6; 13:19; Rom. 1:20; 8:19-23, 39; Gal. 6:15; Col. 1:15.*
Although the stories of creation (two stories in *Gen.*, *chs. 1 and 2*) come first in the Bible, the O.T. people knew God first and primarily as the One who saved them and entered into covenant with them. Only later did they develop the understanding of God as creator of all the world. Other accounts of creation are given in parts of *Job; The Psalms; Isa.*, *ch. 40.* (See *Adam; Genesis.*)

creditor. One who makes a loan. In O.T. times Israelites were to lend to their brothers without interest, but they did take something in pledge, or a third person offered surety. At intervals, all debts were supposed to be canceled. Yet in some cases, creditors took the debtor or his children into slavery when the debt was not paid. *Ex. 22:25; Deut. 15:2; 2 Kings 4:1.*
In N.T. times Roman law allowed a creditor to have his debtor sent to jail for nonpayment. *Luke 7:41.*

cross. A stake or pole set upright in the ground with a crosspiece attached to make a T or X shape, on which a condemned person was hung to die. *Mark 15:21-24; John 19:17-19.*
In N.T. letters, often means the suffering and death of Christ. *1 Cor. 1:17-18; Gal. 6:14; Eph. 2:16.* (See *crucify.*)

crucify. In N.T. times, to execute by nailing to a cross. Crucifixion was used by many ancient nations. The Romans used it for slaves and foreigners, but not for citizens of the Empire. The condemned person was scourged before carrying his cross to the place of execution, usually outside the city. Death from starvation and thirst was usually slow. *Matt. 20:17-19; 27:22-23, 26.* (See *Golgotha.*)

cubit. A unit of measurement for length, based on the distance from the tip of the middle finger to the elbow, or two spans, about eighteen inches. *Gen. 6:15; Ex. 25:10; 1 Sam. 17:4; Matt. 6:27.* The following table shows measurements of length used in both O.T. and N.T. times.

4 fingers = 1 handbreadth
3 handbreadths = 1 span
2 spans = 1 cubit

cult prostitute. A woman, or sometimes a man, who engaged in sexual intercourse as a part of the official worship of some of the gods, Canaanite and others, of the O.T. nations. *Deut. 23:17; 1 Kings 14:23-24; Hos. 4:14.* (See *high places.*)

cummin. A spice. The seeds of the cummin plant were used for seasoning food in the way that poppy seed is used today. *Isa. 28:25, 27; Matt. 23:23.*

cup. Usually shallow, bowl-like, and handleless; made of pottery or metal and used for water or wine. *Gen. 40:21; 2 Sam. 12:3; Jer. 25:15; Matt. 26:27; Mark 9:41.*
Also used figuratively with abstract words to mean something one experiences, as **cup of salvation** in *Ps. 116:13.* See also *Isa. 51:17; Ezek. 23:33; Mark 10:38.*

cupbearer. An officer of a royal court who served the king's wine. He was often a person of considerable importance, and had administrative duties beyond those of waiting on table. Originally the duty of the cupbearer was to test the wine so that no one could poison the king. *2 Chron. 9:3-4; Neh. 2:1.*

curds. Goat's milk churned with clots from a previous churning. Milk was used only in the form of cheese or curds. *Gen. 18:8; Judg. 5:25; 2 Sam. 17:29; Isa. 7:21-22.*

curse. To express a wish that evil will come upon a person; the opposite of bless. In ancient times, words were believed to have power; thus a curse was not thought of as an idle wish but was considered to be almost magical. *Ex. 22:28; Deut. 27:15-26; Josh. 6:26; Judg. 21:18; Gal. 3:10.* (See *God, or gods, do so to me and more also; oath.*)

custodian. In Roman households of N.T. times, a slave who accompanied a boy to and from school until he was sixteen years old. *Gal. 3:24.*

Cyprus (sī'prəs). In N.T. times, an island in the Mediterranean Sea off the coast of Syria, and a province of the Roman Empire. The island bears the same name today. Timber and copper were the chief products. *Acts 4:36; 11:19-20; 13:2-4; 15:39; 21:16; 27:4.* (See map Plate XV, F-4.)

Cyrene (sī rē'nĭ). In N.T. times, a city in northern Africa in the area then called Libya. *Matt. 27:32; Acts 2:10; 6:9; 11:20; 13:1.* (See map Plate XV, D-4.)

49

Cyrus (sī'rəs). Ruler of the Persian empire, which he founded when his forces overcame the Chaldeans at Babylon in the sixth century B.C. He called himself " king of the world." Cyrus reversed the policy of deportation practiced by the Assyrians and Chaldeans, and sent back to their own lands any of the deportees who wanted to return. *2 Chron. 36:22-23; Ezra 1:1; 4:3-5; Isa. 44:28; 45:1-14.* (See Time Line.)

D

Damascus (də măs'kəs). A city in Syria, one of the oldest in the world, located on three important caravan routes of the ancient world. In the time of David and Solomon, Damascus was the center of an Aramean kingdom and was a rival of Israel. Like Samaria, it was captured by the Assyrians in the eighth century B.C. In N.T. times it was in the Roman province of Syria. There were Christians in Damascus from very early times. *2 Sam. 8:5-6; 1 Kings 20:34; 2 Kings 16:10-17; Acts 9:1-2, 19b-25; Gal. 1:17.* (See, for O.T. times, map Plates II, E-3; V, D-3. See, for N.T. times, map Plate XV, G-4.)

Dan (dăn). One of the twelve sons of Jacob; also the tribe descended from him, **Danites,** and the territory they occupied. This area, including the town of Gezer, was only partly occupied by the Danites, who pushed north to the area around a town they renamed Dan. *Gen. 30:5-6; Num. 1:38-39; Josh. 19:40-48; Judg. 13:2.* (See map Plate IV, B-5 [the tribal territory], D-2 [the town].)

Dan (dăn). O.T. town in the northern part of Canaan below Mt. Hermon. It was considered the northern limit of the area given to the Israelites, and received its name from the tribe of Dan, which captured it. The phrase **from Dan to Beer-sheba** means the length of the land. *Gen. 14:14; Judg. 18:27-29; 1 Sam. 3:20; 1 Kings 12:26-30; 1 Chron. 21:2.* (See map Plate IV, D-2.)

dance. In O.T. times, performed by women on joyous occasions, such as the welcome for a victorious fighter and harvest festivals, or as a part of worhip. *Ex. 15:20; Judg. 21:16-21; 1 Sam. 18:6-7; 2 Sam. 6:14-15; Ps. 149:3.*

Daniel, The Book of. O.T. book written by an unknown author during the Greek rule over the Jews (about 168 B.C.) to encourage the faithful to have hope in the eventual triumph of God in history. The setting of the book is the time of the exile. The stories and visions in it comprise a type of secret language intended to make sense to those who would read them as symbols of persons and powers in the history of that time. Such writing is called " apocalyptic " (meaning " revealing "), and is represented in the Bible by the books of Daniel and The Revelation. *Matt. 24:15.* Others.

daric (dăr'ək). A gold coin of the Persian empire in O.T. times, equal to about five dollars; named for the emperor Darius. *1 Chron. 29:7* (darics were not in use in David's time, but were familiar to the writer many years later); *Ezra 2:68-69; Neh. 7:70.* (See *money.*)

Darius (də rī'əs). King of the Persian empire whose reign began about 522 B.C. In general history, Darius is known for his attempt to make Greece a part of his empire and his defeat at the battle of Marathon. *Ezra 4:4-5; Hag. 1:1; Zech. 1:7.* The Darius in The Book of Daniel is another person and has not been identified with certainty as any historical person. (See Time Line.)

David (dā'vǐd), meaning "beloved." The second king of Israel, about 1000 B.C., who enlarged the kingdom, moved the capital to Jerusalem, and strengthened the armed forces. In later times, David was looked on as the ideal ruler who would return, or it was believed that a descendant of his would arise, to restore the kingdom of Israel. Stories in *1 Sam., ch. 16 to 1 Kings, ch. 2;* see also *Ruth 4:18-22; Jer. 30:9; Ezek. 34:23; Matt. 1:1; Luke 1:32; 2:11; Acts 2:29-36.* (See Time Line.)

day. In O.T. times, reckoned from sunrise to sunset to distinguish it from night, and divided into four general periods: sunrise, the heat of the day, the cool of the day, and sunset. Not until after the exile in Babylon did Hebrews use a twelve-hour system for dividing the day. The sabbath was the only day given a name; the others were numbered. *Gen. 3:8; 18:1; Ex. 16:1; 2 Kings 25:3; Jer. 31:35.* (See *dial; hour; watch.*)

day of the Lord. A phrase used by the prophets of O.T. times for the future time when God would be fully revealed and would judge all people.

Isa. 2:12-21; Joel 1:15; Amos 5:18-20; Zeph. 1:7.
In the N.T. it is called the **day of judgment**, *Matt. 10:15* (see *Rom. 2:16* for explanation), and the **day of the Lord Jesus,** *2 Cor. 1:14; 2 Thess. 2:2;* or the **day of Christ**, *Phil. 1:10;* or **the Day,** *1 Cor. 3:13.*

deacon; deaconess, meaning "servant." An officer in the early churches. Like the persons described in *Acts 6:1-6,* their duties probably were to care for the poor and needy. *Rom. 16:1; Phil. 1:1; 1 Tim. 3:8-12.* (See *church* for a list of some of the other officers.)

death. (See, for customs relating to burial, *anoint; embalm; mourning* [list of related words]; *sepulchre; tomb.* See, for ideas about life after death, *fell asleep; Hades; hell; immortal; Paradise; resurrection; Sheol* [and list of other O.T. words]; *slept with his fathers.* See also *necromancer.*)

Deborah (děb'ə rə). A woman who was one of the leaders of the Israelites during the time of the judges. With Barak she fought against the Canaanites. She was also called a prophetess, meaning that she was inspired by God. *Judg. 4:4-24* (stories of Deborah); *Judg., ch. 5* (the same in poetry). The fifth chapter of Judges is considered to be one of the oldest parts of the O.T., probably dating from the twelfth century B.C. (See Time Line.) Other.

debt; debtor. In O.T. times Israelites were supposed to make loans to fellow members of their tribes without making any charge. Usually the agreement was witnessed by others and a pledge was taken from the debtor, or a third person provided surety. Debts were usually repaid quickly or written off every few years, but in some cases debtors were forced to sell themselves or their children into slavery as payment. Such slavery was supposed to be ended at intervals, also. *2 Kings 4:7; Neh. 10:31; Prov. 22:26; Hab. 2:6-7.*

In N.T. times the prevailing practices were based on Roman law, which permitted seizure and imprisonment of a debtor who could not pay. *Matt. 18:23-35.*

Decapolis (dĭ kăp′ə lĭs). In N.T. times, a federation of ten cities which dominated an area mostly southeast of the Sea of Galilee; part of the Roman province of Syria. The cities were Greek, having been built or rebuilt during the time of the Greek empire. *Matt. 4:25; Mark 5:20; 7:31.* (See map Plate XIV, D-3.)

decree. A ruling by a king, made public in writing, and by proclamation and reading aloud to the people; same as edict. *2 Chron. 30:5-6; Ezra 5:13; Isa. 10:1; Luke 2:1; Acts 17:6-7.*

Dedication, feast of the. An annual celebration of the rededication of the temple in Jerusalem about 165 B.C. *John 10:22.* (See *feast.*)

defile. To make unclean. *Num. 19:20; 2 Sam. 1:21; 2 Kings 23:13; Isa. 59:3; Matt. 15:10-20; Heb. 9:13-14.*

Demas (dē′məs). Member of the early church who worked for a time with Paul, but later, perhaps, gave up his work. *Col. 4:14; 2 Tim. 4:10; Philemon 24.*

demon. In the O.T. especially, a god. *Deut. 32:17; Ps. 106:37;* also *1 Cor. 10:20.*

Usually, in the N.T., an evil or unclean spirit believed to be the cause of illness, insanity, or disaster. *Matt. 7:22; Mark 1:32; 5:2* (unclean spirit); *Luke 8:29; 11:14-15.* Demons do not appear in the Gospel of John.

demoniac. A person possessed by a demon or demons; for example, see *Mark 5:1-20.*

denarius (dĭ nâr′ĭ əs). Roman silver coin in N.T. times, worth about seventeen cents. It was sometimes a day's

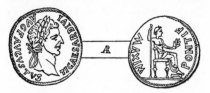

Silver denarius with image of
Tiberius Caesar

pay for a laborer. The coin bore a picture of the ruling emperor. *Matt. 18:28; 20:2; Mark 6:37; 14:5.* The denarius is the coin in *Matt. 22:15-22.* (See *money*, in N.T. times.)

deportation. A common practice of empires in O.T. times, especially of the Assyrians and the Chaldeans, was to remove conquered peoples from their homelands and to replace them with peoples deported from other places. Described in *2 Kings 17:6, 24.* In *Matt. 1:11-12,* " deportation " means exile of the Jew in O.T. times in Babylon. (See *captivity; exile.*)

Derbe (dûr'bĭ). City in N.T. times in the Roman province of Galatia; often mentioned with Lystra. Paul visited the city twice. *Acts 14:5-6, 20; 16:1; 20:4.* (See map Plate XV, F-3.)

destroyer. A personification of destruction or death, similar to a modern way of speaking of death as the Grim Reaper. *Ex. 12:23; Job 15:21; Jer. 15:8; 1 Cor. 10:10.*

Deuteronomy (doo'tə rŏn'ə mĭ), meaning " second law." An O.T. book written in the form of a speech by Moses. Like many O.T. books, it was formed from numerous writings and traditions, some of which had been in existence long before they were incorporated into a book. Parts of Deuteronomy are probably the book that was found in the temple in the time of Josiah, 622 B.C. *2 Kings, chs. 22 and 23.* A priest or priests later added to it books from other sources. Jesus quoted *Deut. 6:4-5* as the most important commandment. (See *Genesis* for an account of the writing of the first five books of the Bible.)

devil. A personification of evil, used in the N.T. to mean Satan. *Luke 4:5; John 8:44; Eph. 4:27; Heb. 2:14.* (See *Satan* for explanation and other names.)

devote. In O.T. warfare, to dedicate spoil or booty to God. Usually this meant total destruction of all things and persons taken. Sometimes part was given to a sanctuary. A reason for this practice is given in *Deut. 20:16-*

18. See also *Josh. 6:18; 1 Sam. 15:21; 1 Kings 20:42; Micah 4:13.* (See *vow.*)

dial. Sundial; probably a series of steps, each of which marked the time of day according to the shadow cast by a stick or another object nearby. *2 Kings 20:11; Isa. 38:8.* (See *day; hour.*)

dill. Seeds, like caraway, used for seasoning foods and for medicine. *Isa. 28:27; Matt. 23:23.*

disciple. In the N.T., a learner or a follower of a teacher. There were disciples of the Pharisees, *Matt. 22:15-16,* and John the Baptist had disciples, *John 1:35.* The disciples of Jesus were numerous. *Luke 6:13.* From them he chose twelve to work with him. The lists of Jesus' twelve disciples are in *Matt. 10:1-4; Mark 3:14-19; Luke 6:13-16; Acts 1:12-13.* These lists do not agree with one another. The differences are accounted for by the use of different names for the same person (for example, Bartholomew and Nathanael; Thaddaeus and Judas the son of James).
In the book of The Acts, " disciple " also means a member of the church. *Acts 20:1; 21:16.* (See *Christians* for list of other names for members of the church.)

Dispersion. N.T. term for the scattering of the Israelites into other lands from the time of the exile on. Some exiles from Samaria and Judah of O.T. times had not returned to their own land. Later, many Jews had moved to various cities of the Greek empire. In the time of the Roman Empire, there were colonies of Jews in almost all parts of the Empire. Each colony had its synagogue, but all Jews paid taxes to the temple in Jerusalem and went there, if possible, for the major feasts. *John 7:35.* Paul in his travels usually went first to speak in the synagogues of the scattered Jews. The people listed in *Acts 2:5-11* were Jews of the Dispersion who were in Jerusalem for the feast of Pentecost. In *James 1:1* and *1 Peter 1:1* it means Christians residing in different places.

distribution, daily. In the early church, the giving of bread to the widows and other needy persons of whom the believers took special care. *Acts 6:1;* see also *Acts 4:34-35.*

divine, v.; divination. A form of magic in which future events were foretold by such things as the way oil spread on water or the appearance of the inner organs of sacrificed animals. The practice was forbidden to the Israelites. *Gen. 44:5, 15; Num. 22:7; Deut. 18:10; Judg. 9:37; Acts 16:16.* (See *magic.*)

divorce. A man could divorce his wife by giving her a written statement, a **bill of divorce,** and sending her away. The statement read, "She is no longer my wife and I am no longer her husband." This statement was the opposite of the marriage vow. Women could not divorce their husbands. *Deut. 24:1-4; Jer. 3:8; Mark 10:2-12.*

dragon. Large sea animal. *Ps. 74:13; Isa. 27:1.* The description in *Ezek. 29:3-5* seems to fit the crocodile. In the book of The Revelation, "dragon" is a symbol of the power of evil at war with God. *Rev. 12:9.* (See *Leviathan.*)

dream. Sometimes the means by which messages came from God to men. The interpretation of dreams, as in the story of Joseph, *Gen. 40:12-19,* was practiced by most ancient peoples. *Gen. 28:10-15; Num. 12:6; 1 Sam. 28:6; Matt. 1:20; 2:12-13; Acts 16:9-10* (vision). (See *vision.*)

dresser of sycamore trees. Workman who pierced the unripe fruit to force insects out. *Amos 7:14.* (See *sycamore;* also *vinedresser.*)

dross. The accumulation of impurities of metal, especially of silver, that settles at the bottom of a refining furnace. *Ps. 119:119; Prov. 25:4; Isa. 1:22; Ezek. 22:18.* (See *furnace* for list of related words.)

dyed. Although Bible references are few, we know from archaeological sources that the Hebrews in O.T. times were famous for dyed goods. The work was carried out in homes rather than in factories. In some cases whole towns seem to have been given over to the industry. Thread was dipped in stone vats of dye and in lime or potash to fix the color, then laid out to dry. *Judg. 5:30; Job 38:14.* (See *weave* for list of words related to the making of cloth.)

E

earth. Descriptions in the Bible are largely poetical, but they represent a view of the earth common to most peoples of ancient times. The earth, that is, the dry land, was thought of as a flat mass supported on pillars, which were mountains grounded in the seas, or the deep, that lay under the earth. The **four corners of the earth** refers to the four directions. Above the earth was the domelike firmament. The stars on the other side of the firmament showed through openings in it. From the waters above the firmament, the rain and snow fell through windows. Heaven was beyond the firmament and the waters. Sheol was somewhere beneath the earth, but not definitely located. *Gen. 1:1, 6-10; Ex. 20:4; Job 9:6; Ps. 24:1-2; 69:34; Isa. 11:12; 42:5.* See illustration opposite page 66.

east, people of the. In general, non-Israelite nations east of the Jordan River in O.T. times; used of different groups — sometimes the people of Aram, sometimes Edom and Moab, sometimes nomadic tribes of the desert. *Gen. 29:1; Judg. 6:3; 1 Kings 4:30; Isa. 11:14.*

Ecclesiastes (ĭ klē'zĭ ăs'tēz), meaning "preacher." Also called The Preacher. O.T. book attributed to Solomon in the way in which ancient writers often gave their books well-known authors. It was probably written between 300 and 100 B.C. The theme of the sayings that make up the book is, " All is vanity " (*ch. 1:2*). Ecclesiastes belongs to a type of writing known as wisdom literature and represents a philosophy that was current in late O.T. times.

edict. A ruling by a king, made public in writing and publicly read aloud. Same as decree. *Ezra 6:11; Esth. 3:12-15* (describes how an edict was proclaimed in the Persian empire); *Heb. 11:23.*

Edom (ē'dəm). A name for Esau, the brother of Jacob. Also the O.T. people descended from him and the land they occupied to the east and south of Canaan. Although **Edomites** and Israelites were related, they were often enemies. David conquered the Edomites in order to gain control of their mines and the port of Ezion-geber. Another name for the territory of Edom was Seir. *Gen. 32:3; 36:9; Num. 20:14-21; 2 Sam. 8:13-14; 2 Kings 8:20-22; Amos 1:11.* (See *Esau;* map Plates III, G-3; IV, C-8 — Seir, Edom.)

Egypt. One of the two oldest civilizations of history (the other one centered in the land between the Tigris and Euphrates Rivers), Egypt had a great influence on O.T. history. The center of Egypt was the land along the Nile River in Africa, but at times the Egyptian empire extended into Asia. During the time of the patriarchs, Egypt controlled Canaan. Jacob's family went there to live in a time of famine. His descendants were enslaved by the Pharaohs and escaped under the leadership of Moses. In later times, Egyptian forces often threatened or invaded the Israelites. One of the factors that made David's kingdom possible was the weakness of Egypt at that time. *Gen. 12:10; 46:6-7; Ex. 1:8-14; 14:5-31; 2 Chron. 12:2-3; 2 Kings 23:29-30; Matt. 2:13; Acts*

2:10. (See map Plates II, B-4 [inset], D-3; III, B-5.)

elder. In the O.T., the head of a family or tribe who had various kinds of authority, such as governing, judging, and taking special part in worship. In *Num. 11:16-17* is a story of how elders helped Moses govern. How they judged is shown in *Ruth 4:2-12.* See also *Ex. 3:16; 24:1; Sam. 8:4-5.*
In N.T. times there was a council of elders in each Jewish community or synagogue, similar to the council in Jerusalem, the members of which were known as elders also. *Matt. 21:23; Mark 7:5; Luke 7:3; 9:22.*
The early churches had elders (also called bishops), probably much like the Jewish elders, who governed and also taught. *Acts 14:23; 15:2; 1 Tim. 5:17; Titus 1:5; 1 Peter 5:1-5.*

elect, *n.* In the N.T., the chosen, or those to whom God had made himself known and with whom he entered into special relationship. *Matt. 24:22; Rom. 8:33; Titus 1:1.* Christians believed that they were the continuation of the covenant people of O.T. times, that is, the people of Israel, whom God had chosen (See *children of God; son of God.*)

Eli (ē'lī). Priest of the sanctuary at Shiloh during the time of the judges. He was also considered a judge, in the sense of governing rather than of leading in war. Samuel trained for the priesthood under Eli. *1 Sam., chs. 1 to 4; 1 Kings 2:27.*

Elijah (ĭ lī'jə). A prophet in the Northern Kingdom, Israel, in the ninth century B.C., during the reign of Ahab. He fought against the worship of Baal and the unjust actions of the king. According to the later prophet Malachi, Elijah would return before the day of the Lord. *1 Kings, chs. 17 to 19; 21; 2 Kings 1:1 to 2:12; Mal. 4:5-6; Matt. 11:13-14; Mark 8:27-30.* (See Time Line.) Others.

Elisha (ĭ lī'shə). A prophet of the ninth century B.C., in the Northern Kingdom, Israel; pupil and successor to Elijah, continuing his teacher's struggle against the worship of Baal. *1 Kings 19:19-21; 2 Kings, chs. 2 to 13; Luke 4:27.* (See Time Line.)

embalm. Egyptian process for preserving bodies of the dead. From the Egyptian mummies we have learned a great deal about life then. Egyptians also buried persons of importance with many objects from everyday life that were thought necessary in the life after death. The Hebrews used a process of purification with spices, but did not embalm bodies. *Gen. 50:2-3, 26.*

emperor. The ruler of the Roman Empire in N.T. times; same as Caesar. *Acts 25:21, 25; 1 Peter 2:13, 17.* (See *Rome* for list of words related to Roman Empire.)

enrollment. In the O.T., a listing by ancestry, thus usually **enrollment by genealogies.** *1 Chron. 5:1, 17; Ezra 2:62; Neh. 7:5.* (See *census; genealogy; register.*)
In the N.T., a census taken by order of the Roman Government for purposes of taxation, usually taken every fourteen years. *Luke 2:1; Acts 5:37.*

ensign. O.T. tribal symbol set on a pole; same as banner, standard. *Num. 2:2; Isa. 11:10.* In *Ezek. 27:7,* a ship's flag. (See *banner* for description.)

enthroned. O.T. figure of speech describing God as king of his people; often **enthroned on the cherubim** or **enthroned above the cherubim.** *1 Sam. 4:4; 2 Kings 19:15; Ps. 9:7; 29:10; 123:1; Isa. 37:16.* (See *ark; cherubim; king.*)

Epaphras (ĕp'ə frăs). A member of the church at Colossae who preached in Colossae, Laodicea, and Hierapolis, and was in prison with Paul. *Col. 1:7-8; 4:12-13; Philemon 23.*

Epaphroditus (ĭ păf'rə dī'təs). A member of the church in Philippi who delivered a gift from the church to Paul when he was imprisoned in Rome. On his return trip, Epaphroditus probably carried Paul's letter to the Philippians. *Phil. 2:25-30; 4:18.*

ephah (ē'fə). O.T. measure for dry substances, equal to a little over one bushel by modern measurements. *Ex. 16:36; Ruth 2:17; Ezek. 45:10-11; Amos 8:5; Zech. 5:7* (a container). (See *homer* for table of dry measures.)

Ephesians, The Letter of Paul to the (ĭ fē'zhənz). N.T. book written by Paul (though this is less certain than is the case with other letters) around A.D. 60, perhaps to several churches. The subject of the letter is the church as part of God's plan.

Ephesus (ĕf'ə səs). Seaport city in the Roman province of Asia in N.T. times, a center of worship of the goddess Artemis. The main trade route from Rome to eastern lands passed through Ephesus. The outdoor theater there seated twenty-five thousand people and can still be seen among the ruins of the ancient city. *Acts 18:19-21, 24-28; 19:1 to 20:1; 1 Cor. 15:32; 2 Tim. 1:18.* (See map Plate XV, E-3.) See illustration opposite page 66.

ephod (ē'fŏd). A garment worn by a priest when carrying out his official duties. It is described in *Ex. 28:4-14.* See also *1 Sam. 22:18; 2 Sam. 6:14.* It was sometimes used to inquire of God because it was close to the Urim and Thummim contained in the breastplate. *1 Sam. 23:9-12; 30:7-8.* Perhaps also an idol or used as an idol. *Judg. 8:27.*

Ephraim (ē'frĭ əm). A son of Joseph; also, with Manasseh, one of the twelve tribes of Israel. Also the territory of the **Ephraimites,** usually **hill country of Ephraim.** *Gen. 41:50-52; Num. 1:32-33; Josh. 16:4; 2 Sam. 20:21; 1 Kings 12:25; 1 Chron. 6:67; Ps. 78:9.* Occasionally a name for the Northern Kingdom, Israel. *Isa. 9:9; 28:1,3; Hos. 4:17; 7:11.* (See map Plate IV, C-4.)

Epicurean (ĕp'ə kyōo rē'ən). In N.T. times, one of the two main schools of philosophy of the Greek-Roman world, founded by Epicurus in the fourth century B.C. The central teaching of the philosophy was that attaining happiness is the aim of life. *Acts 17:18.* (See *Stoic.*)

Esau (ē'sô). Son of Isaac, twin

57

brother of Jacob, to whom he sold his birthright. He was an ancestor of the Edomites. Stories in *Gen., chs. 25; 27; 33; 36:1, 6-8;* also *Mal. 1:2-5; Rom. 9:13; Heb. 11:20; 12:16.*

Esther, The Book of. O.T. book. The name is taken from the main character of the book. The story was written probably in the third century B.C. to explain the origin of the feast of Purim. The setting of the story is the court of a Persian king in the fifth century. Esther, a Jewish woman, becomes queen and saves the Jews from being persecuted.

eternal life. In the N.T., a phrase meaning a new relationship to God involving the whole self. In the Gospel of John it means the same as the kingdom of God or the kingdom of heaven in the other Gospels. *Mark 10:17; John 3:14-16; 4:13-14; 6:68; Gal. 6:8.*

Ethiopia (ē'thǐ ō'pǐ ə). A nation south of Egypt corresponding roughly to the country of Sudan today. In the O.T. it is also called Cush. The Ethiopians were famous in ancient times as merchants. *2 Chron. 14:9-13; Ps. 68:31; Isa. 20:3-5; 45:14; Acts 8:26-39.* (See map Plate II, B-4 [inset], E-4 — Cush.)

eunuch. An emasculated man; often in O.T. times, a chamberlain, especially in the women's quarters of a king's palace. *2 Kings 9:30-32; Esth. 2:3; Jer. 38:7; Matt. 19:12* (probably means " remaining unmarried "); *Acts 8:27.* (See *chamberlain.*)

Euphrates (ū frā'tēz). The large river on the western boundary of the area called Mesopotamia today. It joins the Tigris River and flows into the Persian Gulf. In the O.T., often called " the River." In ancient times, irrigation canals along the banks made rich farming lands. A number of ancient cities, such as Babylon and Ur, were on the Euphrates. *Gen. 15:18; Josh. 1:4; 1 Kings 4:24; 1 Chron. 18:3; Jer. 46:10.* (See map Plates II, F-2; IX, C-2.)

evangelist, meaning " messenger of good tidings." Traveling preacher in the early church. *Acts 21:8; Eph. 4:11; 2 Tim. 4:5.* (See *church* for list of other officers.)

Eve (ēv), meaning " life." In the Genesis stories of creation, the first woman, and the wife of Adam. *Gen. 1:27; 2:18-23; 3:20; 2 Cor. 11:3; 1 Tim. 2:12-14.* (See *Genesis* for general background.)

exile. In the O.T., often referring to the time when the people of the Southern Kingdom, Judah, and Jerusalem were taken captive to Babylon until their release, 587 to 538 B.C. In exile the Jews lived fairly independent lives in colonies around the city of Babylon. Some of them prospered so much that they preferred to stay in Babylon rather than return to Jerusalem, when the Persian emperor Cyrus gave them permission to do so. *2 Chron. 36:20; Ezra 6:19; 8:35; Neh. 1:3; Jer. 40:1; 52:28-30* (a description); *Ezek. 1:1; 3:15.* (See *captivity; deportation;* Time Line.)

Exodus (ĕk'sə dəs), meaning " going

out." O.T. book that tells how the Israelites became the people of God, starting with their slavery in Egypt and ending with the encampment at Mt. Sinai. See also *Heb. 11:22.* (See *Genesis* for an account of the writing of the first five books of the Bible.)

exorcist. In N.T. times a person who, supposedly, drove out evil spirits by words or magic acts. *Acts 19:13-20.*

expiation. The act of covering sin, or taking it away from the sight of God. *Num. 8:7; 1 Sam. 3:14; Rom. 3:23-25; Heb. 2:17; 1 John 2:1-2.* (See *atonement.*)

Ezekiel (ĭ zē′kyəl). Prophet at the time of the exile in Babylon, sixth century B.C. He probably lived and taught at Telabib, one of the colonies of Jews near Babylon. (See Time Line.)

Ezekiel, The Book of. O.T. book containing some of the prophet Ezekiel's sermons and prophecies, very likely written by the prophet himself. He taught concerning God's judgment on his people and the possibility of a future restoration of their kingdom.

Ezion-geber (ĕ′zĭ ən gē′bər). O.T. seaport at the southern end of the Arabah on the Gulf of 'Aqaba (modern name); originally in the territory of Edom, but captured by David. It was a center for the smelting of iron and copper from the mines of the Arabah. Solomon based his fleet of commercial ships there. Archaeolo-gists have excavated the ancient furnaces used in smelting and other parts of the refineries. *Num. 33:35-36; Deut. 2:8; 1 Kings 9:26; 2 Chron. 20:35-37.* (See map Plate III, G-4.)

Ezra (ĕz′rə). A priest and scribe who led a group of Jews back to Jerusalem from exile in Babylon, about 450 B.C., and supervised the rebuilding of the city. *Ezra, chs. 7 to 10; Neh., ch. 8.* (See Time Line.) Others.

Ezra, The Book of. O.T. book, a continuation of the books of the Chronicles; written by the same author, who is known as the Chronicler, in the fourth century B.C. Originally the books of Ezra and Nehemiah were one book. Ezra tells about the return of two groups of exiles from Babylon to Jerusalem. Parts of the book written in the first person were probably taken from the memoirs of Ezra.

F

faith. A relationship with God characterized by complete confidence and trust in him. Specifically in the N.T., acknowledgment of Christ's Lordship. Chiefly used in the N.T. *Ps. 78:22; Hab. 2:4; Matt. 23:23; Acts 16:5; Rom. 4:13; 5:1; Eph. 2:8.*

family. In O.T. times, the family might include more than one wife, concubines, the daughters until they married, the sons and their wives, and the servants. The father was the head of this community. In later O.T. times and in N.T. times it was no longer the custom to have more than one wife. *Gen. 37:2; 46:5-7* (description); *Ruth 2:1; 1 Sam. 9:21; 2 Chron. 19:8.* Sometimes used in a wider sense, as in *Ps. 22:27; Amos 3:2.*

fast. To go without food and water for a set period of time. In early O.T. times, Israelites fasted as a sign of mourning or repentance, sometimes individually, other times as a group. *Judg. 20:26; 2 Sam. 12:16-17; 1 Kings 21:8-9; Ezra 8:21-23.* In later O.T. times, after the exile, there were appointed days of fasting to commemorate such events as the capture of Jerusalem. (See *atonement.*)
In N.T. times, fasting was a common practice. *Matt. 6:16-18; 9:14-15; Luke 18:10-14.* Very strict Jews fasted on Tuesday and Thursday of each week. Early Christians apparently did not take over this practice, although they fasted on such occasions as the appointing of officers. *Acts 13:2-3; 14:23.* Later the twice-a-week fast was revived and was the origin of the Wednesday and Friday fasting (from meat) still observed by some Christians especially during Lent.

father. The person having authority over members of a family. *Deut. 5:16; Matt. 23:9.* Also used for an ancestor, *Gen. 28:13,* or an originator, *Gen. 4:20; Rom. 4:16-18.* Sometimes a title given to another person in recognition of his authority. *1 Sam. 24:8-11; 2 Kings 2:11-12; Job 29:16.*
In the N.T., used by Jesus in speaking of God. *Matt. 6:32; Luke 6:36; John 16:28.* Also so used by Paul and other writers of N.T. letters. *Eph. 5:20; 2 Thess. 1:1; 1 John 3:1.*

fatherless. One of the groups of the needy, with widows and sojourners, for whom O.T. laws required special consideration. *Ex. 22:22-24; Deut. 14:28-29; Job 29:12; Ps. 146:9; Isa. 1:17, 23.*

fathom. In N.T. times, a measurement for depth of water, equaling the distance from the tip of one outstretched hand to the other, about six feet. *Acts 27:28.*

fatling. An animal, such as an ox, a sheep, or a cow, especially well fed and in good condition, used for sacrifice. *1 Sam. 15:9; 2 Sam. 6:12-13; Ps. 66:15; Isa. 11:6; Ezek. 39:18.*

fear of God; or **fear of the Lord.** Recognition of the difference between God and man, or of God's holiness; awe. *Deut. 6:13; Josh. 24:14; 2 Sam. 23:3; 2 Chron. 19:7; 26:5; Ps. 33:8; Luke 1:50; 1 Peter 2:17.* (See *holy.*)

feast; usually **appointed feasts.** A time of rejoicing. The feasts were observances of events in Israelite history, or harvest celebrations and the like observed by most ancient peoples. Usually a feast included a sabbath, an assembly, and sacrifices. *Ex. 23:14-16* (a list of some of the feasts); *Ps. 42:4* (description); *Isa. 1:14; Hos. 2:11; Nahum 1:15; Matt. 26:3-5; John 7:2, 37.*

feasts. The three major feasts each year were:

passover, also called unleavened bread (in the N.T. the words are capitalized). *Ex. 23:15; 34:25; 2*

Chron. 8:13; Ezra 6:22; Ezek. 45:21; Mark 14:1; John 13:1.

weeks, called Pentecost in the N.T. *Deut. 16:10; 2 Chron. 8:13; Acts 2:1; 1 Cor. 16:8.*

booths, also called tabernacles (capitalized in the N.T.) and ingathering. *Ex. 23:16; Lev. 23:34; 2 Chron. 8:13; Ezra 3:4; John 7:2.* In N.T. times, every male Jew was required to be at the temple in Jerusalem for each of the three major feasts. There were other, minor, feasts, such as the feast of the Dedication, Purim, new moon, sabbath year, and jubilee year. (See names of feasts, both major and minor, for further information.)

Felix (fē'lĭks), Antonius. Roman governor of Judea, A.D. 52–60. He had a reputation as a cruel governor. *Acts 23:23 to 24:27.*

fell asleep. N.T. expression for "died." *Acts 7:60; 1 Cor. 15:20-21; 1 Thess. 4:14.* (See *slept with his fathers* for a similar O.T. expression.)

festal garments. Clothing worn for a celebration or other special occasion. No particular garments are meant, but they were probably more elaborate and costly than everyday clothes. *Gen. 45:22; Judg. 14:12; Isa. 3:22.*

Festus, Porcius (fĕs'təs, pôr'shəs). Roman governor of Judea, A.D. 60–62 successor to Felix. *Acts 24:27 to 26:32.*

fig. Common item of food, eaten fresh, dried, or pressed into cakes. Fig cakes were also used for medicinal

purposes. The trees were usually grown singly or in small groups, not in orchards. The ripe fruit was gathered from June on. *Num. 13:23; 1 Kings 4:25; 2 Kings 20:7; Isa. 28:4; Matt. 7:16; John 1:48.* (See *sycamore.*)

finger. Measurement of length equal to the width of one finger, about three fourths of an inch. *1 Kings 7:15; Jer. 52:21.* (See *cubit* for table of other measurements of length.)

finger of God. Symbol of God's power. *Ex. 8:19; Deut. 9:10; Ps. 8:3; Luke 11:20.*

firmament. O.T. word for part of the sky, thought of as a sheet of metal or a curtain that held back the upper waters. In it were placed the sun, moon, and stars. Windows allowed the rain to pour through from the upper seas. *Gen. 1:6-7; Ps. 19:1; 150:1.* (See *earth.*)

first-born. The eldest son. The first offspring of a domesticated animal was called a **firstling.** Among people of O.T. times, both were considered to belong to the gods, and therefore were to be sacrificed. Some peoples, such as the Canaanites, did sacrifice children. The Israelites redeemed first-born children by making a payment or substituting an animal to be sacrificed. The first-born also had birthright privileges. *Ex. 13:11-15; Num. 18:15-18; Deut. 21:15-17; Luke 2:22-24; Col. 1:15.*

fisherman. Fishing was a major oc-

cupation in N.T. times, when there were commercial fisheries on the Sea of Galilee and the Jordan River that supplied the markets in Jerusalem and also export markets. Fish were caught in nets, by spear, or by line from small boats or from shore. Other tasks of the fisherman were sorting fish and mending nets. *Matt. 4:18-22; 17:27; Luke 5:4-7; John 21:3-8.*
For descriptions of fishing in O.T. times, see *Job 41:1, 7; Isa. 19:8; Hab. 1:15.* (See *boat; hook; net.*)

flagon. Large, pitcherlike container of metal or earthenware for liquids. *Ex. 25:29; Num. 4:7; Isa. 22:24.*

flask. Small bottle for oil, water, or perfume, made of earthenware or of carved alabaster. *2 Kings 9:1-3; Jer. 19:1; Matt. 25:4; Luke 7:37.*

flax. Linen plant grown in Canaan and, especially, in Egypt. The stalks were dried and made into fiber by processes of soaking, combing, and spinning. *Ex. 9:31; Josh. 2:6; Isa. 19:9; Ezek. 40:3.* (See *linen.* See *weave* for list of words related to the making of cloth.)

flesh. N.T. word for the weakness of human nature in contrast with God's power, or when not animated by the Spirit of God. *John 1:14; 8:15; Rom. 7:5; Gal. 5:16-24; Eph. 2:3.*
Also, especially in the O.T., meat, as in **fleshpot,** a cooking pot for meat. *Ex. 16:3.*

flute. A pipe of one, two, or several reeds used for joyous occasions or used to accompany laments in mourn-

ing. *1 Sam. 10:5; Isa. 5:12; Jer. 48:36; Matt. 9:23.*

footmen; or **foot soldiers.** Members of the infantry, the main division of any ancient army. They were armed with bow and arrow, and dagger; or sword and shield; or lance (spear) and shield; or sling. *1 Sam. 4:10; 2 Kings 13:7; 1 Chron. 18:4.*

footstool. Steps or footrest of the throne of a king in ancient times. An interesting Egyptian one is decorated with carvings of all the peoples Egypt had conquered; thus the king sat with his captives literally under his feet. *1 Chron. 28:2; 2 Chron. 9:18; Ps. 110:1; Isa. 66:1; Matt. 5:34-35.* (See *throne.*)

ford. Shallow place at which a river could be crossed by wading. Such places were vulnerable to enemy attack and hence always well defended. Bridges were not used in Bible lands until the time of the Roman Empire. *Josh. 2:7; 1 Sam. 13:6-7; Jer. 51:31-32.*

forgive. To cover or remove sin or guilt, restoring the relationship between God and man or between men. *Gen. 50:17; Deut. 21:8; Ps. 79:9; Matt. 6:12; Luke 5:21, 24; Acts 2:38; Col. 1:14.*

fornication. Sexual relationship between unmarried persons. *Matt. 15:19; John 8:41.*

fortified city. City defended by walls. Most cities of O.T. times were walled. Towers afforded lookout places, and gates were usually guarded and barred at night. When the Israelites conquered Canaan, they found fortified cities, some of which they rebuilt after taking them. (It was the custom then to destroy completely any city that was conquered.) Archaeological evidence shows that the Israelites at that time were not the good builders the Canaanites had been. Later they built some fortified cities of their own. *Deut. 1:28; 3:5; 1 Sam. 6:18; 2 Sam. 20:6; Hos. 8:14.* (See, for other details, *city; wall.* See also *siege.*)

fortress. A fort or fortified place, often outside a city. Fortresses of the time of the two kingdoms were walled enclosures built on hilltops, with rooms inside for the storage of arms and for troops. Walls were made of blocks of stone, with sloping banks of earth below. *2 Sam. 24:7; 2 Kings 8:12; 2 Chron. 17:12; Isa. 34:13.* Also used as a figure of speech describing God. *Ps. 91:2.* (See *citadel.*)

Forum of Appius (ăp'ĭ əs) **and Three Taverns.** In N.T. times, stopping places between Puteoli, where ship passengers to Rome disembarked, and the city of Rome, about forty miles away. *Acts 28:15.* (See map Plate XV, B-2 — Tres Tabernae and Appii Forum, the names in Latin.)

fountain. A spring, as distinguished from a storage well or a cistern. In such place-names as Endor, the prefix " en " means fountain. *Deut. 8:7; 1 Sam. 29:1; Hos. 13:15.* (See *water* for list of related words.)

frankincense. Powder made by grinding the white resin of a tree; burned as incense. It was imported from Arabia. *Ex. 30:34; Lev. 2:1; Isa. 43:23; 60:6; Matt. 2:10-11.*

freedman. In N.T. times, a former slave who had been released. *Acts 6:9; 1 Cor. 7:22.*

fringe. Tassels at the corners of a cloak. See *Deut. 22:12.* To Jews of N.T. times, a reminder of the commandments of God. *Matt. 9:20; 23:5; Mark 6:56.*

frontlet. A band or ornament worn on the forehead when at prayer, and like the fringe, a reminder of the commandments of God. *Ex. 13:9, 16; Deut. 6:4-9; 11:18.* (See *phylacteries.*)

fuller. A craftsman who finished new cloth or, in N.T. times, also a cleaner and dyer of clothes. Treated cloth was laid out to bleach in the sun. *2 Kings 18:17; Mal. 3:2* (soap in O.T. times would have been lye or ashes); *Mark 9:2-3.* (See *weave* for list of words related to the making of cloth.)

furlong. In N.T. times, a Greek measurement of distance, about two hundred yards. *Matt. 14:24.*

furnace. In O.T. times, used for smelting metal from ore, chiefly copper and iron, or for refining precious metals. Small furnaces were circular or square, about nine feet in width. The large ones excavated at Eziongeber had several rooms. In the walls were two rows of flues, one of which carried warm air from room to room, the other being used for a draft. Bellows were used to make a draft in small furnaces. The plant at Ezion-geber was situated so that a steady natural wind from the desert provided a draft. *Deut. 4:20; Ps. 12:6; Prov. 17:3; Ezek. 22:17-22; Matt. 13:42.* (See, for metals commonly used, *bronze; copper; goldsmith; iron; silver.* See, for methods of producing metals, *dross; refine; smelt; smith.*)

G

Gabriel (gā'brĭ əl). A messenger from God; an archangel. *Luke 1:11-23; Dan. 8:16.* (See *angel.*)

Gad (găd). One of the twelve sons of Jacob; also the tribe descended from him, sometimes called **Gadites,** and their territory east of the Jordan River. *Gen. 30:10-11; Num. 1:24-25; 1 Sam. 13:6-7; 1 Chron. 5:11; 12:8, 14.* (See map Plate IV, D-5.) Other.

Galatia (gə lā'shə). In N.T. times, a province of the Roman Empire in what is now the country of Turkey. Important cities were Iconium, Derbe, Lystra, Antioch of Pisidia. *Acts 16:6; 18:23; 1 Cor. 16:1; Gal. 1:2; 1 Peter 1:1.* (See map Plate XV, F-3.)

Galatians, The Letter of Paul to the (gə lā'shənz). N.T. book, a letter written by Paul to the churches in Galatia, about A.D. 51, to counteract the effect of visiting teachers who were saying that Christians must keep all of the Jewish law.

galbanum (găl'bə nəm). Spice used in incense, probably made from gum of a fennel plant grown in Arabia, Persia, and India. *Ex. 30:34.*

Galilee (găl'ə lē). In O.T. times, part of the territory of the tribe of Naphtali, of which several cities were given by Solomon to Tyre. Many Canaanites remained in the area, so that it had only a minority of Israelites. *Josh. 21:32; 1 Kings 9:11; Isa. 9:1.* (See map Plate IV, C-3 — Naphtali.)
In N.T. times a division of the Roman province of Syria, with a governor (called a tetrarch, *Luke 3:1*) at Tiberias, the capital. Of the 350,000 people, about 100,000 were Jews. The area was noted for fish, oil, and grain. Galileans spoke with an accent different from that of Judeans. *Matt. 2:22-23; 26:69-75; Mark 1:9, 28, 39; Luke 4:31; 17:11; John 4:46; 7:1; Acts 9:31.* (See map Plate XIV, C-3.)

Galilee, Sea of. A freshwater lake on the Jordan River in the area of Galilee. The lake is about thirteen miles in length and seven miles wide. The hills rise steeply from the shores. The surface of the lake is more than six hundred feet below sea level. Many of the towns on its shores in N.T. times were fishing ports. *Matt. 4:18; Mark 7:31; John 6:1.* Also called lake of Gennesaret, *Luke 5:1,* and Sea of Tiberias, *John 6:1.*
In the O.T., Sea of Chinnereth or Chinneroth. *Deut. 3:17; Josh. 12:3.* (See map Plates IV, D-3 — Chinnereth; XIV, D-3 — Galilee.)

gall. Bitter or poisonous substance. *Job 20:14; Lam. 3:19; Matt. 27:34; Acts 8:23.*

Gallio (găl'ĭ ō), Junius Annaeus.

Proconsul of the Roman province of Achaia in N.T. times, with headquarters at Corinth around A.D. 50. *Acts 18:12-17.*

Gamaliel (gə mā'lĭ əl). In N.T. times, a Pharisee, a member of the council at Jerusalem, and famous in Jewish history as an interpreter of the law. He was Paul's teacher. Gamaliel died around A.D. 50. *Acts 5:34-39; 22:3.*

garrison. O.T. fortress or body of troops stationed for defense, often on borders. *1 Sam. 14:6-15; 2 Sam. 8:6, 14; 1 Chron. 11:16; 2 Chron. 17:1-2.*

gash. To cut oneself as a sign of mourning or as part of the worship of a god. O.T. laws prohibited the practice, probably because it was connected with the worship of gods. *Jer. 41:4-5; 47:5; 48:37-38; Hos. 7:14.*

gate. Usually of a city wall. In O.T. times the gate was elaborately con-

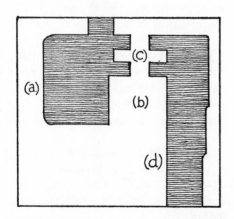

Plan of city gate at Mizpah. (*a*) Outside wall. (*b*) Stone benches. (*c*) Double gates, forming courtyard. (*d*) Guards stationed on wall.

structed, often with inner and outer gates, sometimes built at an angle to the wall so that approaching soldiers had to expose their unprotected (unshielded) sides. A tower over the gate housed a watchman. At night, gates were closed and barred. The space inside the gate was usually the market place. The elders of the city sat there, or in the space between double gates, to hear cases brought to law. *Deut. 3:5; Josh. 20:4; Ruth 4:1-12; 2 Sam. 18:24; 1 Kings 22:10; Amos 5:10, 12, 15.* (See *judge; wall.*)

Gath (găth). A Philistine city, one of five that resisted the Israelites, until conquered by David. Later the city had its own kings. Goliath was from Gath, and other **Gittites** seem to have been large people, descendants of the Anakim. *Josh. 11:22; 1 Sam. 17:4, 52; 1 Chron. 18:1; 2 Chron. 26:6* (Uzziah). (See map Plates IV, B-5; V, B-5.)

Gaza (gā'zə). An ancient city on the main road between Mesopotamia and Egypt, at the edge of the desert and at the juncture of a trade route from southern Arabia. It is still called Gaza today. In O.T. times it was one of the five Philistine cities of the coast that fought the Israelites. Because of its location at the meeting of several trade routes, Gaza was always a commercial center. *Judg. 16:1-2; 1 Sam. 6:17; 1 Kings 4:24; Amos 1:6-7; Acts 8:26.* (See map Plates IV, A-5; V, B-5; XV, F-4.)

Geba (gē'bə). O.T. city northeast of Jerusalem, scene of battles between the Philistines, and Saul and David;

considered the northern boundary of the Southern Kingdom, Judah. *Judg. 20:33; 1 Sam. 13:3, 16; 2 Sam. 5:25; 2 Kings 23:8.* (See map Plate IV, C-5 [Geba would be between Gibeah and Michmash].)

genealogy. A listing of persons according to their families and ancestry. There are many such lists in the Bible. The O.T. Israelites considered them of importance in establishing property rights and other matters that depended on inheritance, such as the priesthood. Some very old lists, such as those in Genesis, give the supposed origins of the nations. *Gen. 10:32;* see also *vs. 1-31.* Some of the lists are not accurate but have been arranged, in artistic patterns. The genealogy of Jesus Christ in *Matt. 1:1-17* is an example. *1 Chron. 5:17; Ezra 2:62; 8:1; Neh. 7:5.* (See *census; enrollment; register; tribe.*)

In the N.T., the listing of angels or beings who were intermediaries between God and men according to the Gnostic beliefs. *1 Tim. 1:4; Titus 3:9.*

Genesis (jĕn'ə sĭs), meaning "origin" or "in the beginning." O.T. book about the beginnings of the universe and of history, and about the fathers of the Hebrew people, Abraham, Isaac, and Jacob. The stories in the first part of the book are more legend than history. That is, they are answers to certain deep questions, such as, "How did life begin?" and "Why is there evil in the world?" But they are not records of actual persons and events. Genealogies and lists in the first few chapters of Genesis show ancient beliefs about the origins of different peoples. Beginning with the material about Abraham, however, the stories are considered to have a historical basis.

The first five books of the Bible, often called the Pentateuch, had a common origin made up of many different parts. One part consists of a history of Israel written in the Southern Kingdom, Judah, shortly after the death of Solomon. The writer used stories that had been passed down orally from generation to generation, songs and poems, lists, and some written materials. A writer in the Northern Kingdom, Israel, composed a similar history using the same traditions and perhaps some other material, but seeing them from a slightly different point of view. The two histories were put together in such a way as to preserve both. This fact explains why some stories are told twice in different ways. Later, at the time of the exile in Babylon, a third writer or writers added still another version of the history and re-edited all that had been written before. The five books reached their final form about 400 B.C.

Gennesaret (gĕ nĕs'ə rət). A name for the Sea of Galilee in N.T. times; also an area on its shores. *Mark 6:53; Luke 5:1.* (See map Plate XIV, C-3 — Plain of Gennesaret.)

Gentile. N.T. word for a person who was not a Jew. Same as nations. *Matt. 5:47; Mark 10:42; Acts 11:1; Rom. 2:14; I Cor. 1:23; Gal. 2:14.* (See *nations.*)

gerah (gĭr'ə). O.T. measurement of weight, one twentieth of a shekel.

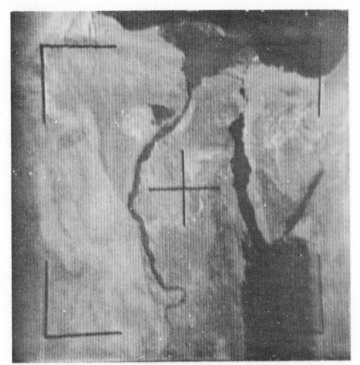

earth: View of Bible lands taken from the Tiros V satellite on its sixteenth orbit around the earth, June 20, 1962. Shown are the Red Sea, the Nile River, a part of the Mediterranean Sea, Egypt, the Sinai Peninsula, and part of the Arabian Peninsula.

Ephesus: Ruins of the theater at Ephesus. The street in New Testament times ended at the sea. Since then the harbor has gradually filled in with silt.

Lachish: Assyrian wall sculpture showing an attack on Lachish by Sennacherib's forces. Soldiers and siege machine are shown moving up to the city walls.

scroll: A scroll of The Book of Isaiah found in 1947 in caves of the Wadi (brook) Qumran near the Dead Sea. The scroll probably dates from the first century B.C.

Ex. 30:13; Num. 18:16; Ezek. 45:12. (See *money; weigh.* See *shekel* for table of other weights.)

Gethsemane (gĕth sĕm'ə nĭ), meaning " oil press." In N.T. times, a garden on the Mount of Olives across the brook Kidron from Jerusalem. *Matt. 26:36; Mark 14:32; John 18:1* (not named). (See map Plate XVI, F-5.)

giants. Probably the very early people of Canaan, descendants of whom were still living there when the Israelites took over. Perhaps these people were larger in stature than the Israelites. Or it may be that the Israelites were overly impressed with the fortified cities they found in Canaan. See *Deut. 1:22, 28.* In the O.T., the Anakim, the Rephaim, and the Nephilim, and also the people of Gath, are spoken of as giants. *1 Chron. 20:4-8.*

Gibeah (gĭb'ĭ ə), meaning " hill." An O.T. town north of Jerusalem, capital of the kingdom of Israel under Saul. Located on a highway, Gibeah was on the route taken by invaders and therefore always fortified. A fortress from the time of Saul has been excavated there. *Judg. 19:10-15; 1 Sam. 10:26; 14:16; 22:6; Hos. 10:9.* (See *citadel;* map Plate IV, C-5.)

Gibeon (gĭb'ĭ ən). O.T. town northwest of Jerusalem. During the conquest of Canaan the inhabitants resisted the Israelites by trickery. Later the town was taken from the Philistines by David. *Josh. 9:3-21; 1 Chron. 14:16; 16:39-40; 2 Chron. 1:3; Jer.*

28:1; Neh. 3:7. (See map Plate IV, C-5 [Gibeon would be between Gibeah and Beth-horon Lower].)

Gideon (gĭd'ĭ ən). One of the judges who led the Israelites after the conquest of Canaan and before the kingdom was founded. He fought against raids by the Midianites. Also called Jerubbaal. *Judg. 6:11 to 8:35; Heb. 11:32.* (See Time Line.)

Gilead (gĭl'ĭ əd). An O.T. tribe or family related to the tribe of Manasseh. Also an area east of the Jordan River around the Jabbok River. *Gen. 31:21; Num. 26:30; Judg. 5:17; 11:1; 2 Kings 10:32-33.* The **balm of Gilead** was a medicine made from the gum of an evergreen tree. *Gen. 37:25; Jer. 8:22.* (See map Plate I, D-4.)

Gilgal (gĭl'găl). O.T. town; there were probably several towns of the same name. The Israelites made their first encampment in Canaan there after crossing the Jordan River under Joshua's leadership. Saul was proclaimed king at Gilgal. In later times a sanctuary there was denounced by the prophets as idolatrous. *Josh. 4:19-20; 1 Sam. 7:15-16; 11:14-15; Hos. 9:15; Amos 4:4-5.* (See map Plate IV, C-5.)

gird. To put on, as clothing, or to fasten on, as a sword. To **gird up your loins** or **loins girded** refers to tucking the ends of the coat into a girdle in order to move more freely, and thus to get ready for action. *Gen. 24:32; Ex. 12:11; Deut. 1:41; 2 Sam. 3:31; Neh. 4:18; Job 38:1-3; Luke 17:7-8; John 13:3-4.*

girdle. Piece of cloth or leather worn about the waist over the coat or, sometimes, over the cloak. Both men and women wore girdles. Sometimes the coat was bloused over the girdle to shorten it, or the ends were tucked up into it for greater freedom of movement. Pockets in the girdle made of slits or folds in the material were used for carrying knives, food, or coins. *Ex. 39:29* (priest's); *2 Kings 1:8; Isa. 11:5; Matt. 3:4; Mark 6:8* ("belts"); *Acts 21:11.* (See *gird.* See *coat* for other information about clothing.)

glean. To gather grain or fruit left over after the work of harvesting. In O.T. times Israelites were to leave gleanings for the poor, the fatherless, and the widows. *Deut. 24:19-21; Ruth 2:2-23; Job 24:6; Micah 7:1.*

glory. Splendor or great worth. *Ex. 14:4; 1 Chron. 16:24; Ps. 29:3; 96:8; Jer. 9:23; Matt. 6:29; Luke 2:14; John 11:4; 17:4-5; Acts 11:18; Eph. 1:12.*
glory of the Lord. In the O.T., the presence of God, often seemingly visible. *Ex. 16:10; Num. 20:6; 2 Chron. 5:14; Ps. 57:5; Isa. 35:2.*

goad. A pole with a sharpened end or metal tip, used for guiding oxen. *Judg. 3:31; Eccl. 12:11; Acts 26:14.*

goat. Raised with sheep, though often in separate flocks. Used for milk (curds), meat, wool (woven into tent cloth), skins; also used in sacrifices. *Gen. 30:32; Ex. 35:26; Lev. 3:12; 1 Sam. 19:13; Prov. 27:27; Matt. 25:32.*

God. In terms of the Bible, no definition can be made. God was known to people of O.T. times as the One who rescued, and entered into covenant with, his chosen people, and he was known in their history through judges, kings, and prophets. In the N.T., he was made known through Jesus Christ.
The name of God in Hebrew was Yahweh. Other names were used, some of them closely related to the titles of gods. It was the practice to refrain from saying the actual name of God; thus, in O.T. books there was added a word to use in place of the name. It is translated "LORD." In addition, many other titles were used, among them: Ancient of Days, *Dan. 7:13;* Creator, *Rom. 1:25;* deliverer, *Ps. 70:5;* Everlasting God, *Gen. 21:33;* Father, *Jer. 3:19; Matt. 6:6; 2 Cor. 1:2;* God of Abraham, *Ex. 3:6;* God of hosts, *Amos 4:13;* Maker, *Isa. 17:7;* Mighty One of Jacob, *Gen. 49:24; Isa. 49:26;* Redeemer, *Jer. 50:34;* Rock, *Deut. 32:4; Ps. 31:3;* Savior, *2 Sam. 22:3; Isa. 49:26;* Sovereign Lord, *Acts 4:24.* Many other titles and figures of speech are used. (See, for two examples, *enthroned; fortress.*)

God, or **gods, do so to me and more also.** Part of a curse, meaning "may God do to me what I want to do to you if I am not able to do it." Or, sometimes, the "do so" was not specified but meant something too awful to put into words. *1 Sam. 3:17; 2 Sam. 3:9; 1 Kings 2:23; 19:2; 20:10.*

God-fearing; or **you that fear God.** In N.T. times, Gentiles who were partial converts to the Jewish faith. *Acts 10:22; 13:16, 26.* (See *proselyte.*)

gods. The deities or idols worshiped by the nations surrounding Israel in O.T. times. Some of them are listed in *1 Kings 11:5, 7, 33*. A reason for sacrificing to the gods is given in *2 Chron. 28:22-23*, and a similar appeal was made by the Assyrians to the besieged Jerusalemites, *2 Chron. 32:10-15*. The difference between God and the gods is described in *2 Chron. 32:19*. (See, for worship of the gods, *Asherah; Baal; cult prostitute; gash; high places; idol; image; oak; pillar; shrine; teraphim; tree, under every green*. See also *adultery; harlot*.)

goldsmith. A craftsman who made jewelry or idols. *Neh. 3:8, 31-32* (probably members of a guild); *Isa. 40:19; Jer. 10:9, 14*. Some other uses of gold are given in *Gen. 24:22; 41:42; 2 Sam. 1:24; 8:7; 1 Kings 6:21-22; 2 Kings 25:15; 2 Chron. 4:19-22; Acts 3:6*. (See *furnace* for list of words related to production of metals.)

Golgotha (gŏl'gə thə), meaning "skull." In N.T. times, a hill outside the walls of Jerusalem where executions were carried out. Today it is not known for certain where the hill was located. *Matt. 27:33; John 19:17;* also *Luke 23:33; Heb. 13:12*.

Goshen (gō'shən). In O.T. times, a part of northeastern Egypt between the Nile delta and what is now the Suez Canal. This land was not valued by the Egyptians. Jacob and his family were allowed to settle in it. *Gen. 46:28-34; 47:4-6; Ex. 8:22*. (See map Plate III, C-3 — Land of Goshen.) In The Book of Joshua, Goshen refers to an area in Canaan.

gospel. Good news. See *Luke 2:10; 4:16-19* for explanation. Also *Matt. 4:23; Mark 1:1; Acts 8:40; Phil. 1:12-14; 1 Thess. 2:9*. From the second century on, the name given to the four N.T. books about Jesus Christ.

governor. In the O.T., various officials, usually one designated by a king to rule over an area. *Gen. 42:6; Ezra 5:3; Neh. 5:15; Jer. 51:28*. In N.T. times, a Roman-appointed ruler over part of a province; same as tetrarch. *Matt. 27:2; Luke 2:2; 3:1; Acts 23:24*.

grace. The unearned love of God, who calls men into relationship with him. The O.T. equivalent is " steadfast love." *John 1:14; Acts 15:11; Rom. 5:17; Eph. 1:2; Phil. 1:7; 1 Peter 4:10*.

granary. Place for storing threshed grain. In O.T. times, the grain was placed in large jars stored in an allocated part of a house or in a pit or a dry cistern. *Jer. 50:26; Joel 1:17; Matt. 3:12; Luke 3:17*. (See *harvest* for list of words related to harvesting.)

grape. Common fruit grown in vineyards; eaten fresh or boiled down into a sweet syrup, but chiefly used in the making of wine. *Gen. 40:10-11; Lev. 19:10; Judg. 9:27; Isa. 5:1-2; Jer. 25:30; Luke 6:44*. (See *vineyard* for list of words related to methods of growing.)

graven. Carved or engraved; used to describe images. In contrast to " molten." *Ex. 20:4; 32:4; Judg. 18:14; Job 19:24; Isa. 30:22; 49:16*. (See *molten*.)

Great Sea. Ancient name for the Mediterranean Sea. *Num. 34:6; Josh. 1:4; Ezek. 47:10.* Also called the western sea, *Deut. 11:24,* and the sea, *Josh. 5:1.* (See map Plate III.)

greaves. Armor worn to protect the legs from ankle to knee. *1 Sam. 17:6.* (See *armor* for list.)

Greece. Seldom mentioned in the Bible, Greece was the ruling power in the world from the fourth to the first centuries B.C. and, therefore, ruler of the Jews. Many Jews were influenced by the Greek culture. The party of the Pharisees in N.T. times had originated in protests against Greek influence. When the Romans came into power, following the Greeks, they retained or copied much of Greek culture. Thus the world of N.T. times is often called the Greek-Roman world. *Dan. 11:2; Zech. 9:13; Acts 20:2.* (See Time Line. See *Rome* for list of words describing the Greek-Roman world of N.T. times.)

Greek. In N.T. times, a person who was not a Jew, but was part of the Greek-Roman world, and therefore civilized and not a barbarian. *Mark 7:26; John 7:35; Rom. 2:9; Gal. 3:28; Col. 3:11.* (See *Gentile.*)
Also the international language of the N.T. world. *John 19:20; Acts 21:37.* The books of the New Testament were written in the common, everyday Greek, known as Koine, which differs from the language of Greek literature.

grind. To make grain into meal or flour by rubbing between two stones.

Usually done by women early in the morning for the daily baking of bread. *Isa. 47:2; Jer. 25:10; Matt. 24:41.* (See *mill.* See *bread* for list of words related to bread-making.)

guest room. Large houses had a separate room for guests, sometimes built on the roof. In N.T. times, guest rooms in Jerusalem were rented or loaned to out-of-town Jews who came to the feasts. Same as upper room. *2 Kings 4:10* (description); *Mark 14:14; Luke 22:11-12; Philemon 22.* (See *hospitality; house.*)

H

Habakkuk (hə băk′ək). A prophet in the Southern Kingdom, Judah, from about 609 to 598 B.C., during the reign of Jehoiakim, when the Chaldeans were threatening Judah.

Habakkuk, The Book of. O.T. book, a collection of the teachings of the prophet Habakkuk. The book takes up the problem of why the catastrophe of conquest by an enemy should befall the Israelites.

Hades (hā′dēz). N.T. word for the place beneath the earth where it was believed the dead lived. *Matt. 11:23; Acts 2:27.* The equivalent O.T. word is Sheol. Over the years, details were added to the vague idea of Sheol. By the time of Christ, many Jews believed that there would be a resurrection of the dead. Hades, in the beliefs of that time, had two parts: Paradise for the good (some thought of Paradise as above the earth), and hell, a place of punishment. (See *death* for list of words related to beliefs about life after death.)

Hagar (hā'gär). A servant of Sarah by whom Abraham had a son, Ishmael. *Gen., ch. 16; 21:9-21; Gal. 4:24.*

Haggai (hăg'ī). A prophet who returned from exile in Babylon to Jerusalem at the time of the rebuilding of the temple. *Ezra 5:1.* (See *Zechariah.*)

Haggai, The Book of. O.T. book based on teaching of the prophet Haggai. The prophecies are dated in the book itself as having been made in 520 B.C. They are about the rebuilding of the temple.

hair. In O.T. times both men and women wore their hair long. Women bound theirs or wore a veil for covering. To **round off the hair** or to **cut the corners of their hair** meant to follow the style of non-Israelite peoples. *Lev. 19:27; Num. 6:18; 2 Sam. 14:25-26; Isa. 3:24; Jer. 9:26.*

Hallelujah (hăl'ə lōō'yə). An exclamation meaning " Praise the Lord! " used in the book of The Revelation; same as *Ps. 106:1. Rev. 19:1, 3, 4, 6.*

hallow. To make holy or to set apart. *Ex. 20:11; Lev. 16:19; 22:32; Ezek. 20:20; Matt. 6:9.*

Ham (hăm). Youngest son in the stories of Noah. As given in Genesis, the sons (descendants) of Ham were different peoples of ancient times. *Gen. 5:32; 10:1, 6-20.*
land of Ham, as in *Ps. 106:22,* and other uses of Ham in The Psalms,

means Egypt. (See *Genesis* for general background.)

Hamath (hā'măth). O.T. town north of Damascus captured by Solomon, but later, in the time of the two kingdoms, an independent state. The phrase **entrance of Hamath** (of uncertain meaning) was a way of speaking of the northern boundary of Israel. *Josh. 13:5; 1 Kings 8:65; 2 Kings 14:28; 19:13; 2 Chron. 8:4; Ezek. 47:15.* (See map Plates V, D-1; VII, D-1.)

hammer. Probably in early O.T. times, a stone used in the hand. Later, a stone attached to a handle; of different sizes, used for working metals, driving tent pegs, breaking up rocks, and in building. *Num. 8:4; Judg. 4:21; 1 Kings 6:7; Isa. 41:7; Jer. 51:20.*

hamstring. To disable an ox or a horse by cutting a tendon in the thigh; often done in O.T. warfare. *Gen. 49:6; Josh. 11:6; 2 Sam. 8:4.*

handbreadth. Measurement of length equal to the width of a hand measured across the palm at the base of the fingers. In O.T. times, four fingers equaled a handbreadth, or nearly four inches as we measure. *Ex. 25:25; 1 Kings 7:26; Ps. 39:5; Ezek. 40:5.* (See *cubit* for table of other measures of length.)

handmaid. A female slave or servant, or a self-title used by a woman in speaking to a superior, such as a king. *1 Sam. 28:21; 2 Sam. 14:12; Ps. 86:16; Luke 1:38, 48.*

Haran (hâr'ən). A brother of Abraham. Also a city northeast of Damascus on the Euphrates River, in Aram; a caravan stop on an ancient trade route. *Gen. 11:31; 27:43; 28:10; 2 Kings 19:12; Ezek. 27:23; Acts 7:2.* (See map Plate II, F-2.) Others.

harlot. A woman who earns her living by engaging in sexual intercourse. In the O.T., to **play the harlot** means to forsake God and to worship the gods of the nations. *Gen. 34:31; Ex. 34:15-16; Josh. 2:1; Judg. 8:33; Jer. 3:6; Hos. 4:12; Matt. 21:31-32.*

harp. A small stringed musical instrument that could be carried about in the hand; chiefly used in worship. *1 Sam. 10:5; 2 Chron. 20:28; Ps. 71:22; 150:3; Isa. 5:12; Amos 6:5; 1 Cor. 14:7.*

harvest. The season beginning with the barley harvest in April or May, continuing through the wheat harvest in May and June, to the harvesting of fruits, such as figs and grapes, in August and September. It was a time of rejoicing, with the observance of several feasts. *Lev. 19:9-10; 1 Sam. 6:13; 2 Sam. 21:9; Jer. 8:20; Matt. 9:37; John 4:35.* (See, for words related to harvesting processes, *chaff; glean; granary; reap; sheaf; sickle; sift; threshing floor; winnow.* See *wheat* for list of words related to general farming. See, for harvest festivals, *booths, feast of; weeks, feast of.*)

heads of families; or heads of fathers' houses. Same as elder in the O.T. *Num. 7:1-3; Josh. 22:30; 2 Chron. 19:8; Ezra 2:68.* (See *elder,* in O.T. times.)

heap. In addition to usual meanings, in O.T. times a pile of stones made as a witness to a covenant, or put over a grave to mark it as an unclean place. *Gen. 31:46, 48; Josh. 8:29; 2 Sam. 18:17.*

heathen. People who do not worship God; similar to nations and Gentiles. *Ps. 79:1; 1 Cor. 12:2; 1 Thess. 4:5; 3 John 7.* (See *nations.*)

heaven. All of the region above the earth including the firmament; specifically, the area or areas beyond the firmament. The phrase **heaven and earth** meant the universe to O.T. people. The phrases **highest heaven** and **heaven of heavens** mean all the expanse of heaven. *Gen. 1:8; 14:19; Deut. 10:14; 1 Kings 8:27; Job 22:12-14; 26:11; Isa. 48:13; Matt. 3:16-17.* In the N.T., as in the O.T., heaven is considered the dwelling place of God, *Matt. 6:9, 14,* and is therefore not always definitely located, but sometimes means the presence of God, as in *Matt. 6:20.* There were popular beliefs that heaven was divided into several parts, as in *2 Cor. 12:1-4* or *Eph. 4:10.* (See *earth; firmament.*)

Hebrew, meaning "one from the other side [of the Euphrates River]." Refers to Abraham's coming from the east into Canaan. In the O.T., a name for the Israelites. *Gen. 14:13; Ex. 2:11; Deut. 15:12; 1 Sam. 4:6; Jer. 34:9;* also *Phil. 3:4-6.* Also the language in which most of the books of the Old Testament were written.

Hebrews. In the N.T., Jewish Christians who were not from a Greek-speaking background, as were the Hellenists. *Acts 6:1.*

Hebrew, the language. In the Gospel of John and the book of The Acts, Aramaic, the language that had replaced Hebrew in common usage, is meant. *John 19:20; 20:16; Acts 22:2.*

Hebrews, The Letter to the. N.T. book, a letter written by an unknown author probably near the end of the first century A.D. to Christians who wished to return to Jewish ways of worship. The writer used many references to O.T. books to show that Jesus Christ was the true high priest, replacing the priests of earlier times.

Hebron (hē′brən). O.T. town in the hill country south of Jerusalem about nineteen miles. Originally a Canaanite city-kingdom, it was conquered by the Israelites and rebuilt. For a time it was the capital of Israel under David. *Gen. 13:18; Josh. 10:36-37; 20:1-2, 7* (with another name); *1 Kings 2:11; 2 Chron. 11:5, 10.* (See map Plate IV, C-5.)

hell. N.T. name for a place of punishment under the earth where it was believed the dead lived. *Matt. 5:22; James 3:6.* Footnotes give the word " Gehenna," a name for the valley of Hinnom. (See *Hades* for explanation of view of death in N.T. times and for words with similar meaning; *Hinnom, valley of,* for origin of " Gehenna.")

Hellenists. In the N.T., Jewish Christians from a Greek-speaking background. *Acts 6:1; 9:29.*

helmet. Leather cap to protect head,

ears, and cheeks of a soldier. Probably in O.T. times, metal helmets were used only by kings and leaders, often for ceremonials or for display. Some drawings of O.T. Israelite soldiers show helmets like pointed caps. *1 Sam. 17:5, 38; Ps. 60:7; Isa. 59:17.* The helmet of the Roman soldier in N.T. times was made of heavy metal. *Eph. 6:17; 1 Thess. 5:8.* (See *armor.*)

Hermes (hûr′mēz). In N.T. times, a Greek god, an eloquent speaker who served as messenger for the chief god, Zeus. *Acts 14:12.*

Hermon, Mount (hûr′mən), meaning " sacred mountain." A large, snow-capped mountain at the southern end of the Lebanon mountains and the northeastern limit of the Israelites' territory in O.T. times. The Jordan River rises on the slopes of the mountain. *Deut. 3:8; Josh. 11:16-17; Judg. 3:3* (probably means it was a center of Baal worship); *1 Chron. 5:23; Ps. 42:6; 89:12.* (See map Plate IV, D-2 [note other names].)

Herod (hĕr′əd). Family name of a number of rulers of Judea and other areas in N.T. times. They were Idumeans who had become Jews. They were appointed rulers by the Roman authorities. Herods who appear in the N.T. are:

Herod the king, who ruled in Judea (and Galilee and Samaria) from 40 to 4 B.C. He is the Herod mentioned in the stories of Jesus' birth. *Matt., ch. 2; Luke 1:5.* (See Time Line.)

Herod the tetrarch was a son of Herod the king, ruler in the territories of Galilee and Perea from 4 B.C. to A.D.

73

39. He is the Herod mentioned as ruler at the beginning of Jesus' mission, and throughout the rest of his life; also the one to whom Pilate sent Jesus at the time of his trial. *Matt. 14:1; Mark 6:14; Luke 3:1; 9:7-9; 23:7; Acts 4:27.*

Herod the king, the Herod in the book of The Acts, ruled over an area about equal to that of his grandfather, the first Herod the king. His reign began in A.D. 37. *Acts 12:1-3; 13:1.*

Other members of the Herod family mentioned in the N.T. are Philip the tetrarch, *Luke 3:1,* and Agrippa, *Acts 25:13.* (See *Agrippa.*)

Herodians (hĭ rō'dĭ ənz). In N.T. times, Jews who were supporters of the Herods and therefore of the rule of the Romans. *Matt. 22:16; Mark 3:6; 12:13.*

hewers of wood. In O.T. times, servants of very low standing whose work was gathering firewood. *Deut. 29:11; Josh. 9:21* (the story begins with *v. 3*).

Hezekiah (hĕz'ə kī'ə). King of the Southern Kingdom, Judah, from 715 to 687 B.C., during the time of the prophet Isaiah. Alarmed by the conquest of Samaria and the Northern Kingdom, Israel, Hezekiah tried to make alliances with other nations against the Assyrians, but he was forced to pay tribute to them. *2 Kings, chs. 18 to 20; Isa., chs. 36 to 39; Jer. 26:18; Matt. 1:9-10.* (See *conduit; king;* Time Line.) Others.

high places. Places for worship of the gods, chiefly on hills in O.T. times.

Occasionally a place for worship of God, *2 Chron. 33:17,* made over from a Canaanite place of worship. A high place consisted of a circular, leveled-off area enclosed by a stone wall, with an altar and a pillar or an Asherah be- or temple. Priests presided at the high places, and cult prostitutes were associated with them. *Num. 33:50-52; 1 Sam. 9:11-13; 1 Kings 3:2, 4; Hos. 10:8.* Also **on every high hill,** as in *Jer. 3:6.* (See *gods* for list of related side it. Sometimes there was a house words.)

high priest. Head of the priests who had charge of the temple and the services; he acted as the representative of all the people of Israel before God. In O.T. times he was supposed to be the head of the Aaronite family, but kings sometimes appointed high priests. In N.T. times the high priest was appointed by the Roman rulers. *2 Kings 12:10; 22:8; Hag. 1:12; Matt. 26:57; John 11:49; Acts 4:5-6; 23:1-2; Heb. 6:19-20.* In the O.T., also called **chief priest,** *2 Chron. 19:11* (not the same as chief priests in the N.T.); **chief officer of the house of God,** *1 Chron. 9:11;* **ruler of the house of God,** *Neh. 11:11.* (See *priest.*)

highway. A caravan route, little more than a well-worn track. The Romans in the first century A.D. constructed the first paved roads in Bible lands. *Num. 20:17; Judg. 20:31; Ps. 84:5; Isa. 33:8; Luke 14:23.* (See *King's Highway; road.* See, for some of the highways of ancient times, map Plate III.)

hill country. One of the main geographical divisions of Canaan, consisting of a north-south range of rocky mountains east of the coastal plains. This area was the main one occupied by the Israelites in O.T. times, and the three districts of N.T. times — Judea, Samaria, and Galilee — were located in it. The mountains rise to heights of four thousand feet above sea level. The area was noted for tree crops, but there were also some plains used for farming. The east-west passes in the mountains were points of defense in O.T. times. *Gen. 31:21; Num. 14:44-45; Josh. 10:6; Judg. 2:9; 1 Sam. 13:2; Jer. 32:44; Luke 1:65.* (See *Canaan* for description of main geographical areas; map Plate I.)

hin. In O.T. times, a unit of measure for liquids, equal to a little more than a gallon in modern measurements. *Ex. 29:40; Ezek. 4:11.* (See *cor* for table of liquid measurements.)

Hinnom, valley of; or **valley of the son of Hinnom** (hǐn'əm). Located south of Jerusalem, a center of worship of the god Molech, to whom children were sacrificed by fire. *Josh. 18:16; 2 Chron. 28:3; Jer. 19:2; 32:35.* It was such a place of horror that by N.T. times the name (in Greek, Gehenna) and the nature of the valley were used to describe the place of punishment after death. The word "Gehenna" occurs in footnotes for *Matt. 5:22* and *Mark 9:45* as an alternate reading for hell. (See map Plate XVI, B-6.)

Hiram (hī'rəm); also **Huram** in the Chronicles (*2 Chron. 2:3*). A king of the city of Tyre in the time of David and Solomon, with both of whom he was friendly. By agreements with Solomon he supplied lumber and workmen for the building of the house of God in Jerusalem. *2 Sam. 5:11; 1 Kings 5:1-12; 9:10-14.* Other.

hire, *n.* Wages or payment. *Ex. 22:15; Isa. 19:10; Hos. 9:1.*

hireling. A servant who was paid wages. *Job 7:1-2; Isa. 16:14; Mal. 3:5; John 10:12-13.*

Hittites (hǐt'īts). O.T. people of several small states in the area now known as Turkey. There were also colonies of Hittites in Canaan; thus they were one of the peoples whom the Israelites drove out when they conquered the land. *Gen. 23:3-16; Deut. 7:1; Josh. 1:4; 11:1-5; 2 Sam. 11:3-27; 2 Chron. 1:17.*

In general history, "Hittites" usually refers to a well-developed empire about the time of the patriarchs, generally credited with the discovery and use of iron. (See map Plate II, E-2 — Old Hittite Empire.)

Hivites (hǐv'īts). O.T. people who were living in various cities and towns of Canaan when the Israelites conquered it. *Deut. 7:1; Josh. 9:1-2; Judg. 3:3; 2 Sam. 24:7; Isa. 17:9.*

holy. Separate or set apart. A holy day is one that is different from any other day. God is holy because he is different from and separate from all beings. *Ex. 20:8; Lev. 21:6; Isa. 6:3; Matt. 7:6; 2 Cor. 7:1; 1 Thess. 4:7.* (See *common*, the opposite of holy.)

holy place. One of two inner rooms

in the tabernacle and the temple. The holy place was the larger room separated by a veil or door from the most holy place, which was the innermost room. Also, in some N.T. references, the temple itself. *Ex. 26:31-35; Lev. 6:16; 1 Kings 8:8; 2 Chron. 29:5-7; Ps. 74:4; Matt. 24:15; John 11:48; Acts 6:13; Heb. 9:1-14.*

Holy of Holies. A name for the most holy place. *Heb. 9:3.* (See *temple* for description.)

Holy Spirit. N.T. name, equivalent to O.T. Spirit of God, but also thought of as a being distinct from the Father and the Son, and sometimes referred to as "he." *Matt. 1:18; Mark 1:10; Luke 4:1; John 14:25-26; Acts 2:1-4; 2 Cor. 13:14; Eph. 1:13-14.*

homer. O.T. measure for dry substances, equal to about ten bushels by modern measurements. It was equivalent to the liquid measure called the cor. Probably the word "homer" originally meant the load an ass could carry. *Lev. 27:16; Isa. 5:10; Hos. 3:2.* The following table shows the relationships between different dry measures:

10 omers = 1 ephah
10 ephahs = 1 homer

hook. Used by fishermen. *Job 41:1-2; Matt. 17:27.* Also put in the noses of animals or of captive persons in order to lead them by ropes. *2 Kings 19:28; 2 Chron. 33:11.* (See *pruning hook* for another kind of hook.)

Horeb (hō'rĕb). A name for Sinai, the mountain at which the Israelites

under Moses encamped for a long time. *Ex. 3:1; Deut. 1:2; 5:2; 2 Chron. 5:10; Ps. 106:19.* (See *Sinai, Mount;* map Plate III, F-5.)

horn. In the O.T., animal horn used as a bugle or trumpet, or as a flask. *Josh. 6:13; 1 Sam. 16:1; 1 Kings 1:39.* Also used in several figurative expressions, usually as a symbol of strength or power. *Ps. 18:2; 75:1-5, 10; 89:24; 132:17; Jer. 48:25;* also *Luke 1:69.*

horns of the altar were projections on the four corners. To lay hold of them meant to plead for mercy. *1 Kings 1:51; 2:28; Ps. 118:27.*

horse. Among Israelites of O.T. times, horses were used more in warfare than for farming or transportation. Solomon was the first to import them. *1 Kings 10:26-29; Job 39:19-25; Ps. 33:17; Nahum 3:1-3.*

horsemen usually means chariot troops, not mounted troops. *Ex. 14:9; 1 Sam. 8:10-11; 2 Sam. 10:18; 2 Chron. 1:14; Hos. 1:7.*

Hosanna (hō zăn'ə). An exclamation meaning "Save us!" Same as *Ps. 118:25.* During the feast of tabernacles in O.T. times, processions of worshipers sang this verse while waving branches. *Matt. 21:9; Mark 11:9; John 12:13.*

Hosea (hō zā'ə), meaning "salvation." A prophet in the Northern Kingdom, Israel, beginning in the reign of Jeroboam II, about 750 B.C. *Rom. 9:25.* (See Time Line.)

Hosea, The Book of. O.T. book containing the teachings of the prophet

Hosea that were collected after his death. The first part of the book compares God's love for the people of Israel with that of a husband who takes back his unfaithful wife. The second part is a summary of the prophet's teaching.

Hoshea (hō shē′ə), same as Hosea, meaning "salvation." The last king of the Northern Kingdom, Israel. He was under the control of the Assyrians, but attempted to rebel. As a result, Shalmaneser V, of Assyria, besieged Samaria and took Hoshea captive. *2 Kings 15:30; 17:1-6; 18:9-12.* (See *king;* Time Line.) Others.

hospitality. Among ancient peoples of Bible lands, the care of travelers was a duty, and hospitality was extended even to fleeing criminals or enemies because of the difficulties of travel and the lack of any public accommodations such as hotels. There are descriptions in *Gen. 19:1-3* and *Judg. 19:13-21* of how a traveler might find a place to stay for the night.
In N.T. times the few inns were very bad, and thus hospitality was commended to Christians as a duty, especially toward traveling church teachers. *Rom. 12:13; 1 Tim. 3:2; 5:9-10; Heb. 13:2; 1 Peter 4:9.* (See *guest room.*)

host. An army or a large group of people. *Ex. 7:4; 12:17; Num. 10:15; 1 Sam. 17:20; Eph. 4:8.*
host of heaven sometimes means the sun, moon, and stars, as in *Gen. 2:1* and *Deut. 4:19.* Because ancient peoples worshiped the sun and the moon,

the expression also means the gods of the nations, as in *2 Kings 21:5; 23:5; Acts 7:42.* The phrase sometimes refers to angels, as in *1 Kings 22:19; Ps. 148:2; Luke 2:13.*
Lord of hosts, as a title for God, is related to this last use. *1 Sam. 1:3.*
Also one who entertains, as in the modern meaning.

hour. In O.T. times, until the exile in Babylon, the day was not divided into equal hours.
In N.T. times, time was divided into twelve hours in the day and twelve hours in the night. The third hour was nine o'clock in our way of reckoning time. The sixth hour was noon or midnight; the ninth hour, three o'clock. *Matt. 20:3, 5-6; Luke 23:44; John 11:9; Acts 2:15.* (See *day; watch.*)

house. For most families a one-story, one-room building of sun-dried brick or stone, with a flat roof. The interior included a lower area for the animals and a raised area that was the living quarters for the family. Often a number of small houses were grouped around a courtyard. Some houses were built with a court alongside. The word is also used for a palace. *Deut. 22:8; Josh. 2:15; 1 Sam. 19:9; 2 Sam. 5:11; 2 Kings 11:19; Amos 3:15.* (See, for other details, *guest room; parapet; roof; upper room; window.* See, for furnishings, *bed; couch; lamp; pallet; table.* See, for other household goods, *basket; cup; flagon; jar; kneading bowl; mill; oven; skin of water; water jar.*)
Also means family, as in **house of Jacob,** *Ex. 19:3;* or **house of David,** *1 Kings 12:19; Luke 2:4.*

house of God; or **house of the Lord.** A sanctuary or temple, especially the temple in Jerusalem built by Solomon, and later rebuildings of it. *1 Sam. 1:24; 1 Kings 3:1; 5:5; 7:51; Ezra 5:17; Matt. 12:4; 21:13.* (See *temple* for description.)

Most of the O.T. books were written after the temple in Jerusalem was supposed to have taken the place of all other worship centers. Information about other temples was suppressed in these writings. However, we know that there were other houses of God, and that many of them continued in use after the temple was built. Probably the early Israelite temples were like those of the Canaanites at the high places: one-room buildings with an altar outside.

householder. In the N.T., the head of a household, either the master or a steward. *Matt. 13:27; 20:1; Mark 14:14.*

hunter. O.T. people hunted for food or to destroy predators. Hunting as a sport was practiced only by kings, especially the Assyrians. The hunter used bow and arrow, sling, and traps. *Gen. 25:27; 27:3; 1 Sam. 26:20; Jer. 16:16.* Some methods of hunting are described in *Job 18:8-10; Jer. 5:26; Ezek. 19:4.*

hymn. A song of praise or of meditation. The main hymns in the O.T. are the psalms; others are found in *Ex. 15:1-18; Judg., ch. 5; 1 Sam. 2:1-10.* See also *Matt. 26:30* (the " hymn " was probably from *Ps. 113 to 118*); *Acts 16:25; 1 Cor. 14:26; Eph. 5:19.* Examples of early Christian hymns are believed to be found in *Phil. 2:6-11* and *1 Tim. 3:16.* (See *psalm.*)

hypocrite. In the N.T., used, not with its modern meaning, but to mean " one who does not believe." The O.T. word " godless " is its equivalent. *Matt. 6:2, 16; 23:13-15; Mark 7:6; Luke 6:42.*

hyssop. Branches of a small bush used for sprinkling as part of a ceremony of cleansing. *Ex. 12:22; Ps. 51:7; John 19:29; Heb. 9:19.*

I

Iconium (ī kō′nǐ əm). City in the Roman province of Galatia in N.T. times, visited by Paul. It is now Konya, in the country of Turkey. *Acts 13:51 to 14:6; 2 Tim. 3:10-11.* (See map Plate XV, F-3.)

idol. A likeness or image of a person or animal representing a god. A description of the making of an idol is given in *Isa. 44:9-17.* See also *Deut. 29:16-17; Ps. 96:5; Acts 17:16; 1 Cor. 8:1-4; 10:7.* (See *gods* for list of related words.)

Idumea (ĭd′yŏŏ mē′ə). In N.T. times an area south of Judea, corresponding to Edom in O.T. times. *Mark 3:8.* (See map Plate XIV, B-6.)

image. Likeness. *Gen. 1:27; Col. 1:15.* In the O.T., graven and molten images were representations of gods in human or animal form used in worship. Among the excavations in Palestine have been found numerous small figurines, often of a female goddess, probably Asherah. These were evidently charms, or, perhaps, household images. *Ex. 20:4; Deut. 9:12; 1 Sam. 19:13-16; 1 Kings 15:13; Ps. 106:19-20; Isa. 48:3-5.* (See *gods* for list of related words.)

immortal. Having never-ending life. Used in the N.T. only of God. *Rom. 1:23; 1 Tim. 1:17; 6:15-16.*
immortality has been made possible for men through Christ's death and resurrection. The word does not mean the continued existence of a soul after the death of the body, but is closely related to the meanings of eternal life and resurrection in the N.T. *Rom. 2:7; 1 Cor. 15:53-54; 2 Tim. 1:10.* (See *death* for list of words related to beliefs about life after death.)

incense. Made of powdered gums and spices, burned as an offering to God or to the gods. Many ancient nations used incense in worship, for it was believed that the deity would enjoy the fragrance. *Ex. 30:34-38; 1 Kings 9:25; Ps. 141:2; Hos. 11:2; Luke 1:8-11.* (See *odor, pleasing.*)
altar of incense. An altar for the burning of incense in the holy place of the temple in Jerusalem. *Ex. 30:1-10; Luke 1:11.* Other nations in O.T. times used incense altars also, and a number of such altars, small enough to be carried about, have been found in archaeological excavations in Palestine. *2 Chron. 14:5;* see also *34:25; Jer. 48:35.* (See *temple* for location.)

ingathering, feast of; also called feast of booths, or of tabernacles. A festival celebrating the end of all the harvests, thus coming at the end of the year in O.T. times. The harvest celebration was combined with memories of the journey of the Israelites from Egypt to Canaan. *Ex. 23:16; Deut. 16:13.* (See *feast.*)

inheritance. In the O.T., a portion of the land of Canaan thought of as God's gift to the Israelites and divided among the tribes. *Lev. 27:24; Num. 36:7; Josh. 13:28; Ps. 105:11.* (See *allotment.*)

iniquity. Same as sin. *Lev. 26:39; 2 Sam. 24:10; Ps. 51:9; Ezek. 18:19-20; Matt. 23:28; 2 Cor. 6:14.* (See *sin.*)

ink. Made of lampblack, the carbon deposit from the burning of oil, mixed with resin. Ink was carried in dried form and dissolved in water as needed. Some of the ink of ancient times is still readable on papyri and potsherds. *Jer. 36:18; 2 John 12.* (See, *Lachish.* See *write* for list of related words.)

inn. In N.T. times, a rough shelter for travelers and their animals. Guests provided their own bedding and food, and fodder for the animals. Sometimes there was a resident manager; often there was not. Some villages provided guest houses or rooms. *Luke 2:7; 10:34.* (See *guest room.* See *hospitality* for O.T. customs.)

inquire of God; or **inquire of the Lord.** To find out God's will or the possible outcome of some venture, such as war, by asking a seer or prophet, or a priest. The Urim and Thummim were used by the priest to inquire of God. *Ex. 18:15-16; 1 Sam. 9:8-9; 1 Kings 22:5-6; 2 Chron. 34:19-21; Ezek. 20:1.*

iota (ī ō'tə). The letter *i*, the smallest in the Greek alphabet. *Matt. 5:18.*

iron. Before the time of David, iron was not commonly used, copper and bronze being more widely used. Some of the peoples around the Israelites used iron — for example, the Canaanites — so that some iron implements may have been obtained as booty. At one time the Philistines controlled the manufacture of iron and forced the Israelites to come to them for sharpening what iron tools they had. Iron was used for farming tools, weapons, builder's tools and nails, chains, gates, and bars. Ore was taken from the Lebanon mountains. *Josh. 17:16; 1 Sam. 13:19-22; 1 Chron. 22:3; 29:7; Amos 1:3; Acts 12:10.* (See *furnace* for list of words related to the production of metals.)

Isaac (ī'zĭk), meaning "God laughs." The son of Abraham whom God had promised him; father of Esau and Jacob. *Gen. 17:15-21; 21:1-12; chs. 22, 24, 26 to 28; Ex. 3:16; Matt. 22:32; Gal. 4:28; Heb. 11:9.* (See Time Line.)

Isaiah (ī zā'ə), meaning "God has saved." A prophet in the Southern Kingdom, Judah, from the reign of Uzziah, about 742 B.C., to that of Hezekiah, around the close of the century. The prophet's teachings were concerned with the political situation of the time — with the alliances being made between Judah and other powers against the Assyrians. Isaiah urged that God's people should trust in Him and not in their own power. *2 Kings 19:19; ch. 20; Matt. 4:14; John 12:37-41.* (See Time Line.)

Isaiah, The Book of. O.T. book containing prophecies of Isaiah and some history in *chs. 1 to 39*, which were compiled after the death of the prophet. *Chapters 40 to 55* seem to have been based on the teachings of a prophet who lived during the exile in Babylon. He was concerned to teach the exiles that God, whom they had known in their own history, was the creator of the world and ruler over all nations and all history. *Chapters 56 to 66* are believed to have originated with a third prophet, or perhaps several prophets, from a time later than that of Isaiah. The Book of Isaiah is frequently quoted in the N.T. *Matt. 3:3; Luke 4:17-19; Acts 8:28.*

Ishbosheth (ĭsh bō'shĭth). A son of Saul whom some of the Israelites made king after his father's death. He ruled about two years until overcome by David. *2 Sam., chs. 2 to 4.*

Ishmael (ĭsh'mĭ əl). A son of Abraham and Hagar, the servant of Sarah. The story seems to be one of those in Genesis which explain the origins of nations, in this case, the **Ishmaelites,** a wandering nation in north Arabia who were related to the Israelites. *Gen., chs. 16; 17:15-21; 21:8-21; 25:12-18; 37:25; Judg. 8:24.* Others.

isles. In the O.T., the islands of the Mediterranean Sea, usually thought of

as kingdoms distant from Canaan. *Ps. 72:10; Isa. 40:15; Ezek. 26:18.*
Those mentioned by name in the N.T. are Cyprus, *Acts 11:19;* Cauda, *Acts 27:16;* Malta, *Acts 28:1;* Rhodes, *Acts 21:1;* and Cos, *Acts 21:1.* (See map Plates II and X for ancient names; map Plate XV for names in N.T. times, some of them in use today.)

Israel (ĭz'rā əl), meaning "God strives" or "God rules." A name given to Jacob. *Gen. 32:22-32; 35: 9-10; 46:8, 29.*
children of Israel; Israelites; people of Israel; sons of Israel; also **Israel.** The descendants of Jacob and his twelve sons; the people of God. *Ex. 1:9; 32:4; Judg. 6:2-3; 1 Sam. 4:1; 2 Sam. 7:26; 2 Chron. 7:3; Ps. 22:23; John 1:47, 49; Acts 2:22; Rom. 11:1.* (See *people of Israel; tribe.*)
The name applied to the whole people became the name of the kingdom under Saul, David, and Solomon (more especially in modern usage), *1 Kings 11:42.* (See *king;* Time Line; map Plate V.)
Used to designate a group of tribes that came to differ with the tribe of Judah, first over the support of Ishbosheth rather than of David after the death of Saul. *2 Sam. 2:10; 5:1-5; 1 Kings 12:12-20.*
The name of the Northern Kingdom, formed after the death of Solomon, when the tribes that differed with Judah refused to accept Rehoboam as king. Jeroboam was the first king of this nation. Its capital was, eventually, the city of Samaria. The kingdom lasted about two centuries, until the Assyrians captured Samaria and took the people to areas in the east, replac-ing them with colonies of people from other areas. *1 Kings 15:9; 2 Kings 17:1, 21-23.* (See *king;* Time Line; map Plates V and VI.)

Issachar (ĭs'ə kər). One of the twelve sons of Jacob; also the tribe or people descended from him and their territory, southwest of the Sea of Chinnereth (Galilee). *Gen. 30:18; Num. 1:28-29; Judg. 5:15; 1 Chron. 12:40; 2 Chron. 30:18.* (See map Plate IV, C-3.) Other.

Italy. In N.T. times, similar to the area of the country Italy today. Rome, the capital of the world of that time, was located there. Other towns of Italy mentioned in the N.T. are Rhegium, Puteoli, Forum of Appius, and Three Taverns. *Acts 18:2; 27:1, 6; Heb. 13:24.* (See map Plate XV, B-2 — Italia.)
Italian Cohort. A division of the Roman Army made up of soldiers recruited from Rome and Italy, not from the provinces, as was the case in many cohorts. It was stationed in Caesarea in the time of Paul. *Acts 10:1.*

ivory. In O.T. times, a valuable import from India and Ethiopia, the possession of which was a sign of great wealth. It was used for carvings and inlays to decorate furniture and houses, and for small statues, games, cosmetic jars, and other luxury items. *1 Kings 10:18, 22; Ps. 45:8; Ezek. 27:6; Amos 3:15; 6:4.*

J

Jabbok (jăb'ək). A tributary of the Jordan River, rising to the east and flowing through a deep canyon. In O.T. times it was the boundary of the territories of the Amorites and Ammonites, and later of the tribe of Gad. *Gen. 32:22; Num. 21:24; Deut. 2:37; Judg. 11:13.* (See map Plate IV, D-4.)

Jacob (jā′kəb); also called Israel. Son of Isaac, twin brother of Esau. He deceitfully obtained his brother's birthright and thus became head of the family. His twelve sons and their descendants became the twelve tribes of Israel, that is, the people of God. Sometimes the name is used, as is Israel, to mean the whole people. Stories in *Gen., chs. 25 to 49.* See also *Ex. 19:3; Ps. 46:7; Isa. 44:1; Luke 1:33; Acts 7:8; Heb. 11:9.* (See *Israel;* Time Line.)

James. The brother of Jesus. The brothers of Jesus did not support him during his lifetime, but they are listed among the believers after the resurrection. *Mark 6:3; John 7:5; Acts 1:14.* James held an important position in the church at Jerusalem, probably as head of the elders. *Acts 12:17; 21:18; Gal. 1:19; 2:9, 12.*

James, The Letter of. N.T. book, a letter by an unknown author to Christians in general, not to any one church; written probably toward the end of the first century. The writer describes the practical things that a Christian must do.

James the son of Alphaeus. One of the twelve disciples of Jesus. It is possible that Mary the mother of James, in *Mark 15:40* and *16:1,* was the mother of this disciple. *Matt. 10:3.* (See *dis-*

ciple for Bible references to lists of the twelve.)

James the son of Zebedee. One of Jesus' twelve disciples, a brother of John and a fisherman with Peter and Andrew. *Matt. 4:21-22; Mark 9:2-10; 14:33; Luke 5:10; Acts 12:1-3.* (See *disciple* for Bible references to lists of the twelve.)

Japheth (jā′fith). One of Noah's three sons. In the Genesis stories of the origins of nations, he is the ancestor of people to the northwest of Canaan. *Gen. 5:32; 9:18-19; 10:1-5.* (See *Genesis* for general background.)

jar. Earthenware container used for dry or liquid substances, such as meal and oil. Women used two-handled jars to carry water from the well. Large jars of twenty-gallon capacity were used for storing wine. Some of these, made with pointed bottoms, were thrust into the earth or held in

Jar-handle stamps, probably on jars used for collecting taxes in quantities of wine and oil

racks. Among the jars found in archaeological excavations of O.T. sites are some marked with seals on the handles, indicating the owners or showing the vessel's contents in standard measures, such as the bath. *Gen.*

24:14-20; 1 Kings 14:3; Matt. 26:7; Luke 22:10; John 2:6; 4:28. (See *potter; water jar*.)

javelin. O.T. weapon, a small spear used for throwing; probably made of wood, at least in early times. *Josh. 8:18; 1 Sam. 17:6; Job 39:23; Ps. 35:3.* (See *weapon* for list.)

jealous. In addition to the usual meaning, in the O.T., the word means "having a strong, single-minded devotion." *Deut. 6:15; 1 Kings 19:10.*

Jebus (jē′bəs). The ancient name for Jerusalem when it was controlled by the **Jebusites,** a Canaanite tribe. After David captured the city, the few Jebusites left continued to live there with the Israelites. *Judg. 19:10; 1 Chron. 11:4-9; 21:18; Neh. 9:8.*

Jehoiakim (jǐ hoi′ə kǐm). King of the Southern Kingdom, Judah, in the time of Jeremiah the prophet, sixth century B.C. He owed his throne to the Egyptian Pharaoh and was later subject to Nebuchadnezzar, king of Babylon, by whom he was taken captive at the beginning of the siege of Jerusalem. *2 Kings 23:34 to 24:15; 2 Chron. 36:5-8; Jer. 1:3.* (See *king; Time Line*.)

Jephthah (jĕf′thə). A Gileadite warrior who was a judge over the Israelites in the time between the conquest of Canaan and the founding of the kingdom. *Judg. 10:17 to 12:7; Heb. 11:32.* (See *Time Line*.)

Jeremiah (jĕr′ə mī′ə). A prophet

in the Southern Kingdom, Judah, in the last years before its capture by the Chaldeans, about 620 B.C. to 580 B.C. Jeremiah was interested especially in the political situation of Judah, its alliances with other nations, the threat from the empires to the east. Foreseeing the disaster that was about to come, the prophet urged God's people to change their ways and to return to Him. *2 Chron. 35:25; 36:12, 21-22; Matt. 2:17-18; 16:13-14.* (See Time Line.) Others.

Jeremiah, The Book of. O.T. book, a collection of the prophet Jeremiah's teachings and some history of the times, parts of which are probably based on the scrolls that Baruch prepared from Jeremiah's dictation.

Jericho (jĕr′ə kō). An ancient city in the southern Jordan valley, important in both O.T. and N.T. times. Before or at the time the Israelites entered Canaan, it was a fortified city. (Archaeological evidence seems to show that Jericho was destroyed a century before the conquest of it claimed for Joshua.) *Josh., chs. 2; 6; 2 Kings 2:4.*
In N.T. times, Jericho was located on an important trade route. The tax collector's office there was for collecting duty from merchants using the highway. Jericho was 825 feet below sea level. A traveler literally went "down" from Jerusalem to Jericho. *Mark 10:46; Luke 10:30; 19:1-27; Heb. 11:30.* (See map Plates IV, C-5; XIV, C-5.)

Jeroboam (jĕr′ə bō′əm). First king

83

of the Northern Kingdom, Israel. He was the son of an officer at the courts of Solomon. Almost all the later kings of Israel are described as following the sins of Jeroboam, which means that they continued the idolatrous worship he started. *1 Kings 11:26-40; 12:12-20, 25 to 14:20.* Also a later king of the same name. (See *king;* Time Line.)

Jerusalem (jĭ rōō′sə ləm). Until the time of David, Jerusalem belonged to the Jebusites, and the Israelites had not been able to take it. David captured it and made it the capital of his kingdom, and by moving the ark there, the center of worship. Solomon further made it the center of worship by building the temple there, and gradually all worship and all the hopes of the people of God became centered in Jerusalem. The city was the capital of the Southern Kingdom, Judah. Conquered and razed by the Chaldeans, it was rebuilt by the Jews who returned from the exile in Babylon. In N.T. times it was the center of religion for Jews in any part of the world, many of whom traveled there for the feasts. The first church came into being in Jerusalem and was recognized as the head church throughout the time of the apostles. *Josh. 15:8; 2 Sam. 5:6-10; 2 Kings 8:16-17; 2 Chron. 36:19; Ezra 1:5; Ps. 137:6; Jer. 3:17; Matt. 16:21; Mark 11:15; Luke 2:41; Acts 1:8; 11:22.* (See *Jebus;* map Plates V, C-5; VI, C-5; XIV, C-5; XVI.)

Jesse (jĕs′ĭ). Father of David. He was a man of the tribe of Judah who lived near Bethlehem. *Ruth 4:17; 1 Sam. 16:1; 17:17; 1 Chron. 10:14; Isa. 11:10; Luke 3:32; Acts 13:22.*

Jesus, meaning " God saves "; from Greek form of the Hebrew Joshua. The given name of our Lord and Savior. **Jesus of Nazareth** is the name by which his contemporaries would have known him. *Matt. 26:71; Mark 1:24; Luke 18:37; John 1:45.* He was recognized as the Christ by his disciples, and throughout the N.T. is called **Jesus Christ,** a combination of his personal name and a title, used as a name. *Matt. 1:1; Mark 1:1; John 1:17; 20:31; Acts 2:36; Rom. 8:39; Gal. 3:26; 1 Tim. 1:1.* Also a common name in N.T. times; others are identified by contexts. (See Time Line.)

Jew, shortened form of Judah. In O.T. times, used only after the exile, to designate one who had gone to Babylon and returned to Jerusalem. All the exiles were Judeans, that is, were from Judah. In N.T. times, the descendants of the returned exiles and the Jews of the Dispersion. *Ezra 6:7; Jer. 34:9; Zech. 8:23; Matt. 27:11; John 4:9; Acts 21:39; Rom. 2:9; Gal. 2:14; Col. 3:11.*

jewelry. Worn by both men and women in O.T. times, including armlets and bracelets, *Gen. 24:22; Num. 31:50;* earrings, *Ex. 35:22; Judg. 8:24;* anklets, usually narrow bands, *Isa. 3:18;* crescents — moon-shaped pendants worn around the neck, *Judg. 8:21; Isa. 3:18;* signet rings, *Gen. 41:42.* Bronze was the metal most often used, but silver, and sometimes gold, were also used to make pieces of jewelry.

Jezebel (jĕz'ə bəl). The daughter of the king of the city of Sidon. Through a political alliance, she became the wife of Ahab, king of the Northern Kingdom, Israel. Because she introduced the worship of Baal, she was opposed by the prophet Elijah. *1 Kings 16:31; 19:1-2; ch. 21; 2 Kings 9:30-37.* Other.

Jezreel (jĕz'rĭ əl). O.T. town southwest of the Sea of Galilee, in the Valley of Jezreel, which slopes down to the Jordan River. It was the location of a battle with the Philistines in the time of Saul. King Ahab of the Northern Kingdom, Israel, had a palace there. *Josh. 17:16; 1 Sam. 29:1, 11; 1 Kings 18:45; 21:1; Hos. 1:5.* (See map Plate IV, C-3.) Also a personal name.

Joab (jō'ăb). Commander of the armies under David. Toward the end of David's life he supported Adonijah as successor to the throne and therefore Solomon, when he became king, had him killed. Stories in *2 Samuel,* and *1 Kings, chs. 1 and 2.* Other.

Job, The Book of (jōb). O.T. book, probably written sometime between the seventh and fourth centuries B.C. An ancient story of a good man was expanded into a dramatic dialogue on the question of why God allows the good person to suffer. *Ezek. 14:14; James 5:11.*

Joel, The Book of (jō'əl). O.T. book of prophecy comparing the day of the Lord to a plague of locusts, and describing the ideal restoration of the Southern Kingdom, Judah. Nothing is known about the prophet, or possibly two prophets, whose teachings the book presents. It was probably written about 400 B.C. Others.

John. One of Jesus' twelve disciples. He was the brother of James and a son of Zebedee, and a fisherman. *Matt. 4:21-22; Mark 3:17; Acts 1:13; 3:1-4, 11; Gal. 2:9.* (See *disciple* for Bible references to lists of the twelve.) Others.

John, The First, Second, and Third Letters of. Three N.T. books, different kinds of letters, written by an elder in one of the early churches who was perhaps the author of the Gospel of John also. The first letter is like a sermon. The second is addressed to a church, and the third to a person who may have been an officer in one of the churches. All were written to combat the teaching (called Gnosticism) that Jesus' bodily life was not important and perhaps not real, because to the Gnostics, anything physical was a handicap to the spiritual things of life.

John, The Gospel According to. N.T. book; an account of the life, death, and resurrection of Jesus Christ, the purpose of which is given in *John 20:30-31.* The writer is not known for certain. Some believe that he was the disciple John; others, that he was a follower of the disciple. Neither is there any certainty about the time the book was written. The Gospel of John is different from the other three, which are called the Synoptic Gospels, because they seem to be based on the same sources and can be put together into one story. The Gospel of John gives information that supplements, differs from, or corrects what is in the Synoptic Gospels, somewhat as though the writer assumed that his readers were acquainted with them. The oldest portion of the N.T. that has been found is a copy of part of John made in A.D. 140.

John the Baptist; or **John the baptizer,** frequently " John " in the Gospels. A preacher who lived in the wilderness and baptized persons in preparation for the coming kingdom of God, which he was announcing. *Matt., chs. 3; 4:12; Mark 6:14-29; Luke 7:18-23; John, ch. 1; Acts 1:5.* (See Time Line.)

John Mark. (See *Mark.*)

Jonah, The Book of (jō'nə). O.T. book written probably in the fourth century B.C. to combat the exclusivism that was popular among the Jews then and to remind them that they had a mission to all the people of the world. The central figure may have been based on a prophet of earlier times. *2 Kings 14:25; Luke 11:29-32.*

Jonathan (jŏn'ə thən). A son of Saul, noted as a warrior, who befriended David when Saul turned against him. *1 Sam. chs. 13; 14; 18 to 20.* Others.

Joppa (jŏp'ə). An ancient town on the Mediterranean coast important in O.T. and N.T. times; now Jaffa. At one time it was the only harbor on that part of the coast, and although thirty-five miles from Jerusalem, Joppa served as Jerusalem's port. Originally a Philistine city, Joppa was conquered by David. In N.T. times there were Christians in Joppa. *2 Chron. 2:15-16; Ezra 3:7; Jonah 1:3; Acts 9:36-43; 10:5-8; 11:4-5.* (See map Plates V, B-4; XV, F-4.)

Jordan (jôr'dən). This river rises twelve hundred feet above sea level at Mt. Hermon and flows south to the Dead Sea (Salt Sea in ancient times), twelve hundred feet below sea level. The valley of the Jordan River is one of the main geographical areas of Canaan. In the Bible, " river Jordan " means the extent from the Sea of Galilee to the Dead Sea. The distance between the two seas by air is sixty miles; the river covers two hundred miles in its wanderings. The land is flat and the climate hot and moist along the river. Easily crossed at several fords, it was always well defended in O.T. times. *Num. 13:29; Josh. 23:4; Judg. 3:28; Ps. 42:6; Mark 1:9; 10:1.* (See *Canaan* for description and list of main geographical areas; map Plates I, D-4; IV, D-4 [time of the judges]; XIV, D-4 [time of Jesus].)

Joseph. In the O.T., a son of Jacob who was sold by his brothers to traders and taken to Egypt, where he became a powerful assistant to the Pharaoh. *Gen. 30:22-24; chs. 37 to 50; Acts 7:9-16; Heb. 11:22.* (See Time Line.)

Also a name for the two tribes Ephraim and Manasseh, which descended from Joseph's sons. *Josh. 16:1-4*. Others.

Joshua (jŏsh'ōō ə), meaning " God saves." Assistant to Moses in leading the Israelites from Egypt to Canaan; as Moses' successor, he led the conquest of Canaan. As in the case of the stories of Moses, the stories of Joshua were very old when they were put in written form, and thus include many tales emphasizing his heroism. Stories in Exodus, Numbers, Deuteronomy, Joshua. See *Ex. 24:13; Deut. 31:3; Josh. 1:1-2; Judg. 2:8-9; Acts 7:45*. (See Time Line.) Others.

Joshua, The Book of. O.T. book that tells the history of the Israelites after the death of Moses, especially the conquest of Canaan and the distribution of the land. Like the first five books of the O.T., it was compiled long after the events it relates, from many sources, some of them dating from the time of Joshua, who is the main character of the book. According to The Book of Joshua, the taking of Canaan was rapidly accomplished. Archaeological investigations do not bear out these stories, and most scholars agree that a much longer time was required.

Josiah (jō sī'ə). A king of the Southern Kingdom, Judah, in the seventh century B.C. During his reign, workmen in the temple found a book (probably parts of Deuteronomy) that had been hidden many years before. The discovery led to major reforms in the worship and life of the people. *2 Kings, chs. 22; 23:1-30; Jer. 1:1-2*. (See *king;* Time Line.) Other.

jubilee. According to O.T. law, every fiftieth year was a special year, during which slaves were to be released and land that had been sold or forfeited for debt was to be returned to the tribe to which it had originally belonged. Fifty years was a unit of reckoning time, used as we today use a century. No evidence has been found that a jubilee year was actually observed in O.T. times. Perhaps it was described as an ideal thing to do. *Lev. 25:8-15; Num. 36:4*.

Judah (jōō'də). One of the twelve sons of Jacob; also the people or tribe descended from him, and their territory, the large area between the Salt Sea and the Philistine areas on the Mediterranean Sea. *Gen. 29:35; Judg. 1:3-4; 2 Sam. 2:4; Ps. 78:68; Heb. 7:14*. (See map Plate IV, B-5.) Others.
The name of the Southern Kingdom, which came into being after Solomon's death, when the former kingdom was divided into two. It was made up of the tribe and territory of Judah and part of Benjamin. The capital was Jerusalem. The kingdom lasted a little over three centuries, until it was conquered by the Chaldeans and its people taken into exile in Babylon. The area then became a province of the Chaldean empire, and later the Persian empire. *1 Kings 12:17; 14:21; 2 Kings 18:1; 25:21; Jer. 52:27; Matt. 2:6*. (See *king;* Time Line; map Plates VI, B-5; VII, B-5.)

Judaism. The religion of the Jews in N.T. times. *Acts 13:43; Gal. 1:13-14*.
Many views and practices of O.T. times remained much the same (for

example, see the things described under *offering; priest; sacrifice; temple; worship*). Nevertheless, the religion of the Jews in N.T. times had some distinctive characteristics. (See, for a general picture of people and practices of Judaism, *captain of the temple; chief priests; council; elder*, in N.T. times; *feast*, in N.T. times; *God-fearing; Hades; Herod; Herodians; law*, in N.T. times; *lawyer; money-changer; Pharisee; proselyte; Rabbi; ruler of the synagogue; Sadducee; Samaritan; scribe; senate of Israel; synagogue; tax* [half-shekel tax]; *tradition; Zealot*.)

Judas Iscariot (jōō'dəs ĭs kər'iət). One of the twelve disciples of Jesus; from the town of Kerioth (Iscariot means "man of Kerioth"). He told the chief priests and elders where they could arrest Jesus. *Matt. 10:4; Mark 14:10; Luke 22:3-6; John 13:21-30; 18:2-3; Acts 1:16.* (See *disciple* for Scripture references to lists of the twelve.)

Judas the son of James. One of Jesus' twelve disciples. *Luke 6:16; John 14:22; Acts 1:13.* Because this Judas is not mentioned in the Gospels of Matthew and Mark, it is believed that he was the Thaddaeus in *Matt. 10:3* and *Mark 3:18.* (See *disciple* for Scripture references to lists of the twelve.) A common name in N.T. times; others can be identified by contexts.

Jude, The Letter of ("Jude" is a variation of "Judas"). N.T. book; a letter written to several or all of the churches, combating the false teach-ing that God's grace allows people to do anything they please. The letter was written toward the close of the first century, after the death of the apostles. The writer may have been a brother of Jesus. *Mark 6:3.*

Judea (jōō dē'ə). In N.T. times a division — with Galilee and Samaria — of the Roman province of Syria, usually ruled by a governor or tetrarch with headquarters in Caesarea, except when Herod was king. The name is a variation of Judah, of O.T. times. Judea was the center of Jewish life in N.T. times because Jerusalem was located there. *Matt. 2:1; Mark 1:5; 10:1; Luke 3:1; John 3:22; Acts 1:8; 9:31; Gal. 1:22.* (See map Plate XIV, C-5.)

judge, *v.* To hear both sides of a dispute between persons and decide between them. In *Ex. 18:13-23* a story is told of how Moses delegated his responsibility for judging to the elders. How judging was done is described in *Ruth, ch. 4.* See also *Deut. 17:12; 1 Sam. 7:15-17; 2 Sam. 15:2-6* (in the days of the kingdoms, the king was the chief judge). (See *gate; witness*.)

Judge. A title given to God in the O.T. and to Jesus in the N.T. Like a human king, God was thought of as the highest judge of men. *Gen. 18:25; Ps. 7:11; 96:10; Isa. 33:22; Acts 10:42; 2 Tim. 4:1.*

judgment. Act of judging or the verdict from judging. Judgment of men: *Lev. 19:15; Zech. 8:16.* Judgment of God: *2 Chron. 20:12; Ps. 9:4; 105:7; John 5:22; Rom. 2:3; 2 Cor. 5:10.*

day of judgment. N.T. expression

similar to "day of the Lord" in the O.T. An expected time when God would finally judge all men. Some descriptions are given in *Acts 17:30-31; 2 Cor. 5:10.* See also *Matt. 11:22-24; 2 Peter 2:9; 1 John 4:17.*

judgment seat. In N.T. times the Roman governor held hearings from a public platform or throne in the courtyard in front of the praetorium. Same as tribunal. *Matt. 27:19; John 19:13; Rom. 14:10; 2 Cor. 5:10.*

judges. War leaders who arose from time to time and led the Israelites against their enemies, in the time following the conquest of Canaan and before the founding of the kingdom. The writer of The Book of Judges summed up the era as a time of anarchy. *Judg. 2:16-19.* The phrase **judged Israel** is used in The Book of Judges to identify these leaders. *Judg. 10:1-3; 2 Kings 23:22.* (See Time Line. See, for some of the judges, *Barak; Deborah; Gideon; Jephthah; Samson.* See also *Abimelech.*)

Judges, The Book of. O.T. book, a continuation of The Book of Joshua, telling about the time between the conquest of Canaan and the founding of the kingdom (until the time of Samuel). Written probably during or after the exile, the book was based on many sources — stories, songs, poems, written materials — some of which were very ancient. (See *judges; Deborah.*)

justice. (See *righteous.*) *Gen. 18:19; Deut. 16:20; Job 29:14; Ps. 37:30; Amos 5:24; Matt. 12:18; 23:23.* Also refers to the administration of laws.

Ex. 23:6; 1 Sam. 7:17; 1 Chron. 18:14.

justify. To make right. *Job 32:2; Ps. 51:4; Isa. 43:9; Luke 10:29; Rom. 3:20-26; Gal. 2:15-21.*

K

Kadesh; or **Kadesh-barnea** (kā'-dĭsh bär'nĭ ə). An oasis south of Canaan where the Israelites, under Moses' leadership, camped for several years on their way from Egypt to Canaan. *Num. 20:1; 32:8; Deut. 2:14; Josh. 10:41; Ps. 29:8.* (See map Plate III, F-3.)

keepers of the threshold. In O.T. times, officials of the temple; probably originally responsible for the entrances, and later had greater responsibilities. *2 Kings 22:4; 25:18.*
gatekeepers. Temple officials, probably those of a lower order, who were in charge of the doors. *1 Chron. 9:17; Ezra 7:7; Neh. 12:45.*

Kidron, brook; Kidron valley (kĭd'-rən). A winter brook and its valley east of Jerusalem between the city and the Mount of Olives. Part of it was used as a public burying ground for the poor. *1 Kings 2:36-37; 2 Kings 23:6; 2 Chron. 30:13-14; Jer. 31:40; John 18:1.* (See map Plate XVI, E-7 — Kidron valley.)

king. In the O.T., the ruler of a city, *Josh. 10:3;* a country, *1 Sam. 8:4-5; 2 Sam. 5:1-3; 2 Chron. 12:13;* or an empire, *Neh. 2:1.* In the N.T., an honorary title given to some Roman-appointed governors such as Herod, *Mark 6:14,* and Agrippa, *Acts 25:24.*

Canaanite king on his throne, from an ivory carving excavated at Megiddo, c. 1200 B.C.

The typical king of ancient times is described in *1 Sam. 8:10-18.* His office was inherited or seized by conquest. In some nations the king was considered a god or the servant of the gods. The signs of a king were his throne and footstool, his crown, a spear and a scepter, his palace, and his chariot. (See, for officials of a king's court and government in O.T. times, *bodyguard; chamberlain; counselor; courier; cupbearer; eunuch; governor; mighty men; overseer; prince; recorder; secretary; servant* [king's servants]; *steward.*)

The title and signs of kingship are often used in the O.T. in speaking of God, *Ps. 29:10; Zech. 14:9,* because he was considered the king of Israel. Any kings of the people were to be his representatives. (See *ark; at his right hand; cherubim; enthroned.*)

By N.T. times the Jews hoped for a king who would be like David and who would give them a kingdom again. *Luke 19:38; John 1:49; 6:14-15.* (See *Christ; Messiah.*)

The kings of O.T. times were as follows. (The names in italics have a separate alphabetical entry in this dictionary.)

The kingdom of Israel
Saul, 1020–1000
David, 1000–961
Solomon, 961–922

The Northern Kingdom, Israel
Jeroboam I, 922–901
Nadab, 901–900
Baasha 900–877
Elah, 877–876
Zimri, 876
Omri, 876–869
Ahab, 869–850
Ahaziah, 850–849
Jehoram, 849–842
Jehu, 842–815
Jehoahaz, 815–801
Joash, 801–786
Jeroboam II, 786–746
Zechariah, 746–745
Shallum, 745
Menahem, 745–738
Pekahiah, 738–737
Pekah, 737–732
Hoshea, 732–724
(Fall of Samaria, 722–721)

The Southern Kingdom, Judah
Rehoboam, 922–915
Abijam, 915–913
Asa, 913–873
Jehoshophat, 873–849
Jehoram, 849–842
Ahaziah, 842
Athaliah, 842–837
Joash, 837–800

Amaziah, 800–783
Uzziah, 783–742
Jotham, 750–735
Ahaz, 735–715
Hezekiah, 715–687
Manasseh, 687–642
Amon, 642–640
Josiah, 640–609
Jehoahaz, 609
Jehoiakim, 609–598
Jehoiachin, 598–597
Zedekiah, 597–587
(Fall of Jerusalem, 587)

kingdom. Area or people ruled by a king. *Num. 32:33; 1 Kings 2:12; 2 Chron. 11:17; 36:20; Matt. 4:8; Acts 1:6.* (See *king* for the three Israelite kingdoms of O.T. times; Time Line.)

kingdom of God; or **kingdom of heaven.** The main theme of Jesus' teaching. A new relationship between God and men, in which God's will controls or rules; begun in Jesus Christ, yet to come fully. In the Gospel of Matthew, " kingdom of heaven " is a way of avoiding the use of the name of God. In the Gospel of John, " eternal life " means the same as " kingdom of God." *Matt. 13:24-52; Mark 14:25; Luke 11:2; 19:11; John 3:5; Acts 14:21-22; Eph. 5:5; Col. 1:13.*

Kings, The First and Second Books of the. O.T. books that relate the history of Israel from the beginning of the reign of Solomon, through the time of the two kingdoms, to the fall of Jerusalem. There are parallels to some of the material in the books of the Chronicles. The writer, or editor, working in the sixth century B.C., compiled his book from many sources,

such as court records and histories, such as the one named in *1 Kings 15:7.* The author's purpose was to show that the end of the Israelite nations had come about because the people forsook the covenant with God.

King's Highway. An ancient travel route from the Red Sea into Syria. The Israelites on their way from Egypt to Canaan wanted to use the route but were prevented from doing so by the king who controlled it. The highway continued in use throughout ancient times and was paved by the Romans in N.T. times. The road, now modernized, is still used today. *Num. 20:17; 21:22.* (See *highway;* map Plate III, G-3.)

kneading bowl; or **kneading-trough.** Shallow container of wood or earthenware, in which were mixed flour and water and a part of the previous day's dough (leavening) for the making of bread. *Ex. 12:34; Deut. 28:5;* also *Gen. 18:6; 2 Sam. 13:8; Jer. 7:18; Hos. 7:4.* (See *bread* for list of words related to bread-making.)

knife. In early O.T. times, a flint blade; or simply a sharpened piece of flint, about six inches long, with a double blade. Later a copper or cast-iron blade was attached to a wooden handle by a prong driven into the wood. Even after the Israelites learned to make metals, metal knives would have been scarce, unless captured as booty from an enemy. *Gen. 22:10; Josh. 5:3; Prov. 30:14.*

Korah (kôr'ə). In the time of the exodus from Egypt, the leader of a

91

rebellion against Moses on the grounds that a member of any family, not just an Aaronite, could be a priest. *Num., chs. 16; 26:9-11; Jude 11.* Later, **Korahites** or **sons of Korah** were helpers in the temple service, *1 Chron. 9:19,* perhaps as a group of musicians, because "Sons of Korah" also appears in the headings of several psalms. *Ps. 42; 49; 87.* Others.

L

Laban (lā'bən). One of the relatives of Abraham who stayed in the region of Paddan-aram. His sister, Rebekah, was married to Isaac, and his daughters, Leah and Rachel, were wives of Jacob. *Gen. 24:29; 28:5; chs. 29 to 31.*

labor, forced. Slavery, especially that enforced on captives. In O.T. times when a king planned an extensive building program, he seized all the foreigners or captives in the country for labor. Sometimes citizens were also impressed, but they did not become slaves. *Josh. 17:13; 2 Sam. 20:24; 1 Kings 9:15-22; 11:28.*

Lachish (lā'kĭsh). O.T. fortified city southwest of Jerusalem, about halfway to Gaza. Originally a Canaanite city-state taken by the Israelites, Lachish was always an important point of defense because it was on the route taken by invaders. Wall carvings discovered in the ruins of a palace at Nineveh show Sennacherib's capture of Lachish, with soldiers and siege machines advancing on the walls of the city and Judean captives bowing before the king. At Lachish itself have been uncovered several letters apparently from the files of a military officer stationed there at about the time of the siege of Jerusalem. The letters were written in iron-carbon ink on potsherds. *Josh. 10:3-5; 2 Chron. 32:9; Jer. 34:6-7.* (See map Plate IV, B-5.) See illustration opposite page 67.

lamb. Used for food and in sacrifices, especially at the feast of Passover. *Ex. 12:3-14; 1 Sam. 7:9; 2 Chron. 35:11; Luke 22:7; John 1:29; 1 Cor. 5:7.*

lament. Loud wailing, a part of mourning for the dead. Relatives or professional mourners, and sometimes musicians, gathered about the body to express their grief, often in poetry. *Gen. 50:10; 2 Sam. 1:17-27; Jer. 16:5; Amos 5:16; Mark 5:38* (description).

Lamentations of Jeremiah, The. O.T. book of poems mourning the destruction of Jerusalem by the Chaldeans in 587 B.C. It is called The Lamentations of Jeremiah because the prophet was supposed to have written the poems. Very likely they were written by several authors and then collected into a book.

lamp. An earthenware saucer; one part of the rim was pinched together to hold a wick. Or a covered saucer with two holes: one for pouring in oil, the other a small spout to hold the wick made of flax. Olive or mineral oil was burned. Usually a lamp was kept burning in a house day and night. *Ex. 27:20; 2 Sam. 22:29; 2 Kings 4:10; Ps. 119:105; Prov. 31:18; Matt. 5:15; Luke 15:8.* (See *house* for list of

other household furnishings.)
Also, in a figurative sense, means " the family of," as in *2 Sam. 21:17; 2 Chron. 21:7.*

lampstand. In the tabernacle or temple, a stand with branches to hold seven lamps. Today this is the symbol of the Jewish religion. *Ex. 25:31-40* (description); *1 Chron. 28:15; Heb. 9:2.*

landmark. In O.T. times, a double furrow or stones used to show the boundary of an allotment of land. *Deut. 19:14; Job 24:2; Hos. 5:10.*

Laodicea (lā ŏd'ə sē'ə). Main city of the area of Phrygia (now part of Turkey) in N.T. times. It was a center of trade and of the manufacture of cloth. A medical school was located there. *Col. 2:1; 4:13-16; Rev. 1:11.* (See map Plate XV, E-3.)

Latin. The language spoken by the Romans in N.T. times; probably used only or chiefly by soldiers and government officials. Greek was the official international language. *John 19:20.*

laver. A large metal basin in the tabernacle or temple, used by the priests for washing before making sacrifices. *Ex. 30:17-19; 1 Kings 7:38.* (See *temple* for location.)

law. In the O.T., instruction, from a Hebrew word meaning " to teach." *Deut. 4:8; Josh. 1:7; Ezra 7:10; Isa. 5:24; Jer. 31:33.* Many judgments and decisions were made on the basis of the ten commandments, which were the heart of the law. Collections of these and of regulations for worship in the O.T. books came to be called generally " the law." This is the N.T. meaning of the word. (See *commandment; ordinance; statute* [three words with related meanings].)

law of Moses. In the N.T., the first five books of the O.T. and the collections of laws in them. *Matt. 22:23-24; Luke 2:22; John 7:19; Rom. 2:17; Gal. 2:16; 3:24.*

the law and the prophets. In the N.T., the books of the O.T. that were accepted at that time by Jewish authorities as scriptures. *Matt. 11:13; Luke 16:16; Acts 13:15.*

lawyer. In N.T. times, a person who specialized in study and interpretation of the law of Moses; similar to a scribe. *Matt. 22:35; Luke 7:30; 10:25; 11:45-52; 14:3.* (See *scribe.*)

lay hands on. In the O.T., often to capture or seize violently. *1 Kings 20:5-6; Esth. 2:21; Luke 20:19.* Also, to make a sign of blessing. *Gen. 48:14; Lev. 3:7-8; 2 Chron. 29:23.* In the Gospels, a sign of blessing or of healing. *Matt. 19:13; Mark 6:5.* Elsewhere in the N.T., a sign of the giving of the Holy Spirit to others by the apostles; used as a dedication of officers. *Acts 8:17; 9:17; 1 Tim. 4:14; 5:22.*

leather. Used for bottles, girdles or belts, shields, tents, sandals, sometimes for clothing or writing material. *2 Kings 1:8; Ezek. 16:10; Mark 1:6.* (See *skin of water; tanner.*)

leaven. Used, as yeast is today, to cause bread dough to rise; usually a

93

piece of dough from the previous day's baking. *Ex. 12:19; Hos. 7:4; Matt. 13:33; Mark 8:15; 1 Cor. 5:6-8.* (See *bread* for list of words related to bread-making. See also *unleavened bread.*)

Lebanon (lĕb'ə nən). A range of mountains north of the Sea of Galilee; in O.T. times the northwest boundary of the land given to the Israelites. Noted for its forests and lumber, especially cedar. Today the area is in the Republic of Lebanon. *Deut. 11:24; Judg. 3:3; 1 Kings 5:6-9; Ezra 3:7; Ps. 37:35; Isa. 40:16; Jer. 18:14.* (See map Plates I, D-1; V, C-3.)

legion. The main division of the Roman Army in N.T. times; about six thousand men, divided into ten cohorts. Officers were tribunes and centurions. In Jesus' time there were three legions stationed in the province of Syria, of which Judea, Galilee, and Samaria were parts. The word came to mean any large number of persons. *Matt. 26:53; Mark 5:9.* (See *Rome* for list of words about the Roman Army.)

lend. (See, for customs related to lending, *creditor; debt; pledge; surety.*) *Deut. 23:19-20; Luke 6:34.*

leper. A person with an infectious, curable skin disease, which is not the same as what is called leprosy today. Lepers were forced to live apart from others and to warn anyone of their presence or approach so that people might avoid them. *Lev.,* ch. 13 (symptoms), especially *vs. 45-46; ch. 14* (treatment); *Num. 5:2; 2 Kings 7:3-15; Matt. 8:1-4; Luke 5:12; 17:12-19.*

letter. In O.T. times, a letter might be written on a clay tablet enclosed in an envelope of clay. It was delivered by a courier. *2 Sam. 11:14-15; 1 Kings 21:8-12; 2 Kings 20:12; 2 Chron. 30:6; Ezra 4:7-22* (two typical letters). (See *Lachish* for example of letters.)
In N.T. times, written on a sheet of papyrus, folded or rolled, and sealed. (Some of the N.T. letters are of the length that would fill one sheet.) The government had courier service; individuals had to hire private messengers or send their letters by traveling friends. *Acts 15:22-23; 23:25-30* (a letter); *Rom. 16:22; Col. 4:16.* The letters of Paul and others in the N.T. follow a typical form used in the Roman world, with greetings, prayers for the person receiving the letter, a formal closing, and the like. The letter in N.T. times was also a literary form, resembling a personal letter but intended for publication. Some of the N.T. letters are of this type. (See *write* for list of related words.)

Levi (lē'vī). In the O.T., one of the twelve sons of Jacob and the people descended from him, called **sons of Levi** or **tribe of Levi,** occasionally **Levites.** No territory was allotted to them, but they were given certain " cities of the priests." *Gen. 29:34; Ex. 2:1; 6:16; Josh. 13:14; Ps. 135:20.* (See *Levite* for another, more common usage.)

Levi (lē'vī). In the N.T., one of the twelve disciples of Jesus; the same as Matthew in *Matt. 9:9-13* and in all of the lists of the disciples. *Mark 2:14-15; Luke 5:27-29.* (See *disciple* for Bible references to lists of the twelve.) Others.

Leviathan (lǐ vī'ə thən). In the O.T., a sea monster, probably the crocodile. *Job 3:8; 41:1; Ps. 104:26.* Also a mythological creature opposed to God. *Ps. 74:14; Isa. 27:1.* (See *dragon.*)

Levite. Often a priest, or an assistant associated with the priests. Perhaps in early O.T. times, all priests were Levites. After the exile, and in N.T. times, Levites seem to have been helpers in the temple. *Ex. 38:21; Josh. 3:3; 1 Kings 8:4; 1 Chron. 16:4; 2 Chron. 5:12; Isa. 66:21; Luke 10:32; John 1:19.*
cities of the Levites. Same as cities of the priests. (See *Levi*, in O.T. times; *city* [cities of the priests].)

Leviticus (lǐ vǐt'ə kəs), meaning " of the Levites." O.T. book, chiefly a manual for priests. Written probably during the sixth to the fifth century B.C., it seems to describe worship after the time of the exile. (See *Genesis* for an account of the writing of the first five books of the O.T.)

libation. A quantity of oil or wine offered to God or the gods with an animal sacrifice. *Ex. 25:29; 29:40-41; 2 Chron. 29:35; Ps. 16:4; Jer. 44:17-19; Hos. 9:4.* (See *offering.*)

Libya (lǐb'ǐ ə). A nation in northern Africa west of Egypt. Parts of the modern countries of Tunisia, Algeria, Egypt, and Sudan make up the area known in ancient times as Libya. Cyrene was the chief city in N.T. times. *2 Chron. 16:8; Ezek. 30:5; Nahum 3:9;* *Acts 2:10.* (See map Plates VIII, A-3; XV, D-5 — Cyrenaica.)

linen. Usually from Egypt, but flax was grown in Canaan also. The priest's garment called the ephod was made of linen. For most people, it probably represented expensive finery. *Gen. 41:42; Ex. 39:2; Judg. 14:12; 1 Sam. 22:18; 1 Chron. 4:21; Prov. 7:16; Isa. 3:23; Luke 23:53; John 19:40.* (See *weave* for list of words related to the making of cloth.)

loaf. Thin, flat, and round. The showbread seems to have been baked in loaves like those of today. *Ex. 29:23; 2 Sam. 16:1; 2 Kings 4:42; Jer. 37:21; Mark 8:14; Luke 9:13; 1 Cor. 10:17.* (See *bake.*)

locust. A grasshopperlike insect often gathering in huge, destructive swarms; also eaten roasted and salted. *Ex. 10:4-6; Ps. 78:46; Isa. 33:4; Joel, ch. 1* (description of a plague); *Matt. 3:4.*

log. O.T. unit of measurement for liquids, about half a quart in modern terms. *Lev. 14:10.* (See *cor* for table of liquid measurements.)

loom. Used for weaving cloth of wool, linen, or goat's hair. Often consisted of two beams pegged into the ground. Upright looms were of two types: two-beamed, at which usually two workers managed the shuttles; or consisting of a beam at the top, with weights to hold down the warp threads. *Judg. 16:14; Isa. 38:12.* (See *weave* for list of words related to making of cloth.)

lord. Anyone in authority over others, as a king or the master of a servant; also a title for such persons. *Gen. 18:3; Josh. 5:14; 2 Sam. 15:21; Matt. 18:27; 20:25* (as a verb).

Lord. In the O.T., a title for God. *Deut. 14:1-2; Josh. 13:33; Ps. 24:10; Isa. 13:4.* (See *God* for other names; *host* for Lord of hosts.)
In the N.T., occasionally the same meaning, *Matt. 1:20; Luke 2:22-23; John 12:13,* but usually a title for Jesus Christ, signifying that he was from God. *Luke 7:19; John 13:13; 20:28; Acts 2:36; 1 Cor. 1:3.*

Lord's supper. The meal eaten together by members of the early church in memory of Jesus' last supper with his disciples. *1 Cor. 11:20;* see *vs. 17-26* for description. (See *break bread.*)

lot. (See *cast lots.*) Probably different-colored stones were shaken in a container and then one was drawn out, or they were poured out on the ground. *Josh. 14:2; 1 Sam. 10:21; Acts 1:26.*
Also, because the lot was cast to apportion the land, the word means portion, both in the sense of land, *Josh. 17:14,* and of one's destiny in life, as in *Jer. 13:25* and *1 Thess. 3:3* (See *Urim and Thummim.*)

Lot (lŏt). Nephew of Abraham who accompanied him to the land of Canaan. *Gen. 11:27, 31; 12:4; 13:5-13; ch. 19; 2 Peter 2:7.*

love. (See, for God's love of man, *covenant; grace; judge; mercy; righ-* *teous; steadfast love.*) *Deut 7:7; Ps. 17:7; Rom. 5:8; 2 Cor. 5:14.*
Man's love of God is his response to God's love. (See *faith; righteous.*) *Deut. 6:5; Matt. 22:37; Eph. 6:24; 1 John 4:20-21.*
Man's love for his fellowman is based on God's love and is inseparable from love of God. (See *mercy; righteous.*) *Lev. 19:18; Mark 12:31; Luke 6:27-36; John 14:23; 1 Cor., ch. 13; Gal. 5:13; 1 John, chs. 3; 4.*

Luke. A Gentile Christian, a doctor, who traveled with Paul. He was the author of a Gospel and of The Acts of the Apostles. *Col. 4:14; 2 Tim. 4:11; Philemon 24;* parts of The Acts in which "we" is used: *chs. 16:10-17; 20:5 to 21:18; 27:1 to 28:16.*

Luke, The Gospel According to. N.T. book about the life, death, and resurrection of Jesus Christ. The purpose is given in *Luke 1:1-4.* With the book of The Acts (see *Acts 1:1-2*), it comprises a two-volume account of the beginnings of the church, written by a Gentile Christian who worked with Paul. The writer used oral accounts and some written sources, including the Gospel of Mark. The book was probably written around A.D. 75.

lute. Small stringed musical instrument consisting of a wooden frame and an uncertain number of strings made of gut. It was not used in worship, but was played mostly by women. *Ps. 92:3; 150:3.*

lyre. A musical instrument with three to twelve strings plucked with fingers or a plectrum. It was used in temple services, and also on other occasions. The frame was usually of

Captives, probably Israelites, playing lyres. From an Assyrian relief

wood, but sometimes of gold or silver. *1 Sam. 10:5; 16:23; 2 Sam. 6:5; 2 Chron. 5:12; Ps. 71:22; Ezek. 26:13.*

Lystra (lĭs'trə). City in the Roman province of Galatia in N.T. times, between Iconium and Derbe. The church there would have been one of those to which the letter to the Galatians was sent. *Acts 14:6, 8, 21; 16:1-2; 2 Tim. 3:11.* (See map Plate XV, F-3.)

M

Macedonia (măs'ə dō'nĭ ə). In N.T. times, a province of the Roman Empire, north of Achaia, in the northern part of what is now the country of Greece. Among the cities of Macedonia were Philippi and Thessalonica, to the churches of which Paul wrote letters. He visited a number of other cities in the province also. *Acts 16:9-10; 19:21; 27:2; 1 Cor. 16:5; 2 Cor. 8:1; Phil. 4:15; 1 Thess. 1:7.* (See map Plate XV, D-2.)

magic. Widely practiced among the ancient nations, forbidden to the Israelites. In *Deut. 18:10-14* there is a list of the forbidden practices, and the reason they are not to be followed is given. *Gen. 41:8; Ex. 7:11; Isa. 3:3; Ezek. 13:18; Acts 13:6-8.* (See, for some types of magic, *augury; divine; medium; necromancer; soothsayer; sorcerer; wise men; wizard.*)

magistrate. In the N.T., a judge, as in *Luke 12:58;* or an officer on the governing council of a Roman city, as in *Acts 16:19-24.*

mail. The coat of mail, or the breastplate, in O.T. times was made of overlapping metal scales attached to a tunic of cloth or leather. Chain armor and solid metal plates were not used until later times. *1 Sam. 17:38; 2 Chron. 26:14; Neh. 4:16; Jer. 46:4; 51:8.* (See *armor.*)

Malachi (măl'ə kī). A prophet in the time following the return of the Jews from exile in Babylon, probably the fifth century B.C. and, possibly, around the time of Ezra and Nehemiah. Nothing is known about the prophet.

Malachi, The Book of. O.T. book containing teachings of the prophet Malachi about the carelessness of people in the prophet's time in matters of faith and worship.

mammon. Riches. *Matt. 6:24; Luke 16:9-13.*

man of God. O.T. term for a prophet. *Josh. 14:6; Judg. 13:6; 1 Sam*

9:6; 1 Kings 17:18; 2 Kings 4:8-10; 2 Chron. 8:14; also 1 Tim. 6:11; 2 Tim. 3:16-17.

Manasseh (mə năs'ə). A son of Joseph; also, with Ephraim, counted as one of the twelve tribes descended from Jacob. Also the tribe's territory along both banks of the Jordan River. *Gen. 41:50-51; ch. 48; Num. 1:34-35; Josh. 4:12; 17:5-6; 2 Chron. 30:10-11; Ps. 60:7.* (See map Plate IV, C-4, D-4.) Others, including a king of the Southern Kingdom, Judah.

manger. A hollowed-out stone or a box made of stones and plaster, used as a feeding place for domestic animals. It was usually located in the lower part of a house, or a cave was used to shelter the animals. *Luke 2:7, 12, 16; 13:15.*

manna, meaning "What is it?" A substance gathered for food during the journey of the Israelites from Egypt to Canaan. There are many theories as to what it may have been: a secretion of certain bushes, for example, or a substance given off by insects. *Ex. 16:3-5, 14-15, 31; Num. 11:6-9; Josh. 5:12; Ps. 78:24; John 6:31, 49; Heb. 9:4.*

mantelet. A portable shelter behind which besiegers moved to attack a city's walls. *Nahum 2:5.*

mantle. A full, sleeveless, outer garment; a cloak. The mantle which the prophet Elijah put on Elisha was a symbol of Elisha's prophetic calling. *Ex. 22:26-27; 1 Kings 19:19; 2 Kings 2:13; Isa. 59:17; Matt. 24:18; Mark*

14:63; Luke 22:36. (See *coat* for list of other items of clothing.)

Mark; or **John Mark.** A member of the church at Jerusalem, one of Paul's fellow workers, probably the writer of the Gospel of Mark. His mother's home may have been the meeting place of the first church in Jerusalem. *Acts 12:12, 25; 15:37-39; Col. 4:10; 2 Tim. 4:11; Philemon 24.*

Mark, The Gospel According to. N.T. book about the life, death, and resurrection of Jesus Christ; probably written by John Mark on the basis of recollections of the disciple Peter. It was the first Gospel written, around A.D. 65, and was used as source material by the writers of both Matthew and Luke.

market place. In the Gospels, as in O.T. times, the space inside the gate of a town or city, where goods were sold and people gathered for business or for exchange of news and gossip. *Ps. 55:11; Matt. 20:3; Mark 12:38.* In the book of The Acts, the central, open place of a Greek-style city. *Acts 16:19; 17:17.* (See *city*, in N.T. times; *square of the city*.)

marriage. A long betrothal preceded marriage. The wedding was not a religious ceremony but a family celebration of several days' length. On the first day, the bride was dressed at her own home. The groom, with his friends, went from his father's house to the bride's. She and her friends accompanied the groom's party to his home. The words of the vow were, "She is my wife and I am her hus-

band from this day forever." *Gen. 34:11-12; Ex. 22:16; Ps. 78:63; Matt. 22:2-9; John 2:1-11.*
It was the custom that when a man died one of his brothers or a near relative would marry the widow, if possible, to continue the family line and to preserve property rights. *Deut. 25:5-10.* This custom is reflected in The Book of Ruth and in *Matt. 22:23-33.*

Mary. The mother of Jesus. Aside from the stories of Jesus' birth and childhood, *Matt., chs. 1; 2; Luke, chs. 1; 2,* the N.T. tells us only that Mary was present on at least two occasions during Jesus' years of work, that she was at his crucifixion, and that she was with the disciples after Christ's resurrection. *John 2:1-10; Luke 8:19-21; John 19:25-27; Acts 1:14.*
Five other women named Mary appear in the N.T. They are usually identified or can be identified by other details in the context.

Maskil (măs′kĭl). A word in the titles of several psalms, the meaning of which is not clear. It may mean a psalm for meditation or a psalm that teaches. *Ps. 42; 52 to 55; and others.*

mason. A workman in stone or brick. At the time of the building of Solomon's temple, the Israelites were not skilled at masonry and so hired workmen from Tyre to help. Some of the things a mason might have been called on to build are: walls, sheepfolds, millstones, cisterns and water tunnels, houses, tombs, olive presses and wine vats. *2 Sam. 5:11; 1 Kings 5:18* (builders); *2 Kings 12:11-12; Ezra 3:7.* (See *axe; brick; hammer;*

mortar; quarry; stonecutter.)

master. A person in authority over others, usually the owner of slaves, or the head of a household, or a king; also a title used in speaking to such people. *Gen. 24:27; Judg. 19:11; Isa. 37:4; Matt. 24:45-51; John 13:16.*
Master. In the Gospels and in some of the N.T. letters, a title given to Jesus Christ. *Matt. 26:25; Mark 9:5; Luke 9:49; Eph. 6:9.*

Matthew. One of the twelve disciples of Jesus. He was a tax collector stationed in Capernaum, perhaps to collect customs from merchants traveling on the road to Damascus. Also called Levi in the Gospels of Mark and Luke. *Matt. 9:9; 10:3; Acts 1:13.* (See *disciple* for Bible references to lists of the twelve.)

Matthew, The Gospel According to. N.T. book about the life, death, and resurrection of Jesus Christ. The writer used as sources the Gospel of Mark, a collection of sayings made by the disciple Matthew, and some other materials. He wrote his book around A.D. 80. Like the writers of the other Gospels, he was not concerned to put his materials together into an accurate, historical account, but rather he was concerned to put them into a form for teaching new disciples and answering the questions of believers. He especially wished to show how Jesus Christ was the fulfillment of prophecies and predictions made in O.T. times.

meal. A coarse type of flour made by grinding the whole kernels of wheat or barley. Flour was made from the inner kernels only and was more expensive. *Gen. 18:6; Num. 5:15; 2 Sam. 17:28; 1 Kings 17:12; Isa. 47:2; Luke 13:21.* (See *bread* for list of words related to bread-making.)

measure. In addition to the usual meanings, a definite unit or several units of measurement of which the quantity is unknown today. *Ex. 29:40; Ruth 3:15; Hag. 2:16; Matt. 13:33; Luke 16:6-7.* (See, for O.T. dry measures, table under *homer;* for O.T. liquid measures, table under *cor;* for measurement of length in O.T. and N.T., table under *cubit.* See also *acre.* See, for N.T. measurements of distance, *fathom; furlong; stadia.* See also *mile* and *yard* for equivalents in N.T. terms.)

Medes; Media (mē'dǐ ə). O.T. nation in the northwest part of what is now the country of Iran. The Medes were allied with the Persian rulers who captured Babylon and took over the Chaldean empire during the time that the Jews were in exile. Media was a province in the Persian empire. *2 Kings 17:6; Ezra 6:2; Isa. 13:17; Jer. 51:11; Acts 2:9.* (See map Plate X, C-2.)

medium. A person who divined, or used other magic practices to foretell events. *Deut. 18:10-11; 1 Sam. 28:3, 7; 2 Kings 21:6; Isa. 8:19.* (See *magic* for list of similar practices.)

meek. Dependent on God (not patient and long-suffering, as the word is used today); not possessing or claiming power over others. *Num. 12:3; Ps.*

37:11; Isa. 11:4; Matt. 5:5; 2 Cor. 10:1; Eph. 4:2.

Megiddo (mə gǐd'ō). O.T. town in north-central Canaan, located on an important mountain pass. It was a fortified city under the Canaanites. In later times Solomon fortified the city and had extensive stables there for over four hundred war horses. The remains of the stables have been excavated by archaeologists. Megiddo is an example of a chariot city. *Josh. 12:21; 1 Kings 9:15; 2 Kings 23:29-30.* (See map Plate V, C-4.)

Melchizedek (měl kǐz'ə děk'). A king and priest in Abraham's time. He was a symbol of the ideal priest. *Gen. 14:18; Ps. 110:4; Heb. 5:6, 10; 6:20; 7:1-17.*

merchant. Usually a person engaged in international trade. Until the time of Solomon the Israelites carried on little commerce. Certain nations, such as Tyre (Phoenicia in general history), were noted for their trade by sea. The Arameans, Canaanites, and others carried on trade by overland caravans. *Gen. 23:16* (method of paying); *2 Chron. 9:13-14; Neh. 13:20; Isa. 23:2-3, 8; Ezek. 27:3; Matt. 13:45.* (See *caravan; highway; inn; road; ship; trade.*)

mercy. The continued kindness of God to his people which made possible the covenant relationship. Also a similar quality in the relationships of men. *Ex. 34:6; 2 Sam. 24:14; Ps. 23:6; 103:4; 145:8; Matt. 9:13; 23:23; Luke 6:36; 18:13; 2 Cor. 1:3; 1 Tim. 1:2.* (See *grace; steadfast love.*)

mercy seat. The top of the ark of the covenant, the space between the cherubim; thought of as God's throne and therefore representing the presence of God. *Ex. 25:17-22; Num. 7:89; 1 Chron. 28:11; Heb. 9:5.* (See *ark; enthroned.*)

Mesopotamia (měs'ə pə tā'mǐ ə). In the O.T., the valley between the upper Euphrates and Tigris Rivers; same as Aram. *Gen. 24:10; Deut. 23:4; Judg. 3:10; 1 Chron. 19:6.* (See map Plate II, F-2 — Paddan-aram.)
By N.T. times, the Greeks had applied the name to the entire area between the rivers. *Acts 2:9; 7:2.* It is used in this sense today. The area is also known as the Fertile Crescent and as one of the major areas in which civilization first arose.

Messiah (mə sī'ə). A title used by Jews of N.T. times for the king who would be like David and whom God would raise up to restore the kingdom to Israel. *John 1:41; 4:25.* (See, for other names, more commonly used in the N.T. than " Messiah," *anoint* [the anointed]; *Christ; king,* in N.T. times; *son of God* [Son of God; Son of man; Son of David].) Other titles were " Holy One of God," *Mark 1:24;* and " Just One," *Acts 22:14.*

Micah (mī'kə). A prophet in the Southern Kingdom, Judah, in the eighth century B.C. He was a contemporary of Isaiah. *Jer. 26:18.* (See Time Line.) Others.

Micah, The Book of. O.T. book made up of the prophet Micah's teachings about God's judgment on his peo-

ple, *chs. 1 to 3;* and, probably, teachings from other prophets on the same theme, *chs. 4 to 7.*

Michael. In the system of beliefs about angels in N.T. times, an archangel. *Jude 9; Rev. 12:7.* (See *angel.*) Others in O.T.

Michal (mī'kəl). Daughter of Saul and wife of David. *1 Sam. 14:49; 18:20-27; 19:11-17; 25:44; 2 Sam. 3:13-14; 6:16-23.*

Michmash (mĭk'măsh). O.T. town near Bethel, seven miles north of Jerusalem; scene of a battle in which Saul and Jonathan defeated Philistine forces. *1 Sam. 13:2-7, 23; 14:31; Isa. 10:28.* (See map Plate IV, C-5.)

Midian (mĭd'ĭ ən). In O.T. times, an area in the southwest Arabian Desert. The **Midianites** were nomadic people who made raids upon the Israelites while the Israelites were entering Canaan and in the time of the judges. The Midianites were finally defeated by Gideon. *Gen. 37:28; Ex. 2:15-22; Num. 31:7; Judg. 6:1-6; 7:1* (see *vs. 2-23* for description of the battle). (See map Plate III, G-4 — Land of Midian.)

mighty men. Warriors, especially the mercenary troops of King David which comprised his bodyguard; a group distinct from the army, which was made up chiefly of citizens. *Josh. 8:3; 2 Sam. 20:7; 23:8-23.*

Miktam (mĭk'təm). A word in the title of several psalms; of uncertain meaning, perhaps " a psalm of atonement." *Ps. 16; 56 to 60.*

mile. In the N.T., used in the modern meaning, usually explained in footnotes in terms of stadia, the Greek measure of distance used at that time. *Matt. 5:41; Luke 24:13; John 11:18.*

mill. Used in grinding wheat or barley to make meal and flour. In early times, two stones, one slightly concave, the other rubbed over it. Later two round stones, millstones, the top one with a handle. The grain was put between them and the top stone turned. Usually two women worked such a mill, each giving a half-turn to the upper stone. The same principle was used in N.T. times to make large community or commercial mills turned by animal power. *Deut. 24:6; Judg. 9:53; Lam. 5:13; Matt. 24:41; Luke 17:2.* (See *grind; meal.* See *bread* for list of words related to bread-making.)

mina (mī′nə). A weight used in O.T. times for payment before the use of coins; equal to from one to two pounds in modern measurements. *1 Kings 10:17; Ezra 2:69; Neh. 7:71-72; Ezek. 45:12.* (See *money; weight.* See *shekel* for table of weights.)

minister. In the O.T., most often as a verb, meaning to serve, especially at worship or sacrifice. As a noun, a personal attendant. The priest combined both these functions. *Ex. 30:20; Josh. 1:1; 1 Kings 1:4; Ezra 8:17; Ps. 103:21; Ezek. 44:11; Joel 1:9;* also *Matt. 4:11; Luke 1:2; Acts 8:27; Heb. 8:2.*
In the N.T. letters, a deacon or servant. It was an office in the early church that was the origin of, but not the same as, the office of minister today. *Col. 1:7, 23, 25; 1 Tim. 4:6.* (See *church* for list of other officers.)

mint. Similar to the herb today; used as a seasoning. If picked wild, it was not subject to a tithe in N.T. times. Cultivated mint was to be tithed. A tithe would amount to a pinch or two. *Luke 11:42.*

miracle. A sign of God's power in the form of a happening that is different from processes of nature insofar as they are known. *Ex. 7:9; Ps. 78:11; 105:5; Acts 8:13; 19:11; 1 Cor. 12:10; Gal. 3:5.* (See *sign* [signs and wonders].)

Miriam (mǐr′ĭ əm). Sister of Moses, associated with Moses and Aaron in the leadership of the Israelites in their journey from Egypt to the Promised Land, Canaan. *Ex. 15:20; Num., ch. 12; Micah 6:4.*

mirror. A highly polished metal surface. In O.T. times, possessed only by kings and a few wealthy persons, but used more widely in N.T. times. The image in such a mirror was not very clear. *Ex. 38:8; Job 37:18; 1 Cor. 13:12; James 1:23.*

Mizpah (mǐz′pə). Several locations in O.T. times, the most important a town on the border between the Northern Kingdom, Israel, and the Southern Kingdom, Judah. After the fall of Jerusalem, when the area became a province of the Chaldean empire, Mizpah was the capital of the province. *1 Sam. 7:5; 2 Kings 25:23; Jer. 40:6.*

Moab (mō'ăb). In O.T. times, an area east of the Dead Sea. The **Moabites** were considered relatives of the Israelites, descended from Lot. They opposed the Israelites when the Israelites began to take Canaan, and the Moabites invaded Canaan in later times also. During the reign of David they were forced to pay tribute to Israel, but later were independent again. *Gen. 19:37; Num. 22:1; Deut. 29:1; Judg. 3:12-30; 1 Chron. 18:2; 2 Kings 1:1; Jer. 9:26; Amos 2:1.* (See map Plate IV, D-6.)

molten. Made from melted metal poured into a mold; used of images in contrast to "graven." *Ex. 34:17; Deut. 27:15; 1 Kings 7:23; Nahum 1:14.* (See *graven.*)

money. Before 600 B.C., rings, bars, or lumps of metal, usually silver, but also copper and gold, were used as payment. These were of standard weights, but the standards varied from

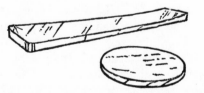

Tongue and circle of gold found at Gezer

nation to nation, and even from one king's reign to the next one. Thus payments were always weighed at the time of the transaction. When coins came into use they bore the same names as the weights they replaced. For example, "shekel" may mean either the weight or the coin. *Gen. 42:25; 43:21; Lev. 25:37; 2 Kings 12:4-5; Jer. 32:10.* (See *weigh.* See *shekel* for table of weights of O.T. times. See also *daric.*)

In N.T. times, coins were widely used, and those of many different nations, including some of Jewish mintage, were in circulation in all parts of the world. *Matt. 25:18; Luke 9:3; 19:23; John 12:6; Acts 8:18.* (See, for money in N.T. times, *copper coin; denarius; penny; pound; shekel,* in N.T. times; *silver; talent,* in N.T. times. See also *banker; money-changer.*)

money-changer. In N.T. times, a person who exchanged coins of any nation for the particular coins needed to pay the half-shekel tax to the temple. Roman or other coinage was not acceptable because it usually carried representations or symbols of the gods. The money-changer collected a commission of three cents on every half-shekel. *Matt. 21:12; John 2:14-15.* (See *shekel,* in N.T. times; *table.*)

month. In O.T. times, based on the moon, the new moon being the first day of the month. The months had alternately twenty-nine and thirty days. Often they were designated by number, but some Canaanite names were used also, and, later, Chaldean names were used. *Gen. 7:11; Deut. 16:1; 1 Kings 12:33; Ezra 6:15; Neh. 1:1; Zech. 7:1.* (See *year.*)

mortar. Mud or clay mixed with straw, pebbles, ashes, or the like, and used to bind stones or bricks in building. *Gen. 11:3; Ex. 1:14; Nahum 3:14.* (See *mason* for list of words related

to brick work and stone work.)
Also a bowl in which spices, grains, and dyes were ground with a pestle. *Num. 11:8; Prov. 27:22.*

Moses (mō'zĭz), Egyptian name, meaning " a son." Leader of the Israelites in their escape from Egypt and journey to Canaan. Throughout the Bible, Moses is considered the founder of the people of God; the lawgiver, that is, the one who taught that God's people must live by his teaching; and the forerunner of the prophets. A summary of his life and work is given in *Acts 7:20-44.* Stories in Exodus, Numbers, Deuteronomy; see also *1 Kings 8:53; Ps. 103:7; Matt. 17:3; Luke 16:29; 1 Cor. 9:9.* (See Time Line.)

Moses' seat. A seat for the ruler or a guest in a synagogue of N.T. times. *Matt. 23:2.*

most holy place. The innermost room of the tabernacle or temple, in which the ark was placed. *Ex. 26:33-34; 2 Chron. 3:8, 10; 5:7; Ezek. 41:4.* (See *temple* for description.)

mound. In O.T. warfare, a ramplike structure built outside a city wall by besieging forces. Used for mounting siege machines. *2 Sam. 20:15; Isa. 37:33; Jer. 6:6; 32:24; Ezek. 21:22.* (See *siege.*)

mourning. See *Jer. 48:37-38* for a general description. Customs followed by the relatives and friends of a dead person included: tearing the clothes, *Gen. 37:34;* wearing sackcloth, *2 Sam. 3:31;* rolling or sitting in ashes, *Jer. 6:26.* In general the person in mourn-

ing neglected his appearance. See *2 Sam. 12:16-23* for a reversal of this custom. Some people shaved their heads or made cuts on themselves. *Deut. 14:1; Jer. 16:6; Amos 8:10.* The relatives and persons hired to mourn made laments over the dead. *Isa. 3:26; Matt. 11:17.* A fast was observed. *1 Sam. 31:13; 2 Sam. 1:12.* The period of mourning might last seven days. *Gen. 50:10.* (See, for customs related to mourning, *ashes; beard; fast; flute; gash; lament; rent his clothes; sackcloth; shave.* See *death* for list of other customs.)
Many of these actions were also used as signs of repentance, a type of mourning for sin. (See *repent.*)

music. Both choir music and instrumental music were used in the temple services. Music was used also for joyous occasions and for dancing, and as a part of mourning. (See, for musical instruments and their uses, *flute; harp; horn; lute; lyre; tambourine; timbrel; trumpet.* See also *hymn; psalm; worship.*)

muster. In O.T. times, before the Israelites had a standing army, volunteer fighters were gathered from the tribes by trumpet call, *Judg. 3:27;* by signals such as banners on hilltops, *Jer. 51:27;* or by messenger, *Judg. 7:24.* See also *Josh. 8:10; 1 Sam. 11:8; 1 Kings 20:15; Isa. 13:4; Jer. 52:25.*

myrrh. Fragrant substance made from the gum of a tree in Arabia; used for perfume, in anointing oil, and in the spices put in shrouds. With wine, myrrh was given to reduce pain. *Gen. 37:25; 2 Chron. 9:24; Ps. 45:8; Matt.*

2:11; Mark 15:23; John 19:39.

mystery. Something formerly secret or unknown, now revealed to some but still hidden from others, and never to be known fully by men. A word borrowed by the apostle Paul from the pagan world to mean God's revelation to men through Jesus Christ. Mystery religions of N.T. times were those in which initiates were taught special secret knowledge. *Rom. 16:25; 1 Cor. 4:1; Eph. 3:9; Col. 1:26-27; 1 Tim. 3:16.*

myths. Stories told to explain the origins of customs, or, as among the Greeks and Romans of N.T. times, stories about the gods. *1 Tim. 1:4; Titus 1:14; 2 Peter 1:16.* (See *Rome* for list of philosophies and religions.)

N

Nahum (nā'əm). A prophet in the Southern Kingdom, Judah, in the seventh century B.C. He was a contemporary of the prophets Zephaniah, Habakkuk, and Jeremiah. (See Time Line.) Other.

Nahum, The Book of. O.T. book containing prophecies of Nahum about the destruction of Nineveh, the capital of the Assyrian empire, which was threatening and conquering all of the world of that time.

name. A person's name had a meaning which was considered to be expressive of his character. A change of name or an additional name indicated a change in character. An example is given in *Gen. 32:27-28.* A person had only his given name. In place of a surname he was sometimes designated by his father's name, with a prefix (Bar-) meaning "son of," *Matt. 16:17,* or by his town, *Mark 1:24.* The name of an individual person in the O.T. may also be the name of a family or a tribe, or even of a whole people or nation. The explanation for this use of names lies in the fact that the basis of Israelite society was originally the tribe, all the members of which were descended from a common ancestor. (For examples, see *Israel; Edom.*) A personal name may also be the name of a place. (See *Dan; Haran.*)

In N.T. times some people had both Hebrew and Greek names, as Simon (Hebrew) and Peter (Greek), or Saul and Paul.

the name of the Lord or **the name of Jesus Christ** means "God's being as revealed to men." **in the name of** means "in his power." *Ps. 7:17; 9:10; 30:4; 118:10; Matt. 6:9; Luke 13:35; John 3:18; Acts 3:6; 5:41.*

for his name's sake means "according to his nature." *Jer. 14:7; Luke 21:17.*

Naphtali (năf'tə lī). One of the twelve sons of Jacob; the people or tribe descended from him; and their territory, northwest of the Sea of Chinnereth (Galilee). *Gen. 30:8; Num. 1:42-43; Josh. 19:32; 20:7; Isa. 9:1; Matt. 4:13.* (See map Plate IV, C-3.)

nard. An expensive perfumed ointment made from the roots of a plant grown in India. *Mark 14:3; John 12:3.*

Nathan (nā′thən). A prophet in the time of David and Solomon. According to the Chronicles, Nathan wrote a history of that time, but it has been lost. *2 Sam. 7:1-17; 12:11-15; 1 Kings 1:8-45; 1 Chron. 29:29; 2 Chron. 9:29.* Others.

Nathanael (nə thăn′ĭ əl). One of Jesus' twelve disciples. The name is used only in the Gospel of John, but it is believed to mean the person called Bartholomew in the other three Gospels. *John 1:45-49; 21:2.* (See *disciple* for Bible references to lists of the twelve.)

nations. Peoples other than the Israelites, not countries like those of modern times, whose boundaries can be shown on a map. A better way to think of nations in ancient times is to imagine a huge desert with different-colored sands shifting about. At one time, the pink sand would be almost everywhere, and there would be only patches of yellow and purple. At another time, yellow would predominate. If each color represented a nation, the desert would show the nations and their changing areas throughout O.T. times. This was true in the land to the east of the Israelites, where especially the Assyrians, the Chaldeans, and the Persians, but also other nations, moved from their own areas to the control of larger areas, and then were pushed back to smaller areas by other nations gaining control. *2 Chron. 36:14; Ps. 106:41; Matt. 28:19; Gal. 3:8.*

nave. In the temple built by Solomon, the holy place. *1 Kings 6:17;*

2 Chron. 3:5; Ezek. 41:15. (See *temple* for description.)

Nazarene. A native of Nazareth. *Matt. 2:23; Mark 14:67.* Also used of Christians. *Acts 24:5.*

Nazareth (năz′ə rĭth). N.T. village in the hills of Galilee, eighty-eight miles north of Jerusalem. *Matt. 2:23; 26:71; Mark 1:24; Luke 4:16-30; 24:19; John 1:46; 19:19; Acts 3:6.* (See map Plate XIV, C-3.)

Nazirite (năz′ə rīt). A person who had taken a vow to be separated to God, or a holy person. Sometimes the vow was taken for life, or it could be taken for a stated period of time. An outline of what the Nazirite had to do is given in *Num., ch. 6.* See *Judg. 13:5; 16:17; Amos 2:11-12;* also *1 Sam. 1:11; Acts 21: 23-24.*

Nebuchadnezzar (nĕb′ə kəd nĕz′ər). A Chaldean king, 605 to 562 B.C., called king of Babylon, the capital of his empire which succeeded that of the Assyrians. He demanded tribute from the Southern Kingdom, Judah. When Judah revolted, he besieged Jerusalem, and captured and destroyed it, taking the people into captivity in Babylon. *2 Kings, chs. 24; 25; Ezra 2:1; Jer. 29:1.* "Nebuchadnezzar" in The Book of Daniel does not refer to the historical person of that name. (See Time Line.)

Neco (nē′kō). A Pharaoh of Egypt in the last years of the Southern Kingdom, Judah, 609 to 593 B.C. He attempted to take the kingdom of Judah; killed the king, Josiah, in battle;

and appointed the next king. He was defeated by Nebuchadnezzar, who then took over the control of Judah. *2 Kings 23:29-35; Jer. 46:2.* (See Time Line.)

necromancer. In O.T. times, one who divined by communicating with the dead, a form of magic forbidden to the Israelites. *Deut. 18:10-11.* (See *shades.* See *magic* for list of related practices.)

Negeb (nĕg'ĕb). A region in the southern part of Canaan west of the Arabah. In O.T. times it was a grazing area inhabited by the Amalekites; in recent years it has been a desert. Now as part of the state of Israel, it is being reclaimed. Beer-sheba and Kadesh-barnea were two of the towns located there. *Gen. 12:9; Num. 13:29; 1 Sam. 27:10; Ps. 126:4; Jer. 32:44.* (See *Canaan* for description of main geographical areas; map Plate I, A-7.)

Nehemiah (nē'ə mī'ə). A Jew who was cupbearer to the Persian king in the fifth century B.C. He went to Jerusalem a century after the first returned exiles and helped Ezra in the rebuilding of the city. (See Time Line.) Others.

Nehemiah, The Book of. O.T. book, originally joined with Ezra as one book. It is an account of Nehemiah's work in Jerusalem. Probably parts of it represent his memoirs, edited, along with other materials, by the same writer who prepared the Chronicles and Ezra.

net. Used for hunting animals and birds, and in fishing. *Ps. 9:15; 140:5; Prov. 1:17; Isa. 19:8; 51:20; Matt. 13:47.* Fishing nets were of two kinds: a cone-shaped, weighted net cast by hand, *Matt. 4:18-21; Mark 1:16-19;* and a large net let out from a boat, *Isa. 19:8; Matt. 13:47; John 21:6.* (See *fisherman.*)

new moon. The beginning of the month, marked by feasting and special sacrifices. *1 Sam. 20:24; 1 Chron. 23:31; Isa. 1:14; Ezek. 46:1-7; Amos 8:4-5; Col. 2:16.*

Nile. The river of Egypt, rising in central Africa and flowing north to the Mediterranean Sea, where it forms a large delta with many waterways. The land of Egypt consisted of the areas along the two banks of the river. The agriculture and all the civilization of Egypt depended on the annual flooding of the river, which literally made the land. The river was considered by the Egyptians to be a god. *Gen. 41:1; Ex. 1:22; Isa. 23:10; Ezek. 29:9; Amos 9:5; Nahum 3:8.* (See map Plate III, C-4.)

Nineveh (nĭn'ə və). The capital city of the Assyrian empire, captured and destroyed in 612 B.C. by the Chaldeans. Located on the east side of the upper Tigris River, Nineveh dated from very early times. It is often represented in the O.T. as a hated place because of the cruelty and oppression of the Assyrians. An emperor of the seventh century B.C. established in Nineveh a library containing many thousands of clay tablets, on such subjects as history, religion, and science. *Gen. 10:11; 2 Kings 19:36; Jonah 1:2;*

NOBLES

3:3; *Nahum 1:1; Zeph. 2:13; Luke 11:30, 32.*

nobles. In O.T. times, leaders of the people; probably the same as elders, not an aristocratic class. *1 Kings 21:8; 2 Chron. 23:20; Neh. 5:7; Jer. 39:6.* (See *elder,* in O.T. times.)

Numbers. O.T. book continuing the story begun in Exodus of the Israelites' journey from Egypt to Canaan. It is named for the numberings of the tribes in *chs. 1 and 4.* (See *Genesis* for an account of the writing of the first five books of the O.T.)

O

oak. Any large tree; in O.T. times often a place that was sacred or that was associated with a person or an event. *Gen. 12:6; Josh. 24:26; Judg. 9:6; Ezek. 6:13; Hos. 4:13.* (See *tree, under every green.*)

oath. A statement affirming that what one says is true, often including an appeal to God as a witness, sometimes including a curse on oneself. When a dispute between two persons could not be decided, the taking of an oath or the refusal to take it was used to find out who was telling the truth. For examples of oaths, see *Job 31:5-8; Ps. 7:3-5; 2 Cor. 1:23.* See also *Gen. 26:28; Ex. 22:10-11; 2 Sam. 19:23; 1 Kings 8:31-32; Acts 23:12; James 5:12;* also *Matt. 5:34-37.* (See *swear.*)

Obadiah, The Book of (ō′bə dī′ə). O.T. book of oracles, from one or several prophets, about Edom, a nation that had long been an enemy of Israel and that had moved into Jerusalem after its conquest by the Chaldeans. The time of the prophecies is not known, but it was probably after the fall of Jerusalem or after the return from exile. Others.

obeisance. The act of showing submission to a king or other person in authority; in O.T. times, usually by lying facedown on the ground before the person. *Gen. 42:6* (description); *1 Sam. 24:8; 1 Chron. 21:21; 2 Chron. 24:17.*

odor, pleasing. In the O.T., the smoke from a burnt offering, considered as pleasing to God. The Israelites held this belief in common with most ancient peoples. *Ex. 29:18; Num. 15:24; Ezek. 6:13;* see also *2 Cor. 2:15; Eph. 5:2.* (See *sacrifice.*)

offering. In the O.T., things given to God are in three general categories: (1) gifts, including food, drink, and incense for God's pleasure, and money to the temple; (2) communion meals eaten with God, usually in thanksgiving; and (3) atonement offerings, which were animal sacrifices. Most of these offerings were sacrifices, or in the case of gifts, parts of a sacrifice. Other ancient nations made similar offerings to the gods. The types of offerings mentioned in the O.T. are numerous and confusing because they differed from time to time. The main kinds and examples are:

burnt offering, *Lev. 1:9; Amos 5.22; Mark 12:33.*
offering by fire (same as burnt), *Ex. 30:20.* (See *odor, pleasing.*)

108

cereal offering (a gift), *Ex. 29:41;*
Amos 5:22.

drink offering (a gift), *Gen. 35:14.*
(See *libation.*)

freewill offering, *Lev. 22:23.*

guilt offering, *Lev. 7:1.*

human offering, *2 Kings 23:10.* (See
first-born; Hinnom, valley of.)

offering of metal or money, *Ex.
35:22; Ezra 8:28.*

peace offering, *Lev. 3:3.*

sin offering, *Lev. 9:2; Heb. 10:18.*

votive offering, *Lev. 22:23.* (See
vow.)

wave offering (waved before the
Lord), *Ex. 29:26.*

(See *bread of the Presence; service.*
See *sacrifice* for further information
and list of related words.)

Og (ŏg). In the time of Moses, a
king of the Amorites in the area of
Bashan; a giant. His defeat by the Israelites was remembered as decisive in
the approach to Canaan. *Deut. 3:1-11;
Josh. 12:4; Neh. 9:22; Ps. 135:11.*

oil. Made from olives, and mentioned with wine and grain as one of
the three chief agricultural products.

Lamp of New Testament times, with
handle shaped like a cross

Deut. 7:13. Used as an offering, *Gen.
35:14; Num. 18:12;* in baking or as a
spread on bread, like butter, *Ex. 29:2;
Num. 11:8;* for lamps, *Ex. 25:6; Matt.
25:3-4;* in perfumed form, for anointing, *Ex. 30:25; 1 Sam. 10:1.* (See *olive*
for methods of making olive oil.)

ointment. Perfume in the form of
scented olive oil. *Eccl. 7:1; Matt.
26:6-13; Luke 23:56.*

olive. Trees were cultivated in the
hill country. In the fall, the ripe fruit
was beaten off the trees with sticks,
placed in vats or presses, and pressed
by foot or by turning a stone. The oil
produced in this way was an important product with many uses. Olives
were eaten fresh or pickled. The
wood of the tree was used for car-
pentry. *Lev. 24:2; Deut. 24:20; 1 Sam.
8:14; Micah 6:15; Rom. 11:17.* (See *oil*
for list of uses.)

Olives, Mount of; or **Olivet.** A hill
east of Jerusalem across the brook
Kidron, at a distance of a sabbath
day's journey. *2 Sam. 15:30; Zech.
14:4; Mark 11:1; 14:26; Luke 19:29;
Acts 1:12.* (See *Gethsemane.*)

omer, from a word meaning
" sheaf." O.T. measure for dry substances, equal to approximately three
quarts in modern measurement. *Ex.
16:18, 22, 36.* (See *homer* for table of
dry measures.)

Omri (ŏm′rī). A king of the Northern Kingdom, Israel, first of a family
that ruled for many years. To the
Assyrians, all kings of Israel, and the
nation itself, were known as Humri.

He moved the capital from Tirzah to the city of Samaria, which he built. His son Ahab's marriage to Jezebel was arranged as one of the alliances Omri made with other rulers to make trade possible and to increase the wealth of the nation. *1 Kings 16:15-28; Micah 6:16.* (See *king;* Time Line.) Others.

Onesimus (ō nĕs'ə məs), meaning "useful." A slave belonging to Philemon, a member of the church at Colossae. Onesimus is the subject of Paul's letter to Philemon. *Col. 4:9; Philemon 10.*

onycha (ŏn'ĭ kə). A spice used in the incense burned in worship; probably made from part of the shell of a mollusk. *Ex. 30:34.*

oracle. A pronouncement or teaching from God. In the O.T., used most often in the introduction to the words of a prophet. *Num. 24:3; 2 Sam. 23:1; 2 Chron. 24:27; Isa. 15:1; Nahum 1:1; Mal. 1:1; Rom. 3:2.*

ordinance. A rule governing conduct or the carrying out of worship. In the O.T., most often used with "statute," also with "commandment." "Ordinance" and "statute" differ somewhat from "commandment," which has a personal note. *Ex. 12:14; Lev. 5:10; 1 Kings 9:4; Ps. 19:9; Luke 1:6; Eph. 2:15.* (See *law* for related words.)

oven. A round pottery jar, from two to three feet in width, inverted over a fire. The bread was baked on pebbles heated beneath the jar or on the inner wall of the jar itself. Dry grass was often used for fuel. *Ex. 8:3; Lev. 2:4; Ps. 21:9; Hos. 7:4; Matt. 6:30.* (See *bake.* See *bread* for list of words related to bread-making.)

overseer. Head of a group of workmen, a taskmaster. *2 Chron. 2:18; Neh. 11:9; Isa. 60:17.*

overseer of his house. The position given by Pharaoh to Joseph was a high one, second to that of the ruler himself and often including much of the actual rule of the land. *Gen. 39:4-6.*

over the household. Used of certain officers of the kings of the Southern Kingdom, Judah, and the Northern Kingdom, Israel. The position was similar to the "overseer of his house." Also called steward. *1 Kings 18:3; 2 Kings 15:5; 18:18; Isa. 22:15.*

ox. Common domestic animal, used to pull plows, carts, and threshing sledges, and to tread out grain; also used for sacrifices. *Ex. 24:5; Deut. 25:4; 1 Sam. 11:7; 1 Chron. 13:9; Job 1:14.* (See *goad; yoke.*)

P

palace. Residence of a king (often "king's house") or of a high official such as a governor; made up of several flat-roofed buildings, sometimes two stories high, arranged around an open court or courts. Sometimes the palace was also the citadel of a town and was therefore surrounded by a wall and towers. The citadel of Saul was also his palace. The palace that Solomon built and other buildings are described

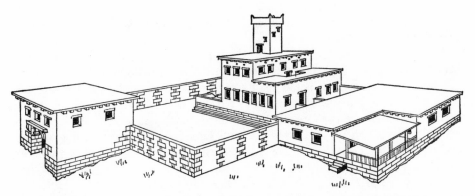

Reconstruction of a palace excavated at Megiddo, dating from 1000 to 800 B.C.

in *1 Kings 7:1-12.* See also *1 Kings 21:1; 2 Chron. 36:7; Isa. 23:13; Hos. 8:14; Matt. 26:3; Mark 15:16.* (See *citadel.*)

pallet. Mat used for sleeping. *Mark 2:4-12; 6:55; Acts 5:15.* (See *bed.* See *house* for list of other household furnishings.)

palm. Shade tree, grown for its fruit, dates, which were used for sweetening. The branches, or leaves, were used for weaving mats and baskets, and for roof coverings. Designs based on palm leaves and fruits were common decorations. *Ex. 15:27; 1 Kings 6:29; Neh. 8:15; Ps. 92:12; John 12:13.*

Pamphylia (păm fĭl'ĭ ə). An area of the southern coast of what is now Turkey, a small Roman province in N.T. times. Paul visited the towns of Perga and Attalia. *Acts 2:10; 13:13; 14:24; 15:38; 27:5.* (See map Plate XV, F-3.)

papyrus. A tall reed grown in Egypt, exported for making paper; also used for making boats and baskets. Paper was made from thin strips of the pith pressed together and polished. *Ex. 2:3* ("bulrushes"); *Job 8:11; Isa. 18:2; 2 John 12* ("paper"). (See *write* for list of related words.)

parable. A figure of speech ("it is like"), extended into a brief story. Examples of parables in the O.T. are *Judg. 9:8-15* and *2 Sam. 12:1-4.* See also *Ps. 78:2; Hos. 12:10.* Parables were used by Jesus to teach about the kingdom of God. *Matt. 13:3-52; Mark 3:23; Luke 13:6.*

Paradise, meaning "a park." In N.T. times, a place to which it was believed the righteous would go after death. *Luke 23:43; 2 Cor. 12:3.* (See *Hades* for N.T. views of life after death.)

parapet. A low wall built around the edges of a roof. *Deut. 22:8.* (See *house; roof.*)

paschal (păs'kəl). The lamb sacrificed at the feast of the Passover. *1 Cor. 5:7.*

111

Passover, feast of the, also called feast of unleavened bread. The annual celebration of the rescue of the Israelites from Egypt. The feast began with a family supper at which a roast lamb was served and the head of the household recited the story of the last night in Egypt. This was followed by seven days in which only unleavened bread was eaten. *Ex. 12:1-20* (description); *2 Chron. 35:1; Mark 14:1; Luke 2:41; John 13:1.* (See *feast.*)

pastor, meaning "shepherd." One kind of leader in the early churches. *Eph. 4:11.* (See *church* for list of other officers.)

patriarch, meaning "father." N.T. name for the early fathers and founders of the people of Israel. *Acts 2:29; 7:8-9; Rom. 9:5; Heb. 7:4.* (See Time Line.)

Paul. The apostle to the Gentiles in the early church, and writer of several N.T. books. "Paul" is the Greek form of the Jewish name Saul (for the king of O.T. times). Paul's family, residents of Tarsus, possessed Roman citizenship. This was a special status given to persons of the provinces as a reward for service to the Empire, or it could be purchased. What happened to Paul after the trip to Rome (told in *Acts, chs. 27 and 28*) is not known. Some traditions say that he was later released and that he traveled again for a few years before he was put to death in Rome. A summary of his early life is given in *Acts 22:3-21;* biographical information is also given in some of the letters. His work and journeys are recounted in *Acts 8:1;*

9:1-30; chs. 13 to 28. (See Time Line.)

Pekah (pē′kə). A king of the Northern Kingdom, Israel, in the eighth century B.C. who formed an alliance with Rezin, of Syria, and invaded Judah. As a result of the siege of Jerusalem, Ahaz, the king of the Southern Kingdom, Judah, sought help from the Assyrian emperor, Tiglath-pileser, and was thereafter forced to pay tribute to the Assyrian overlords. The prophet Isaiah advised against such an alliance. *2 Kings 15:27 to 16:9; Isa. 7:1.* (See *king;* Time Line.)

pen. A tool for engraving. *Job 19:24; Jer. 17:1.* For writing with ink, a pen was made of a split reed and used like a brush. *Ps. 45:1; Jer. 8:8; 3 John 13.* (See *write* for list of related words.)

penny. Roman coin of N.T. times, probably equal to about one fourth of a cent. *Matt. 5:26; 10:29; Mark 12:42; Luke 12:6.* (See *money,* in N.T. times.)

Pentecost (pĕn′tĭ kŏst), **feast of** (N.T.); also called feast of weeks in the O.T. The annual festival held fifty days after the beginning of the barley harvest, or at the end of the wheat harvest, in late May or early June. *Acts 2:1; 20:16; 1 Cor. 16:8.* In the church today the Sunday called Pentecost commemorates the events narrated in *Acts, ch. 2.* (See *feast.*)

people of Israel; or **people of God; my people Israel;** often **the people.** Descendants of Abraham through whom God chose to make himself known in the world. *Ex. 30:31; 2 Sam. 14:13; 2 Chron. 6:6; Ps. 29:11; 47:9; Matt. 2:6; Acts 13:17; 1 Peter 2:9-10.* (See *Israel.*)

peoples. Same as nations. *Deut. 4:27; Ps. 99:1; Micah 4:3; Luke 2:31.*

perfume. A sweet-smelling substance widely used in cosmetics or in making sachets to scent clothing, and in preparing the dead for burial; sometimes carried in small vials in the girdle. Made from spices soaked and boiled, then dissolved in oil to make ointment. Dried spices were put in bags or used in the form of powder or incense. *Ex. 37:29; 1 Sam. 8:13; 2 Chron. 16:14; Prov. 7:17; S. of Sol. 3:6; Isa. 3:20.*

Perizzites (pĕr'ə zīts). One of the peoples living in Canaan before the Israelites conquered it. They are mentioned chiefly in the lists of the peoples driven out by the Israelites; nothing more is known of their history. *Gen. 34:30; Deut. 7:1; Josh. 3:10; 24:11.*

Persia. In O.T. times, the area more or less equivalent to the modern country of Iran. The Persians conquered the Chaldeans in the sixth century B.C. and established an empire that extended from India to Greece. Unlike the Assyrians and the Chaldeans, the Persians followed a policy of tolerance toward dependent peoples. Under them, the Judeans in exile in Babylon were allowed to return to Jerusalem and to rebuild the city. The former Southern Kingdom, Judah, was part of a province in this empire,

called the "province Beyond the River" in Ezra and Nehemiah. Kings of Persia who are mentioned in the Bible are Cyrus, Darius, and Artaxerxes. Cyrus established the capital in Susa. The Persians were overcome by the Greek conqueror Alexander in the fourth century B.C. *2 Chron. 36:20-23; Ezra 4:7, 9; 7:1; Neh. 12:22.* (See *nations;* Time Line; map Plate X.)

Peter; also **Simon; Simon Peter; Cephas.** One of the twelve disciples of Jesus — the most outstanding one, and a leader in the early church. *Matt. 4:18-20; 16:16; Mark 14:54, 66-72; Luke 18:28; John 1:41-42; 18:10; Acts, chs. 2; 3; 9:32 to 11:18; Gal. 2:7-19.* (See *disciple* for Bible references to lists of the twelve; Time Line.)

Peter, The First Letter of. N.T. book, a letter to several churches; probably written by the apostle Peter. It combines teaching about the fundamentals of faith with instructions for living as Christians.

Peter, The Second Letter of. N.T. book, a general letter written sometime after A.D. 100 by an unknown author. The letter seeks to correct false teachings that were being spread at that time.

Pharaoh (fâr'ō). A title given to the rulers of Egypt. The Pharaoh was considered a god and owned all the land in Egypt. Three Pharaohs are mentioned by name in the Bible: Neco, *2 Kings 23:29-35;* Shishak, *2 Chron. 12:2-9* (called king of Egypt); and Hophra, *Jer. 44:30.* The Pharaohs in the times of Joseph and Moses cannot be identified with certainty. *Gen. 41:42; Ex. 2:5; Ps. 135:9; Isa. 30:2; Acts 7:13.*

Pharisee (făr'ə sē), meaning "separated." In N.T. times, a member of one of the major religious parties of the Jews. The party originated in the second century B.C. in protest over collaboration between some Jews and the Greek rulers. The Pharisees emphasized strict and detailed conformity with the law and the traditions. In *Acts 23:6-10* there is an account of a major difference between the Pharisees and the Sadducees. *Matt. 5:20; ch. 23; Mark 2:16; Luke 7:29-30; John 11:46; 18:3; Phil. 3:4-6.* (See *Greece.*)

Philemon, The Letter of Paul to (fī lē'mən). N.T. book, a brief, personal letter from Paul to a Colossian Christian whose slave had run away and was being returned by the apostle. The letter was probably written from Rome around A.D. 62. (See *Onesimus.*)

Philip. One of the twelve disciples of Jesus, from the town of Bethsaida. *Mark 3:18; John 1:43-46; 6:5-7; 12:20-22; 14:8-9.* (See *disciple* for Bible references to lists of the twelve.) Others.

Philip the evangelist. One of the men chosen to serve tables in the first church in Jerusalem; later a traveling preacher. *Acts 6:5; chs. 8; 21:8.*

Philippi (fĭl'ə pī). In N.T. times, a city in northeastern Macedonia. Its port on the Aegean Sea was Neapolis. Although located in a Roman province, it was called a Roman colony because a number of Romans had been settled there by the first emperor. *Acts 16:11-40; 20:6; Phil. 1:1; 1 Thess. 2:2.* (See map Plate XV, D-2.)

Philippians, The Letter of Paul to the (fī lip'ĭ ənz). N.T. book, a letter from Paul to members of the church he had founded at Philippi; probably written when Paul was a prisoner in Rome, around A.D. 63. Paul wrote to thank the Philippians for a gift they had sent him and to encourage them to hold fast to the faith in spite of false teachers.

Philistia (fī lĭs'tĭ ə). In O.T. times, a nation in the western part of Canaan, on the eastern shore of the Mediterranean Sea. The **Philistines** moved from Crete into the coastal area somewhat before the Israelites entered Canaan, and by that time possessed several fortified cities on the main road from Egypt. They attacked the Israelites during the period of the judges. For a time they monopolized the manufacture of iron and made the Israelites dependent on them for the making and sharpening of tools. Both Saul and David fought the Philistines. *Ex. 15:14; Judg. 3:3; 14:4; 2 Sam. 21:15; Amos 9:7.* (See, for Philistine cities, *Ashdod; Ashkelon; Gaza; Joppa.* See also Time Line; map Plates V, B-5; VI, B-5.)

Phoenicia (fī nĭsh'ə). An area to the northwest of Galilee in N.T. times. *Matt. 15:21* ("district of Tyre and Sidon"); *Acts 11:19; 15:3; 21:2.* (See map Plate XIV, C-2.)

Although not mentioned by name in the O.T., the Phoenicians were famous in ancient history as Mediterranean traders and colonizers. The federation of Phoenician cities included Tyre and Sidon. The Phoenician gods El and Baal influenced Israelite worship. Canaanites, driven westward by the Israelites, settled and mingled with the Phoenicians. Thus in the O.T. they are called Canaanites. In *Ezek., ch.* 27, Tyre and its importance as a trading city are described. *Obad. 20.*

Phrygia (frĭj'ĭ ə). In N.T. times, an area in what is now Turkey, divided between the Roman provinces of Asia and Galatia. Cities which Paul visited were Colossae, Laodicea, Hierapolis, and Antioch of Pisidia. *Acts 2:10; 16:6; 18:23.* (See map Plate XV, F-3.)

phylacteries (fĭ lăk'tə rĭz). In N.T. times, small boxes bound on the forehead by Jewish men at prayer. The boxes contained verses of O.T. books written on parchment, such as *Deut. 6:4-5.* See *vs. 6-9,* on which the custom was based. *Matt. 23:5.* (See *frontlet.*)

physician. The Bible word means "bandager." In early times priests had some medical duties, as in the diagnosis and treatment of leprosy. *Lev. 13:1-3.* Physicians in later times used medicines, oils, and ointments to treat patients. In Egypt physicians were also embalmers. *Gen. 50:2; 2 Chron. 16:12; Job 13:4; Mark 5:25-26; Luke 4:23; Col. 4:14.*

pigeon. Used in sacrifices, especially by persons who could not afford the more expensive animals. *Lev. 5:7; Matt. 21:12; Luke 2:22-24; John 2:14.*

Pilate, Pontius (pī'lət, pŏn'shəs). Roman governor of Judea, A.D. 26–36. His headquarters were in Caesarea, but he moved to Jerusalem at feast times, when the city was crowded and riots were likely to break out. *Matt. 27:2; Mark 15:2; Luke 3:1; 13:1; 23:13-16; John 19:19; Acts 3:13; 4:23-28; 1 Tim. 6:13.*

pillar. In O.T. times, a stone, uncut or rounded like a tombstone, set up to commemorate some event or at a place of worship. *Gen. 28:18; Ex. 23:24; 2 Sam. 18:18; 2 Kings 17:10; 2 Chron. 14:3.* Also with the usual meaning of a support for a roof. (See *Asherah; high places.*)

pim. Weight and standard of payment in O.T. times, a fraction of an ounce in modern measurements. *1 Sam. 13:21.* (See *money; weigh.* See *shekel* for table of weights.)

Pit. O.T. word for place beneath the earth where it was believed the dead lived. *Job 33:22; Ps. 28:1; 103:4; Isa. 14:15.* (See *Sheol* for explanation of O.T. views of life after death and for words with same meaning.)

place of honor. At a banquet in N.T. times, the seat on the right hand of the host at the head of the table. Or when several small tables were used, with couches holding three guests each, each place on the couch signified the honor accorded to the guest. In general, the higher places, or those nearer the host, signified the greater honor. *Mark 12:38-39; Luke 14:7-11.* (See *at his right hand; banquet.*)

pledge. In O.T. times, a personal belonging given by a borrower to his creditor as assurance that he would make repayment. Some things might be taken as pledge for only a short time, *Ex. 22:25-27;* some things were not to be taken at all, *Deut. 24:6.* See also *Job 24:3, 9; Amos 2:8.* (See *surety.*)

plow. Pole or forked branch to which a metal plate, the **plowshare,** was attached by a socket and peg. A shaft was attached to the yoke of oxen used to draw the plow. Perhaps in early O.T. times the plow was merely a sharpened stick or had a wooden share. The season of plowing was from October to April. The ancient plow did not turn over furrows, but served more as a harrow. *1 Sam. 13:20-21; 1 Kings 19:19; Prov. 20:4; Isa. 2:4; 28:24; Luke 9:62.* (See *wheat* for list of words related to farming.)

Pontus (pŏn'təs). In N.T. times, an area on the southern shore of the Black Sea (then called Pontus Euxinus); with Bithynia, a province of the Roman Empire. *Acts 2:9; 18:2; 1 Peter 1:1.* (See map Plate XV, F-2 — Bithynia et Pontus.)

pool. A reservoir, usually manmade, for storage of water from rain, springs, or streams. *2 Sam. 2:13; 2 Kings 20:20; Isa. 7:3; John 5:2-9.* (See *water* for list of related words.)

portion. In addition to the usual meaning, in the O.T. the same as " allotment " or " inheritance ": a piece of land. *Deut. 10:9; Josh. 18:10; 2 Chron. 10:16; Ps. 105:11.* (See *lot.*)

potsherd. A piece of broken pottery, often used for writing brief messages or notes. Also sherd. *Job 2:8; 41:30; Isa. 30:14; Jer. 19:2.* (See *write* for list of related words.)

potter. Craftsman who made earthenware items of many types. Clay and water were mixed by treading and kneading. The clay was then put on a wheel turned by a helper or, later, by foot, and formed to the desired shape. Molds and freehand modeling were also used for shaping the clay. The finished product was colored and decorated, then baked in a kiln, usually without glaze. Cooking pots, bowls, cups, jars, flagons, pitchers, and lamps were some of the many household utensils made by the potter. Pottery remains are used by archaeologists to date ruins according to the type of material used in the manufacture and the decorations. *1 Chron. 4:23; Isa. 41:25; 45:9; Jer. 18:1-6; Rom. 9:21.* (See *potsherd.*)

pound. In N.T. times, a Greek unit of money equal to about twenty dollars today. *Luke 19:13.* (See *money,* in N.T. times.)

Also a weight in N.T. times, somewhat less than a pound today. *John 12:3; 19:39.*

praetorium (prē tōr'ĭ əm). In N.T. times, the residence of a Roman governor. Pilate's headquarters in Jerusalem may have been the Tower of Antonia (barracks), where the troops were located. *Matt. 27:27; Mark 15:16; John 18:28; 19:9* (in some uses, the judgment seat in the praetorium); *Acts 23:35.*

praetorian guard. The bodyguard of the Roman emperor, quartered in his

A member of the praetorian guard

palace (praetorium) in Rome. *Phil. 1:13.*

pray. To talk with or commune with God. *Gen. 25:21; 2 Kings 19:15; Ps. 61:1; Jer. 7:16; Matt. 14:23; Luke 11:2-4; John 14:16; Acts 10:1-2; 2 Cor. 1:11.*
Also, in the O.T., to beseech. *Gen. 45:4; 1 Kings 2:17.*

priest. All ancient nations and their gods had priests, usually stationed at the sanctuaries. Among O.T. Israelites in early times, the functions of the priest were to take care of the sanctuary, to inquire of God, to teach, and to take part in sacrifice. In later times the teaching responsibility passed to the prophets and, after the exile, to the scribes. Toward the end of O.T. times, when most descriptions in the Bible were written, the priests had a chiefly sacrificial office. In his sacrificial duties the priest represented God to the people and was the representative of the people before God. Such things as special vestments and anointing had been taken over from the customs having to do with earlier kings. *Gen. 14:18; Ex. 2:16; 19:6; 1 Sam. 1:9; 5:5; 21:1; 1 Chron. 15:14; 2 Chron. 34:14; Jer. 8:10; Hos. 4:4; Luke 1:5; 5:14; John 1:19; Acts 4:1; Heb. 7:23-24; 1 Peter 2:9.* (See *Aaron; chief priests; high priest; Levite; Leviticus; Melchizedek.*)

prince. Often a ruler or king. *1 Sam. 9:16; 2 Sam. 6:21; Isa. 9:6; Hos. 3:4; Luke 11:15; Eph. 2:2.*
princes. In the O.T., men of authority and position, probably in the king's court; somewhat like elders and nobles, not necessarily sons of a king. *2 Kings 24:12-14; 2 Chron. 12:6; Neh. 9:32; Jer. 1:18.*

proconsul. In N.T. times, the ruler of a Roman province who held office for one year by appointment of the senate in Rome. *Acts 13:7-8, 12; 18:12; 19:38.* (See *Gallio.*)

profane. To treat something holy as though it were common, or to make unclean. *Ex. 20:25; Jer. 19:4; Ezek. 22:26; Dan. 11:31; Mal. 1:12; Acts 24:6; 1 Cor. 11:27.*

prophecy. Teaching about the will of God in relation to specific situations. *2 Chron. 15:8; Neh. 6:12.* (See *oracle; says the Lord.*)

In the N.T., also prediction. *Matt. 13:14; 1 Cor. 12:10.*

prophesy. To speak the will of God. In early O.T. times, sometimes in a trance or in ecstasy induced by music and dancing. *1 Sam. 10:5-6, 10-13; 1 Chron. 25:1; Isa. 30:10; Jer. 26:18; 32:3; Matt. 11:13; Acts 2:17-18; 1 Cor. 14:1.*

prophet. A spokesman of God, one who taught God's will not in general doctrines but in terms of the situation of his time. *Deut. 18:18; 1 Sam. 3:20; 9:9; 2 Sam. 7:2; 1 Kings 18:36; 2 Kings 9:1; 19:2; 2 Chron. 36:12; Ezra 6:14; Hab. 1:1; Matt. 2:17; Luke 20:6; 1 Cor. 12:28.* (See *man of God; seer.*)

Also one inspired by a god. In this sense there were prophets of the gods of other nations. Among the Israelites there were prophets of this type also. The **sons of the prophets** may have been a group trained in music and dancing that would bring on an inspired trance. *1 Sam. 10:5; 1 Kings 18:19; 2 Kings 2:5; 2 Chron. 18:9; Jer. 23:30-32; Amos 7:14.*

proselyte. In N.T. times, a convert to the Jewish religion, one who had been circumcised and who accepted all the teachings and requirements. *Matt. 23:15; Acts 2:10; 6:5.* (See *God-fearing.*)

Proverbs, The. O.T. book made up of several collections of sayings, short poems that give advice on how to live wisely. See *Prov. 1:2-6* for a statement of purpose. Some of the proverbs in the book may have come from Solomon, as claimed in the opening verse. In its final form, the book was completed sometime in the fourth or third century B.C.

province. A division of an empire ruled by an appointed official. In the O.T., the provinces of the Persian empire (sixth to fourth centuries B.C.) were ruled by governors or satraps, *Ezra 4:10; Esth. 3:14.* In the N.T., the provinces of the Roman Empire were ruled by governors, tetrarchs, or proconsuls, *Acts 23:34; 25:1.* (See *Rome* for list of words related to governing of the Roman Empire.)

pruning hook. Sicklelike blade attached to a long wooden handle; used in trimming vines or trees. *Lev. 25:3; Isa. 5:6; Micah 4:3; John 15:2.* (See *vinedresser.*)

psalm. A song of praise to God. *Ps. 47:7; Eph. 5:19; Col. 3:16.* Sometimes specifically from The Psalms. *Luke 24:44; Acts 13:33, 35.* (See *hymn.*)

Psalms, The. O.T. book made up of several collections of poems and songs for use in private and public worship. The collections were formed over many centuries and joined in five books, probably during the third century B.C. The meanings of the titles and headings of the psalms are not clear to us today. Some are musical instructions; but we do not know enough about temple music to understand them. Notes about incidents in David's life were probably added later in order to explain why one of the collections bore the name of David. (See *according to . . . ; Ascents, A*

Song of; hymn; Maskil; Miktam; Shiggaion; also *Selah.*)

purification. Ritual of cleansing by washing or by sacrifice after contact with uncleanness. *Num. 31:19-20; Neh. 12:45; Luke 2:22-24; John 2:6; Acts 21:26; Heb. 1:3.*

Purim (pōŏr'ĭm). An annual festival commemorating the events told in The Book of Esther. *Esth. 9:23-28.*

purple. Crimson, the color of royalty and wealth. *Ex. 25:4; Lam. 4:5; Ezek. 27:7; Luke 16:19; John 19:2; Acts 16:14.* (See *Tyre.*)

purse. Small pouch of cloth or of skin for carrying coins, often tucked in the girdle, or the coins were simply carried in a fold of the girdle. *Isa. 46:6; Mark 6:8* (" belts "); *Luke 10:4; 22:35-36.* (See *bag.*)

Q

quarry. Archaeological excavations have discovered how stone was quarried in one place in O.T. times. The workmen used short picks (axes) to hew a channel around four sides of a block of stone. Then wooden wedges were driven into the block at the base. These were moistened until their swelling split the rock and the block could be lifted out. *1 Kings 5:15-18; 6:7; 2 Chron. 34:11; Isa. 51:1.* (See *mason* for list of words related to brick and stone work.)

quart. Greek measure for dry substances in N.T. times, equal to a little

less than a quart in modern measurements. *Rev. 6:6.*

queen of the South. In the N.T., same as queen of Sheba (*2 Chron. 9:1-12*). *Matt. 12:42; Luke 11:31.*

Quirinius (kwĭ rĭn'ĭ əs). Governor of the Roman province of Syria in N.T. times, a military official appointed by the emperor in A.D. 6. *Luke 2:2.*

quiver. Leather case for arrows, often decorated with metal or painted; carried on the back or at the left side, or attached to the side of a chariot. *Gen. 27:3; Job 39:23; Isa. 22:6; 49:2.*

R

Rabbi; Rabboni (răb'ī, rə bō'nī). In N.T. times, a title of respect for a teacher. See *John 1:38; 20:16.* Also *Matt. 23:7-8; John 3:2; 9:2.*

Rachel. Wife of Jacob, and mother of Joseph and Benjamin. Jacob worked several years for her father, Laban, as his marriage payment for Rachel, and then was the victim of Laban's trickery. *Gen., chs. 29 to 33; 35:16-19; 1 Sam. 10:2; Jer. 31:15; Matt. 2:18.*

Rahab (rā'hăb). A prostitute in the town of Jericho who aided the spies of the Israelites when they were conquering Canaan. *Josh., chs. 2; 6:17-25; Heb. 11:31; James 2:25.*
Also a name for Egypt, *Ps. 87:4; Isa. 30:7,* and for a mythical beast, *Job 26:12; Ps. 89:10; Isa. 51:9.*

raid. Type of warfare in O.T. times, a sudden attack using a small number of fighters; much used by nomadic peoples, such as the Midianites, against settled areas. *1 Sam. 13:17; 27:8; 2 Sam. 4:2; 2 Kings 6:23; 1 Chron. 7:21;* also *Judg. 6:2-6* (description).

rain, the early and the later. The two seasons of rain determined the farmer's year. The early rains came in the fall, which was planting time, and in O.T. times, the beginning of the year. The later rains fell in the spring, the main growing season. The summer, harvest time, was dry. *Deut. 11:14; Prov. 26:1; Jer. 5:24; James 5:7.* (See *wheat* for list of words related to farming.)

rampart. Sloping embankment of earth on the outer side of a city wall, kept clear and smooth, even slippery, to prevent the sudden approach of enemy forces. *Lam. 2:8; Nahum 2:1; Zech. 9:3.*

ransom, *n.* (also *v.*). Payment made to free a person or thing, as land that had been sold outside the family to which it belonged. *Num. 35:32; 1 Sam. 14:43-45; Ps. 49:15; Isa. 43:3; Hos. 13:14; Mark 10:45; 1 Peter 1:18-19.* (See *redeem* for more information.)

reap. In early O.T. times the worker used a sickle of flints set in wood. After iron came into use, he probably used a sickle like those of today. He grasped several stalks of grain in his left hand and cut them about halfway up the length, tying the stalks into sheaves. *Lev. 19:9-10;*

Ruth 2:3; 1 Sam. 6:13; Ps. 129:7; Matt. 13:30; Gal. 6:7-8. (See *harvest* for list of words related to harvesting.)

Rebekah (rǐ běk′ə). Wife of Isaac, and mother of Esau and Jacob. *Gen.,* chs. 24 to 27; 29:12; 49:31; Rom. 9:10 (Rebecca).

recorder. An officer of a king's court in charge of arranging audiences and generally keeping the king informed about past decrees and about his people. *2 Sam. 8:16; 2 Kings 18:37; 2 Chron. 34:8.*

Red Sea. In O.T. times, included what are known today as the Red Sea, the Gulf of Suez, the Gulf of ʻAqaba, the Indian Ocean, and the Persian Gulf. The Red Sea that the Israelites crossed in leaving Egypt was probably a small lake, the Sea of Reeds, in the area now crossed by the Suez Canal. *Ex. 10:19; 15:22; 1 Kings 9:26; Ps. 136:13-15; Acts 7:36; Heb. 11:29.* (See map Plate III, F-6.)

redeem. To buy back a person or thing; same as ransom. In O.T. times when a man sold himself into slavery or sold a piece of land because of debts, it was the duty of his nearest relative to buy back the person or the land. First-born children, who were considered to belong to God, were redeemed. For examples of the practice see: *Ex. 13:11-15; Lev. 25:25; Ruth, ch. 4; Jer. 32:8.* For other uses of the word, see: *1 Chron. 17:21; Ps. 19:14; 107:2; 130:7; Jer. 50:34; Luke 24:21; Rom. 3:24; Eph. 1:7; Titus 2:14.*

refine. In O.T. times precious metals

were purified by melting them in large earthenware containers placed in a furnace. The impurities, or dross, settled to the bottom. *1 Chron. 28:18; Ps. 12:6; Isa. 48:10; Jer. 9:7; Mal. 3:2-3.* (See *furnace* for list of words related to the production of metals.)

refuge, cities of. In O.T. times, places in which a murderer could ask for asylum and the right to be judged, instead of being killed by the avenger of the murdered person. The elders of the city might shelter a person who had caused an accidental death, but would hand over to the avenger anyone who had committed intentional murder. In earlier times any sanctuary was a place of refuge; the cities of refuge had sanctuaries. They are also listed as cities of the priests. *Num. 35:9-15; Josh. 20:1-6.* (See *avenger.*)

register. Listing of families by ancestry or of men for military service. *Num. 1:18; 1 Chron. 4:41; Ezra 2:62; Ps. 87:6; Ezek. 13:9.* (See *census; enrollment; genealogy.*)

Rehoboam (rē'ə bō'əm). A son of Solomon, first king of the Southern Kingdom, Judah, founded by the division of Solomon's kingdom. *1 Kings 11:43; chs. 12; 14:21-31; Matt. 1:7.* (See *king;* Time Line.)

religion. N.T. only, usually meaning the carrying out of forms of worship or ritual. *Acts 26:5; 1 Tim. 2:10; James 1:26.*

rent his clothes. In the O.T., a sign of anguish, as in mourning or repentance. *Gen. 37:29; Josh. 7:6; 2 Sam.* *3:31; 2 Kings 22:11; Ezra 9:3; Isa. 37:1.* (See *tore his robes* for N.T. equivalent; *mourning* for list of other customs.)

repent. To turn or to turn back from present actions or intentions. In the O.T., sometimes used of God. In the N.T., **repentance** is the necessary first step in faith. *Ex. 13:17; Job 42:6; Amos 7:3; Matt. 3:2, 8; 11:21; Luke 5:32; Acts 2:37-38; 2 Cor. 7:10.* (See *mourning* for some signs of repentance.)

resurrection. N.T. only. The raising of Jesus Christ from death, a unique event, central in the proclamation of the gospel. *Acts 1:22; 2:24; Rom. 1:4; 6:5; 1 Cor. 15:14; Phil. 3:10; 1 Peter 1:3.*
Also the raising of the dead at the end of time (day of the Lord or day of judgment), a belief held by many, especially the Pharisees, in N.T. times. *Matt. 22:23-33; John 11:24-25; Acts 17:32; 1 Cor., ch. 15; Col. 2:12.* (See *death* for list of words related to beliefs about life after death.)

Reuben (rōo'bən). One of the twelve sons of Jacob; the people and tribe descended from him, also **Reubenites;** and their territory east of the Salt Sea. *Gen. 29:32; Ex. 6:14; Josh. 13:23; 1 Chron. 5:6.* (See map Plate IV, D-5.)

revelation. In the N.T., God's act of making himself known to man, especially in Jesus Christ. *Luke 2:32; Rom. 16:25; 1 Cor. 14:26; Gal. 1:12; Eph. 3:3; 1 Peter 1:13;* also *John 1:18.* (See *word of the Lord.*)

Revelation to John, The. N.T. book written probably toward the end of the first century A.D., when Christians were being severely persecuted. The writer was a church leader who had been banished to the island of Patmos in the Mediterranean Sea. To reassure Christians of God's eventual triumph in history, perhaps also to hide his meaning from outsiders, the writer used many symbols and visions, some of them taken from the O.T. books of Daniel and Ezekiel.

Rezin (rē'zĭn). A king of Damascus in the eighth century B.C. who, with Pekah, of the Northern Kingdom, Israel, attacked the Southern Kingdom, Judah. He was killed when the Assyrians, under Tiglath-pileser, besieged Damascus a few years before they took Samaria. *2 Kings 15:37; 16:5-9; Isa. 7:1.* Other.

righteous, *adj.* Carrying out the obligations of a relationship between men or between God and men. God is righteous because in his steadfast love he keeps his covenant with men. A righteous man is one who maintains relationships. *1 Sam. 24:17; Ps. 1:6; 11:7; 50:6; Amos 5:24; Matt. 5:20; Gal. 3:11.*

righteousness in the writings of Paul in the N.T. also means " right relationship with God," as in *Rom. 4:3; Gal. 3:6.*

River, the. In the O.T., usually the Euphrates River, rising north of Canaan and flowing southeast to the Persian Gulf. With the Tigris River it bounds the area known as the Fertile Crescent, or Mesopotamia. In ancient times the cities of Babylon and Ur were located on the River. *Gen. 15:18; Deut. 11:24; Ps. 72:8; Micah 7:12.* (See map Plate II, F-2.)

beyond the River, as in *Josh. 24:3, 14; Isa. 7:20,* means in Mesopotamia.

the province Beyond the River in Ezra and Nehemiah included Judah (beyond the Euphrates River from the point of view of the Persian rulers), *Ezra 4:10.* (See map Plate X, B-3 — " Beyond the River.")

road. In ancient times a road was made by the constant traveling of people along a route. There were few planned or paved roads, except in cities, until those built by the Romans in the first century A.D. There were many important and old roads in Bible lands. One went from Egypt to Canaan along the coast of the Mediterranean Sea. The King's Highway was another. Roads between Jerusalem and the east, such as were taken by invading armies or by those led into exile in Babylon, went north and east in a long arc to avoid crossing the desert of Arabia. *Deut. 2:27; 1 Sam. 4:13; Job 24:4; Nahum 2:1; Matt. 20:30; Luke 9:57; Acts 8:26.* (See *highway;* map Plate III [see legend: " Roads "].)

robe. A cloak, usually long, often the special garment of a king or priest. *Gen. 37:3; Ex. 28:4; 1 Sam. 24:4; 2 Sam. 13:18; 1 Kings 22:10; Matt. 26:65; John 19:2.* (See *coat* for list of other clothing.)

rod. Same as staff. *Ex. 4:2; Ps. 23:4.* In figurative uses, associated with judgment and punishment. *Isa. 10:5;*

Lam. 3:1; 1 Cor. 4:21; Rev. 2:26-28. (See *staff*.)

Roman citizen. In N.T. times, persons in the provinces became Roman citizens through service to the Empire or through purchase. Citizenship entitled a person to some rights that provincial citizens did not have. For example, the Roman citizen could not be beaten by local authorities and had the right to ask for trial by the emperor in Rome. *Acts 16:37-39; 22:25-29;* also *25:11-12.* (See *Caesar* [appeal to Caesar]; *scourge*.)

Romans. In the N.T., officials of the Roman Empire, such as governors — for example, Pilate — or soldiers. *John 11:48; Acts 16:21; 25:16; 28:17.* (See, under *Rome,* list of words related to government and army.)

Romans, The Letter of Paul to the. N.T. book, a letter from Paul to the church at Rome, which he intended to visit for the first time. The letter was probably written in A.D. 58. It presents a full development of Paul's view of the gospel.

Rome. The capital and chief city of the world in N.T. times. The Roman Empire, ruled by emperors, or Caesars, extended from Spain to the Caspian Sea, and from northern Europe into Africa. The areas outside the city of Rome and outside Italy were divided into provinces ruled by governors appointed by the emperor or by the senate, and occupied by divisions of the Roman Army. The years of peace and unification brought about by the Roman Empire undoubtedly contributed to the spread of the Christian faith, as did the development of travel, both by overland highways and by sea. There was a church in the city of Rome in early times. *Acts 2:10; 18:2; 19:21; 28:14-16; Rom. 1:7; 2 Tim. 1:17.* (See Time Line; map Plate XV [the city is at B-2]. See the following for information about the Roman world of N.T. times: Government and customs: *barbarian; Caesar; cross; crucify; custodian; emperor; freedman; Greece; judge* [judgment seat]; *Latin; magistrate; praetorium; proconsul; province; Roman citizen; Romans; tax,* in N.T. times; *tetrarch; tribunal.* Army: *barracks; battalion; centurion; cohort; legion; soldier,* in N.T. times; *spear,* in N.T. times; *tribune; vinegar.* Architecture: *Areopagus; city,* in N.T. times; *market place; theater.* Philosophies and religions: *Artemis of the Ephesians; Epicurean; Hermes; myths; Stoic; Twin Brothers; Zeus.*)

roof. A house roof was flat, made of beams on which were laid branches covered with a layer of packed earth or clay. Stone rollers were used to keep the surface smooth. An outside staircase gave access to the roof. A **roof chamber** was a guest room, or upper room. The roof was put to many uses and served as an extra room. *Deut. 22:8; Josh. 2:6; 1 Sam. 9:25; 2 Kings 4:10; Neh. 8:16; Jer. 19:13; Mark 2:4; Acts 10:9* ("housetop"). (See *house; parapet*.)

rue. Spice obtained from a small shrub cultivated in Palestine. It was used for seasoning foods and in medicine. *Luke 11:42.*

ruler of the synagogue. In N.T. times, the president who arranged the services in a synagogue. *Mark 5:22; Luke 13:14; Acts 13:15; 18:8.*

rulers. In the N.T., with priests, scribes, and elders, the members of the council, who were, as in *John 3:1,* **rulers of the Jews.** *Luke 23:13; 24:20; Acts 4:5.*

Ruth, The Book of. O.T. book, a story set in the time of the judges; probably written in the fifth century B.C. or later, from a story handed down orally for many generations. It was apparently written in protest against the exclusive attitudes of the Jews in later O.T. times. The woman Ruth appears in Matthew's genealogy of Jesus, *Matt. 1:5.*

S

sabbath, meaning " rest." A day set aside for rest from work, for an assembly, and for special sacrifices. One day each week was a sabbath. It began at sundown on Friday (in our way of reckoning) and lasted until sundown on Saturday. A sabbath day was part of each of the feasts. There was also a **sabbath year,** the seventh year, during which the land was supposed to lie uncultivated, debts were to be settled, and slaves given their freedom. *Ex. 20:8-11; Lev. 23:26-32; Neh. 10:31; Matt. 12:1-8; Luke 13:10-17.*

sabbath day's journey. The distance a person could travel outside a city on the sabbath in N.T. times, according to the interpretations that the scribes had made of the laws, about three fifths of a mile. *Acts 1:12;* see also *Ex. 16:29.*

sackcloth. Coarse cloth woven of goat's hair, of the type used in making bags. It was worn as a sign of mourning or of repentance. Often **sackcloth and ashes.** *2 Sam. 3:31; 2 Kings 19:1-2; Jer. 6:26; Luke 10:13.* (See *ashes.* See *mourning* for list of other customs.)

sacrifice. An offering that included the killing of an animal, all or part of which was burned on an altar; the chief act of worship in O.T. times. Most ancient peoples made sacrifices of many kinds. Among the Israelites some sacrifices were gifts owed to God, such as the animal sacrificed for redemption of the first-born or as a votive offering. Some sacrifices represented a meal in which part of the animal was given to God, part was given to the priests, and part was eaten by the worshiper. These were based on the significance in ancient times of eating together, an act that bound the eaters into a relationship. A sin offering was a sacrifice made to remove uncleanness. Guilt offerings were sacrifices of atonement in cases of sins against other persons. These two kinds of sacrifice were based on the idea of releasing the life (represented in the blood) of the animal. Sacrifice might be made on behalf of a person or of the nation. In later O.T. times the making of sacrifices was restricted to the temple in Jerusalem. Different animals were used: sheep, goats, oxen, sometimes pigeons or turtledoves, and lambs, especially at the Passover. Sacrifices were made every day at the temple, with additional sacrifices made on feast days. *Gen. 31:54; Ex. 3:18;* descriptions of different kinds of sacrifices in Leviticus and Numbers;

Judg. 16:23; 1 Sam. 1:21; 1 Kings 8:62; Ps. 50:14; Ezek. 23:39; Luke 2:24.
In O.T. times some prophets questioned the multiplicity of sacrifices, suggesting that a holy life was more acceptable to God. *Hos. 6:6; Amos 5:21-24* (" offerings "); *Matt. 9:13.*
In the N.T., The Letter to the Hebrews summarizes the view of the early Christians that Christ had redeemed men and that the sacrificial system had come to an end. *Rom. 12:1; Eph. 5:2; Heb. 10:11-14;* also *John 1:29; 1 Cor. 5:7.* (See *altar* and *offering* for other details. See also *beaten oil; fatling; libation; odor, pleasing; paschal; priest; tithe.*)

sacrilege, desolating. In the N.T., something that would defile the temple, such as a pagan idol set up there. *Matt. 24:15; Mark 13:14.* The reference is to an " abomination that makes desolate," mentioned in *Dan. 11:31; 12:11.* Such a thing happened in the second century B.C., when a Greek ruler of the Jews set up another altar in the Jerusalem temple.

saddle. In O.T. times, a piece of cloth or leather girded on the back of an ass. Saddles of the type used today were not used until the fourth century B.C. *Gen. 31:34; 2 Sam. 19:26; 1 Kings 13:27.*

Sadducee (săj′ ə sē). In N.T. times, a member of a religious party of the Jews. Sadducees were generally wealthy and well educated. The Roman Government thought well of them, and the priests appointed by it were of the Sadducee party. They were in the majority on the council

in Jerusalem. They differed with the Pharisees on several points, especially on the question of a resurrection from the dead. In *Acts 23:6-10* some of the points of difference are given. *Matt. 3:7; 16:6; Mark 12:18; Acts 5:17.*

saints. Holy ones. In the O.T., usually the people of God, set apart to serve him. *2 Chron. 6:41; Ps. 31:23; 148:14; Dan. 7:22.*
In the N.T., members of the church, who considered themselves the successors of the people of Israel, or the new people of God. *Acts 9:13; 1 Cor. 1:2; 2 Cor. 9:1; Eph. 1:18; Philemon 7.* A number of saints are named in the closings of N.T. letters by Paul. For example, see *Rom., ch. 16; Col. 4:7-17.* (See *Christians* for other names used for members of the church.)

salt. Mined from the shores of the Dead Sea or evaporated from its waters, salt was used, as it is today, for seasoning and for preserving foods. It was also used in offerings. *Lev. 2:13; Judg. 9:45; 2 Kings 2:19-22; Ezek. 16:4; 47:10-11; Mark 9:50.*
To **eat the salt** with another person meant to be bound to him in a permanent covenant. *Num. 18:19; 2 Chron. 13:5; Ezra 4:14.*

Salt Sea. Ancient name for the Dead Sea, also Sea of the Arabah. The saltwater lake is over twelve hundred feet below sea level, and its floor is many hundreds of feet below. The Jordan River flows into it at the north, but there is no outlet. Its waters contain a much higher percentage of salt than the oceans. In Bible times the sea was probably larger than it is today, but its shape varies frequently. Some cities mentioned in the O.T. are believed to be under the waters of the Dead Sea today. *Num. 34:3, 12; Josh. 3:16; 15:5.* (See map Plates I [physical geography]; IV, C-5 [ancient name].)

salvation; saved. Rescue from danger or death. In the O.T. the salvation that brought the people of God into being was the rescue from Egypt. *Ex. 14:13, 30; 20:2; Deut. 32:15; 2 Chron. 32:22; Ps. 18:35, 46; Isa. 26:1; Jer. 30:10.*
In the N.T., the life, death, and resurrection of Jesus Christ are the acts of God which rescued men. *Matt. 19: 23-30* (indication of how some people thought about salvation in Jesus' time); *Mark 15:31; Luke 19:9; Acts 2:21, 47; Eph. 1:13; 2:5; Phil. 2:12; Titus 3:5.* (See *ransom; redeem; Savior.*)

Samaria (sə mâr'ĭ ə). In the O.T., the capital city of the Northern Kingdom, Israel, from the time of the king Omri until its capture by the Assyrians in 721 B.C. Archaeological excavations have shown that Omri and his son Ahab fortified the city with a double wall and built cisterns within the walls for water supply. Also found there were potsherds from a later time containing names and accounts of taxpayers who brought wine and oil to the king. *1 Kings 16:23-24; 20:1; 2 Kings 13:1; 17:5-6, 24; Hos. 10:5.*
Also used to mean the Northern Kingdom. *2 Kings 17:24; Jer. 31:5.* (See map Plate VI, C-4.)
In N.T. times, a district located between Galilee and Judea; with Judea and Idumea, a division of the Roman province of Syria. The capital, located where the city of Samaria had been, was Sebaste, a city built by Herod. One route from Galilee to Judea went through Samaria. *Luke 17:11; John 4:4; Acts 1:8; 8:1; 9:31; 15:3.* (See *Samaritan;* map Plate XIV, C-4.)

Samaritan (sə mâr'ə tən). In N.T. times, a native of the district of Samaria. The Jews of Judea and Galilee disliked the Samaritans because they were not true Jews. In O.T. times, when Samaria was captured, the Assyrians deported most of the Israelites and moved in colonies of other peoples. Samaritans of N.T. times were the descendants of this mixture of people and therefore not wholly Jewish by inheritance. However, they shared many beliefs with the Jews, with the difference that they worshiped on Mt. Gerizim instead of in Jerusalem. *Matt. 10:5; Luke 10:33; 17:16; John 4:9-42; Acts 8:25.*

Samson (săm'sən). A leader of the Israelites during the period of the judges. The stories about him are based on very old folk tales and contain accounts of many heroic deeds. He led the people in war against the Philistines. Samson was dedicated as a Nazirite at birth. *Judg., chs. 13 to 16; Heb. 11:32.* (See Time Line.)

Samuel, meaning "name of God." A leader of the Israelites in the last years of the time of the judges. He trained as a priest at the sanctuary in Shiloh. He is also called a seer or prophet. The Israelites appealed to him for a king, and he anointed Saul as the first king. Later he anointed David to succeed Saul. Samuel served as a judge (to hear cases) and traveled from his home in Ramah to different towns. The First Book of Samuel (see especially *chs. 1:20; 3:19-21; 7:15-17; 8:4-22; 16:1-13;* also *1 Chron. 9:22; Acts 13:20; Heb. 11:32*). (See Time Line.)

Samuel, The First and Second Books of. O.T. books, originally one book, continuing the story of the people of Israel from The Book of Judges. The books tell about the work of Samuel, and the reigns of Saul and David. Some of the material in them about David is also related in The First Book of the Chronicles. As is true of other O.T. books, the writer of Samuel used many different sources in compiling the book. Often he put in, side by side, two versions of a story. Perhaps parts of the sources consisted of records kept in David's court. Unlike the Chronicles, the book presents what is called a prophetic point of view. That is, it is not interested in worship as much as in the actions of the people and of their kings, and the judgments of God on them. The book was probably written in the seventh or sixth century B.C.

sanctify. In the O.T., to set apart or consecrate for holy use, as a priest or the temple or the furnishings in it, probably by a ritual. *Ex. 29:43; 2 Kings 10:20; 1 Chron. 15:14; 2 Chron. 29:17, 34; 30:17; Joel 1:14.* Also in the general sense, to make holy. *Ex. 31:13; Ezek. 37:28.*

In the N.T. in the latter sense. *John 17:17; Acts 20:32; 1 Cor. 1:2 Eph. 5:26.*

sanctuary. A holy place, such as a temple, a dwelling place for God. Used chiefly of the tabernacle and the temple. *Ex. 25:8; Lev. 10:4; Ps. 73:17; 114:2; Heb. 8:5.*

Occasionally, of the inner part of the temple. *1 Kings 6:19; 1 Chron. 28:10; Ezek. 48:8; Matt. 23:35.* (See *house of God.* See *temple* for a general description.)

sandals. Same as shoes, flat soles of leather or wood bound to the feet with thongs. Some pictures from ancient times show women wearing soft ankle-high boots. An Assyrian carving shows sandals with a covering around the heel and arch, bound by thongs. However, most pictures of O.T. Israelites show them as captives and therefore barefoot. *Isa. 20:2-4.* Sandals were used in a legal transaction. *Deut. 25:5-9; Ruth 4:7.* Apparently sandals were cheap; to be without them was a sign of poverty. *Amos 8:6.* See also *Ex. 12:11; Josh. 9:5; 2 Chron. 28:15; Mark 1:7; Luke 10:4; Acts 12:8.* (See *shoes.*)

Sarah; Sarai, meaning "princess." The wife of Abraham and the mother of Isaac, whom she bore late in life. Isaac was the child promised to Abraham by God. *Gen., chs. 11 to 23; Isa. 51:2; Rom. 4:19; Heb. 11:11; 1 Peter 3:6.*

sardius (sär'dĭ əs). A precious stone of O.T. times, probably a red chalcedony; used in the priest's breastpiece. *Ex. 28:17; 39:10.*

Sargon (sär'gŏn). A king of Assyria, successor to Shalmaneser, who had laid siege to Samaria in the eighth century B.C. According to Sargon's own records, he completed the conquest of Samaria. *2 Kings 17:1-6* (not mentioned by name). Later, also according to his records, he demanded tribute from the Southern Kingdom, Judah. His troops went to Ashdod to put down a revolt. *Isa. 20:1.* (See Time Line.)

Satan (sā'tən). In the O.T., the adversary of men, one who challenges the ways of men or brings them to trial; always subject to God, whose servant he is. *1 Chron. 21:1; Job 1:6-12; Zech. 3:1-2.*
In late O.T. times there arose beliefs in Satan as a definite being, chief of all the evil spirits, the adversary of God in a struggle between good and evil (this idea came from Persian beliefs).
In the N.T., Satan is the source of evil. *Mark 1:13; Luke 22:3; Acts 5:3; 2 Cor. 11:14; 1 Tim. 5:15.* Other names or expressions for Satan are devil, *John 8:44;* the evil one, *Matt. 13:19;* Beelzebul and prince of demons, *Mark 3:22-23;* ruler of this world, *John 12:31;* prince of the power of the air, *Eph. 2:1-2;* Belial, *2 Cor. 6:15.*

satrap (sā'trăp). In late O.T. times, a governor of a province of the Persian empire. *Ezra 8:36; Esth. 3:12; Dan. 3:2.*

satyrs (sā'tərz). In the O.T., gods of the nations, probably in the form of animals. *Lev. 17:7; 2 Chron. 11:15; Isa. 34:14.*

Saul (sôl), meaning "given of God." In the O.T., the first king of Israel, requested by the people, and chosen and anointed by Samuel, probably about 1020 B.C. He was mainly a military leader, fighting against Philistine invasions. His headquarters was at Gibeah. *1 Sam., chs. 9 to 31; 2 Sam., chs. 1 to 4; 1 Chron., ch. 10; Isa. 10:29; Acts 13:21.* Other.

Saul. In the book of The Acts, the Jewish name of the apostle Paul. *Acts 7:58; 8:1-3; 9:1-31; 11:25; 13:7.*

Savior. One who rescues from danger. *2 Kings 13:5; Neh. 9:27.*
In the O.T., usually God. *Ps. 106:21; Isa. 60:16; Hos. 13:4.*
In the N.T., Jesus Christ; occasionally God. *John 4:42; Acts 5:31; Eph. 5:23; 1 Tim. 1:1; 2 Tim. 1:10; 2 Peter 3:18; 1 John 4:14.* (See *salvation.*)

says the Lord; or **thus says the Lord.** An expression used by the prophets to introduce their teachings, indicating that their pronouncements are from God. *Jer. 33:1-2; Amos 1:3, 6, 9, 13, etc.; Micah 3:5.* (See *oracle; prophecy.*)

scales. Device for weighing goods or money; same as balances. *Prov. 16:11; 20:23; Isa. 40:12; Micah 6:11.* (See *balances; money; weigh.* See *shekel* for standard weights.)

scepter. The staff held by a king; one of the signs of his office, symbolizing authority and power. In O.T. times it might have been a long rod with a decorative head or a short mace like a warrior's club. See *Esth. 5:2* for use. Used figuratively in the O.T. for rule or ruler. *Num. 24:17; Ps. 60:7; 89:44; 125:3; Jer. 48:17; Zech. 10:11.*

scourge. To punish by lashing. *Job 5:21; Ps. 91:10; Mark 10:34; Heb. 11:36.*
In N.T. times it was the custom of the Romans to scourge the accused before crucifixion. *Mark 15:15; John 19:1.* It was unlawful to scourge a Roman citizen. *Acts 22:24-29.*

scribe. In the O.T., occasionally one who made a living by writing documents, letters, and the like for others. *Ps. 45:1; Jer. 36:32; Ezek. 9:2* (description). (See *secretary*. See, for list of related words, *write*.)
Chiefly, in both O.T. and N.T., a professional student and interpreter of the law of Moses. The scribes were at first priests who made copies of the law. They came to be of importance during the exile, when they were probably responsible for the collecting and copying of the writings that resulted in many of the O.T. books. Because of their special knowledge they became the wise men and teachers of later O.T. times. *2 Chron. 34:13; Ezra 7:6, 10-11; Neh. 8:9; 13:13.*
In N.T. times the scribes, no longer priests, were influential as teachers and lawyers. A number of them were members of the Jerusalem council. They seem to have been closely related to the Pharisees. *Matt. 5:20; 7:29; 27:41; Mark 2:6; Luke 20:19; Acts 4:5.* (See *lawyer*.)

scripture. A writing. In the N.T., more or less the books of the O.T. as we know them today. (The contents of the O.T. were not officially settled until after the time of Christ.) The word is used to mean one passage, *Mark 12:10; Luke 4:21,* or all the writings together, *Matt. 22:29; Luke 24:27; John 5:39; Acts 18:24; Rom. 15:4; 1 Tim. 4:13; 2 Peter 3:15-16* (written when the letters of Paul were beginning to be considered scriptures also). The writers of the Gospels most often speak of the scripture being fulfilled, meaning that the prophecies in the O.T. which they read as predictions of the Messiah had come to pass in Jesus Christ. *Matt. 26:56; John 2:22; 19:24;* also *Acts 18:28; Gal. 3:8.*

scroll. A book in the form of a roll of papyrus, leather, or parchment attached to sticks. The scroll was rolled from right to left when it was read. The roll was made of sheets from nine to eleven inches by five or six inches, fastened together to a length of thirty feet. On such a scroll the entire book of Samuel (1 and 2 Samuel in our Bibles) could be written in Hebrew. When it was translated into Greek, it required two scrolls. One of the most famous archaeological finds of recent years was the Dead Sea scrolls, dating from the first century A.D., containing some of the earliest copies known of parts of the Bible. These scrolls, of leather and parchment, were encased in copper and sealed in pottery jars. *Isa. 34:4; Jer. 36:2-32.* The phrase " roll of the book " refers to a scroll in *Ps. 40:7,* as does the word " book " in *2 Kings 22:8; Neh. 8:5; Luke 4:17.*

(See *write* for list of related words.) See illustration opposite page 67.

sea. In addition to the usual meaning, a large container for water in front of the temple built by Solomon. It supplied water for the lavers in which the priests washed before making sacrifices. Also **bronze sea** and **molten sea,** indicating how it was made. *1 Kings 7:23-26; 2 Kings 16:17; 25:13, 16.* (See *temple* for location.) For a frequent meaning of **the sea** in the O.T., see *Great Sea.*

seal. A signature in the form of a design impressed on the wax used to close a letter, or on a clay tablet, or on the handles of pottery jars and the like; the seal of a king carried the king's authority. *1 Kings 21:8; Neh. 9:38; Esth. 8:8; Job 38:14; Jer. 32:10-11; John 3:33; Eph. 1:13.* (See *signet* for a description; *write* for related words.)

secretary. An officer in a king's court, scribe for the king and keeper of the records; also with other responsibilities, as secretary of state. *2 Sam. 8:17; 2 Kings 12:10; 2 Chron. 34:18; Isa. 36:3; Jer. 36:12.*

seer, meaning "one who sees [visions]." A prophet, or an early name for a prophet. *1 Sam. 9:9; 2 Sam. 24:11; Isa. 30:10; Amos 7:12.* (See *prophecy.*)

Selah (sē'lə). Of uncertain meaning, perhaps a direction to a choir or to musical instruments. *Ps. 3:2, 4; 7:5; 48:8;* and other places in The Psalms; *Hab. 3:3, 9, 13.*

senate of Israel. In N.T. times, the governing body of the Jews. *Acts 5:21.* (See *council* for description.)

Sennacherib (sə năk'ər ĭb). King of the Assyrians whose reign began about 705 B.C. He sent his troops into Phoenicia and into the Southern Kingdom, Judah, because of an alliance formed by a former king of Babylon against the Assyrians. Several cities of Judah were taken at that time. Sennacherib then besieged Jerusalem but was forced to withdraw his army, perhaps because of an epidemic. *2 Kings 18:13 to 19:37;* cf. *Isa., chs. 36; 37.* (See *Lachish.*)

sepulchre. A chamber or cave used as a family burying place. (See *tomb* for description.) *Gen. 23:6; Neh. 2:3; Matt. 27:61.* (See *death* for list of other customs.)

seraphim (sĕr'ə fĭm). Angels in a vision of Isaiah, or, perhaps, the cherubim in the temple. *Isa. 6:2, 6.*

servant. Anyone who serves another person, ranging from a slave to a king. Often "slave" or "hired" worker. *Gen. 24:2; Ruth 2:5; Matt. 18:26; Mark 9:35; John 15:20; Rom. 1:1.* In speaking to a superior, a person might call himself **your servant.** *Gen. 18:3; 1 Sam. 17:34; 2 Kings 8:13; Ps. 19:13.*

In the O.T., the **king's servants,** or David's servants, for example, were the officers or soldiers of the king's court. *1 Sam. 18:22; 2 Sam. 10:2; 2 Kings 3:11.* Conquered people were servants to the king (and were often forced to be slaves). *2 Sam. 8:6, 14.*

Certain people were called **servants of the Lord**. *Gen. 26:24; Deut. 34:5; 1 Kings 8:66; Ps. 89:20; 105:42; Isa. 41:8* (meaning the people of Israel); *Acts 3:13;* and others. (See *lord; master.*)

service. In addition to the usual meaning, the ritual of attendance on God, or worship, based in part on the idea of O.T. times that when God dwelt among men he was to be served in the way a king was served by attendants. *Ex. 12:25-27; Num. 4:12; Deut. 20:18; 1 Chron. 23:32; 25:6; Neh. 12:45.*

shades. In the O.T., the dead who lived below the earth in a vague state of nothingness. *Job 26:5; Ps. 88:10; Isa. 26:19.* See *1 Sam. 28:8-25* for a story of a medium calling a shade back from the dead. (See *Sheol* for other O.T. ideas about life after death.)

Shalmaneser (shăl'mǝ nē'zǝr). King of the Assyrians from 727 to 722 B.C., who invaded the kingdoms of Judah and Israel. He forced the payment of tribute from Hoshea, king of Israel, and laid siege to Samaria, the capital of Israel. The siege lasted for three years. According to the Bible accounts, Shalmaneser completed the conquest of Samaria, but more probably it was his successor, Sargon, who did so. *2 Kings 17:3-6; 18:9-12.* (See Time Line.)

shave. Men in O.T. times shaved off their beards as a sign of mourning, or at the end of a Nazirite vow, or on being healed of leprosy. *Lev. 14:8; 21:5; Num. 6:18; Deut. 21:12* (a sign of mourning); *2 Sam. 10:4* (a humilia-

tion); *Job 1:20.* The exception is Joseph, *Gen. 41:14,* who was preparing to appear at the royal court of the Egyptians, who were clean-shaven. Probably in N.T. times many men shaved, since it was the custom of the Romans to do so. (See *beard.*)

sheaf. Reaped grain tied into bundles to be taken to the threshing floor. *Gen. 37:7; Lev. 23:10; Deut. 24:19; Ruth 2:7; Amos 2:13; Micah 4:12.* (See *harvest* for list of words related to harvesting.)

shear. To cut the wool from sheep. Shearing was done after the lambing in the spring and was an occasion for feasting. *Gen. 31:19; 1 Sam. 25:2-8; 2 Sam. 13:23; Isa. 53:7; Acts 8:32.*

sheath. Case for a sword, worn on the left side; or a covering for a bow. *2 Sam. 20:8; Ezek. 21:3-5; Hab. 3:9; John 18:11.*

Sheba (shē'bǝ). In O.T. times, a nation in southwest Arabia, noted for its caravan traders. The visit of the **queen of Sheba** to Solomon was probably for the purpose of making a trade agreement. The "hard questions" she asked him may have been riddles often used in formal conversations at that time. *2 Chron. 9:1-12; Ps. 72:15; Jer. 6:20; Ezek. 27:22.* In the N.T. the queen of Sheba is called the queen of the South. (See map Plate II, C-4 [inset].)
Also a personal name.

Shechem (shĕk'ǝm). O.T. city in the hills forty miles north of Jerusalem. It was one of the earliest cities in the area. At the time of the Israelite conquest of Canaan it was a fortified city. Under the Israelites there was a sanctuary at Shechem. Later, Abimelech, losing his position as king of the city, attacked by ambush and destroyed it. Probably Shechem remained as a town, for it became the capital of the Northern Kingdom, Israel, under the first king, Jeroboam. *Gen. 33:18; Josh. 20:7; 21:21; 24:1-28; Judg. 9:18, 34-45; 1 Kings 12:1, 25.* (See map Plates II, E-3; IV, C-4.)

sheep. The main livestock, raised for wool, skins, meat, and milk, and used in sacrifices. The flocks of the people of the patriarchal time were mainly sheep, with some goats. At that time, families and tribes traveled from place to place with their flocks. Later, when the Israelites lived in cities and towns, flocks were pastured outside the towns, but there were always sheep raisers and shepherds. *Gen. 29:2-3; Lev. 1:10; 1 Sam. 16:11; Ps. 78:52; 100:3; Ezek. 34:6; Matt. 18:12; John 10:1-18; 21:17.* (See *shepherd.*)

sheepfold. An enclosure consisting of walls and a gate, and sometimes also a small hut, in which several flocks were herded for the night. One shepherd kept watch. The others came and called their sheep out in the morning to lead them to pasture. *Num. 32:16; 2 Chron. 32:28; John 10:1.*

shekel (shĕk'əl), from a word meaning "to weigh." In O.T. times, a standard weight of metal used as payment before the use of coins; later a coin. A possible reference to coins occurs in *Neh. 5:15.* The standard

weights varied from place to place and from time to time, but the shekel, on the average, was probably about one half of an ounce by modern measurements. *Gen. 23:15-16; 24:22; Ex. 30:13; 1 Sam. 17:5.*
The following table shows the main weights used and their relation to the shekel.

20 gerahs = 1 shekel
50 shekels = 1 mina
60 minas = 1 talent

(See *money; weigh;* also *pim.*)
In N.T. times, a silver or copper coin worth about sixty-five cents; also **half-shekel** coins of Jewish mintage. The half-shekel was the annual tax paid by each male Jew to the temple in Jerusalem. *Matt. 17:24-27.* (See *money,* in N.T. times; *money-changer.*)

Shem (shĕm). A son of Noah. In the Genesis accounts of the origins of peoples, he is the ancestor of the Hebrews, the Arameans, and the Arabs. Today these peoples are called Semites, after Shem. *Gen. 5:32; 6:10; 10:21-31; Luke 3:36.* (See *Genesis* for general background.)

Sheol (shē'ōl). O.T. people believed that the dead lived as shades in a place beneath the earth. *Gen. 37:35; Ps. 139:8.* It was believed that the shades could be called back to earth by necromancy, *1 Sam. 28:7-25,* but the practice was forbidden to the Israelites. These views had changed by the time of Christ. (See *Abaddon* and *Pit,* words meaning the same as Sheol; *death* for list of words related to beliefs about life after death; *Hades* for explanation of N.T. views of death.)

Shephelah (shĭ fē′lə). O.T. name for one of the major geographical divisions of Canaan, an area of low hills and plains between the Mediterranean coastal plains and the Judean hill country, traversed by east-west valleys. It was an agricultural area, olives and grain being the main crops. Also it was a line of defense against the Philistines or other peoples invading from the west. Fortified towns such as Gezer and Lachish were defense points. *1 Kings 10:27; 2 Chron. 26:10; 28:18; Jer. 32:44.* (See *Canaan* for description and list of geographical regions; map Plate I, B-5.)

shepherd. The occupation of the patriarchs was sheepherding. In later times, when the Israelites lived in towns, a member of the family or a hired servant stayed with the flocks in the pasture lands, often for months at a time. *Gen. 29:3; 47:3; Ps. 23; Ezek. 34:1-6; Luke 2:8; John 10:1-18.* Often used figuratively of God and of the leaders of Israel. *Ps. 23:1; Isa. 40:11; Ezek., ch. 34; Zech. 11:17; Heb. 13:20.* (See *goat; lamb; shear; sheep; sheepfold.*)

sherd. A piece of broken pottery; same as potsherd. *Isa. 30:14.*

shield. Two types of shields were in general use among people of O.T. times, and probably Israelite shields were similar. One type was large and rectangular, made of leather on a wooden frame, or in the case of the Assyrians, made of woven wicker. The Assyrians also made very large

shields of this type that covered several archers and were carried by shield-bearers in siege warfare. The second type was small and round, used by foot soldiers. Metal shields were rare, and were probably used only for ceremonial purposes or by kings. " Buckler " is another name for shield. *Gen. 15:1; 1 Chron. 5:18; 2 Chron. 14:8; 26:14; Jer. 51:11.*

shield-bearer. Personal attendant to an important warrior; same as armorbearer. *1 Sam. 17:41.*

Shiggaion (shĭ gā′yŏn); **Shigionoth,** pl. A musical term of uncertain meaning in the heading of *Ps. 7* and *Hab. 3:1.*

Shiloh (shī′lō). O.T. town in the hill country between Bethel and Shechem, somewhat to the east of the road between them. Apparently the town was built by the Israelites during the time of the conquest of Canaan, rather than taken from Canaanites. Joshua made his headquarters there. Also, the tabernacle and ark were placed there in a house of the Lord. In later times it was a city of refuge. *Josh. 18:1, 9; 19:51; Judg. 21:19; 1 Sam. 1:3, 24; 4:4; Jer. 7:12-14.* (See map Plate IV, C-4.)

Shinar (shī′när). O.T. name for the plains surrounding the city of Babylon. *Gen. 11:2; Isa. 11:11; Dan. 1:2.* (See map Plate II, C-4 [inset].)

ship. Until the time of Solomon, the Israelites had little interest in the sea, with the possible exception of the northern territories Zebulun and Asher. *Gen. 49:13; Judg. 5:17.*

In expanding the commercial interests of the kingdom of Israel, Solomon built a fleet of trading vessels. Later kings of the Northern Kingdom, Israel, and the Southern Kingdom, Judah, joined in an attempt to develop ships. *1 Kings 9:26-28; 10:22; 2 Chron. 20:36-37.* Other nations, such as Egypt and Phoenicia, and such cities as Tyre and Sidon, had commercial ships in the Mediterranean Sea and the Indian Ocean. Such ships were small by our standards, usually high-prowed, and propelled by sails and oars. Warships were usually manned by banks of rowers for greater maneuverability. In *Ezek., ch.* 27, we are given a description of Tyre as though it were a ship, with many details of ship-building. The phrase **ships of Tarshish** refers to

Mediterranean sailing ship of Roman Times

any commercial vessels. *1 Kings 10:22; Isa. 2:16.*

The account of Paul's voyage to Rome, *Acts, chs. 27 and 28,* is one of the most complete records of such a trip in N.T. times. The ship was a grain carrier, equipped with two sails. Travelers had to find berths in commercial ships, as there were no passenger ships. The regular route for ships from Rome was across the sea to Alexandria, then along the eastern and northern shores of the Mediterranean and among the islands on the return trip. Often the ships anchored in port at night. No ships sailed in the winter. See *Acts 27:9,* referring to the fast of the day of atonement, in October.

shoes. Shoes were worn only outdoors and were removed when entering a house. *Luke 7:38.* Persons in mourning might go without shoes. *2 Sam. 15:30; Ezek. 24:17.* See also *Ex. 3:5; Josh. 5:15; Acts 7:33;* and *Ps. 60:8; 108:9* (a sign of possession). (See *sandals* for description.)

showbread; also bread of the Presence, and holy bread. Twelve rectangular loaves of bread displayed on a table in the temple or other sanctuary. On the sabbath, new loaves replaced the old ones, which were eaten by the priests. The showbread was a continual offering to God. The bread was unleavened and made of fine flour. *1 Chron. 9:32; 2 Chron. 29:18; Neh. 10:33.* (See *temple* for location.)

shrine. A special place, such as a niche in a wall, for holding an image of a god. *Judg. 17:5; 2 Kings 17:29; Acts 17:24.*

sickle. Tool used in reaping grain. Sickles from early times, found in archaeological diggings, were made of sharpened pieces of flint set in a curved frame of wood. Flint tools were commonly used for a long time after iron began to be used. The iron sickle blade was fastened to a wooden handle by rivets. *Deut. 16:9; 1 Sam.*

13:19-21; Mark 4:29. (See *harvest* for list of words related to harvesting.)

Sidon (sī'dən). A city on the eastern shores of the Mediterranean Sea, about twenty-five miles north of Tyre, with which it is often named in both the O.T. and the N.T. Sidon was an old city before the time of the Israelites. Like Tyre, it was a commercial city and port for a fleet of trading ships that went to all parts of the world of that time. It reached the height of its prosperity about the time of Solomon. Today the city is called Saida. *Gen. 10:19; Josh. 19:28; 2 Sam. 24:6; Jer. 25:22; Joel 3:4; Matt. 11:21; Luke 6:17; Acts 12:20; 27:3.* (See *Phoenicia;* map Plates IV, C-1; XIV, C-1; XV, G-4.)

siege. In O.T. times, a type of warfare carried out against a fortified city. The aim was to surround the city and to break through the walls, or if this was not immediately possible, to seal off the city until lack of food and water forced the inhabitants to surrender. Although used by the Israelites in taking Canaanite cities and by many other nations, this type of warfare was developed especially by the Assyrians. Attacking armies first seized any water supplies outside the city. Then the construction troops (engineers) built a mound (**siegeworks**) to protect troops behind it and to furnish an approach for machines. Battering rams were moved up to the wall. Archers moved forward behind mantelets, or huge shields. Scaling ladders were used by spearmen to gain access to the walls. At the same time, other forces were tunneling under the walls. The defense of the city consisted, first, in the strength of the walls to withstand attack. Archers were stationed on the top of the wall, sometimes using flaming arrows. Other soldiers hurled stones or boiling oil down on the attackers. Chains and grappling hooks might be used to ward off the battering rams. The length of the siege that a city could stand was in large part determined by its water supply. *Deut. 28:52-53; Josh. 10:31; 2 Sam. 20:14-15; 2 Chron. 26:15* (defenses); *Jer. 32:24; Joel 2:7-9* (description); *Nahum 3:14.* The most important sieges in O.T. history were those of Samaria, *2 Kings 17:5,* and of Jerusalem, *2 Kings 24:20b to 25: 30* or *Jer., ch. 52,* both of which resulted in capture and destruction of the cities. (See, for further information, *archers; battering ram; besiege; city; fortified city; gate; mantelet; mound; rampart; shield; tower; wall; watchman.*)

sift; sieve. After grain was winnowed it was gathered from the threshing floor and put through sieves to clean it. A sieve was made of leather straps attached to a rounded wooden frame. *Isa. 30:28; Amos 9:9; Luke 22:31.* (See *harvest* for list of words related to harvesting.)

sign. An action or an object that conveys a meaning. *Ex. 31:16-17; Deut. 6:8; 1 Kings 13:3; Jer. 44:29; Mark 14:44; Luke 2:12; Rom. 4:11.* In the N.T. especially, actions showing the purpose of God. *Matt. 12:38-42; John 4:54; 6:26; Acts 4:16.*

signs and wonders, also with mighty works. Unusual events which, to persons of faith, reveal the purpose of God; to others they may be only wonders. Same as miracles. See *Ps. 77:11-15* for an explanation. In the O.T., chiefly the events of the rescue of the Israelites from Egypt. *Deut. 26:8; Neh. 9:10; Ps. 135:9; Jer. 32:20; Acts 7:36.* See also *Matt. 24:24; John 4:48.* In The Acts and in the letters of the N.T., the miracles of Jesus Christ, *Acts 2:22,* and the works of the apostles in his name, *Acts 2:43; 14:3; 15:12; Rom. 15:19; 2 Cor. 12:12; Heb. 2:4.*

In the last two uses of the word, the important element is always the revealing of God's will, never the miraculous nature of the sign.

signet. A seal, often in the form of a ring, the design on the stone being pressed into wax or clay as a signature. Some signets were like amulets, worn around the neck on a cord. Some were like small stamps, flat on one side, with the design on the other, rounded side. The designs were animals or letters, or sometimes a name. They were made of bone, metal, or gems. *Gen. 41:42* (meaning that the king delegated his authority to Joseph); *Ex. 28:11; Num. 31:50; Jer. 22:24; Hag. 2:23.* (See *write* for list of related words.)

Silas (sī'ləs) in The Acts; **Silvanus** (sĭl vā'nəs) in the letters of the N.T. The first is an Aramaic name; the second, Latin. A worker in the early church with Paul and Peter; a member of the church at Jerusalem. *Acts 15:22 to 17:15; 2 Cor. 1:19; 1 Thess. 1:1; 1 Peter 5:12.*

silver. In O.T. times, considered more valuable than gold. It was the metal most often used in standard weights; also for jewelry, idols, and containers such as cups and bowls. *Gen. 13:2; Ex. 3:22; Lev. 5:15; Num. 10:2; Judg. 5:19; 1 Chron. 28:14; Ps. 12:6; Acts 19:24.*

pieces of silver. In N.T. times there were several types of silver coins of varying values. The amount given to Judas by the priests was probably about twenty dollars. *Matt. 26:15.* In *Acts 19:19* the amount was about nine thousand dollars, doubtless an exaggeration for emphasis. *Luke 15:8.* (See *money,* in N.T. times.)

Simeon (sĭm'ĭ ən). One of the twelve sons of Jacob; also the people or tribe descended from him, also called **Simeonites.** They had no territory of their own, but were merged with the tribe of Judah. *Gen. 29:33; 42:24; Josh. 19:9; Judg. 1:3; 1 Chron. 12:25.* Others.

Simon; Simon Peter; also **Peter; Cephas.** One of the twelve disciples of Jesus. Simon was his original name, a variation of Simeon, to which Jesus added Peter, or Cephas, both meaning "rock." (See *Peter* for more information.) *Matt. 4:18; 16:16; Mark 3:16; Luke 22:31; John 1:42; Acts 10:32.* (See *disciple* for Bible references to lists of the twelve.)

A popular name in N.T. times; other Simons can be identified by details in the context.

Simon the Cananaean (căn'ə nē'ən). Also called **Simon the Zealot** ("Cananaean " means " zealous "). One of the twelve disciples of Jesus, probably a member of the political party called Zealots. *Matt. 10:4; Mark 3:18; Luke 6:15; Acts 1:13.* (See *disciple* for Bible references to lists of the twelve.)

sin. Any action that destroys the basic covenant relationship between God and man, or between men. (See *covet* for an example.) Such actions lead to an inner sickness, also called sin and identified with death, especially in the letters of Paul. *Ex. 34:9; Lev. 5:14; 1 Kings 15:26; Ps. 85:2; Isa. 1:18; Amos 5:12; Matt. 9:5; Luke 17:3-4; Rom. 5:12-13; 1 Cor. 15:3.*
sinners. In the N.T., in addition to meanings related to the above, a term of the Pharisees for those who did not follow their view of the law. *Mark 2:15; Luke 15:1.*

Sinai (sī'nī), **Mount;** also called Horeb. The mountain in Arabia at which the Israelites camped for a long time on their journey from Egypt to Canaan. There the law was given and the people entered into a covenant with God. The location is uncertain, but many scholars believe it was among the granite mountains and desert area of the southern Sinai Peninsula. *Ex. 18:5* (mountain of God); *19:1, 23; 34:32; Lev. 25:1; Neh. 9:13; Ps. 68:8; Acts 7:30.* (See map Plate III, F-5.)

skin of water; skin of milk; skin of wine; or wineskin. The hide of an animal, such as a goat; cured with the openings stopped up, and used as a bottle. *Gen. 21:14; Judg. 4:19; 1 Sam.*

16:20; Job 38:37; Mark 2:22.

skirt. The corners of a cloak or mantle, or the hem of a garment. *Ex. 39:24; 1 Sam. 15:27; Job 38:13; Ezek. 5:3.* The phrase **spread the skirt over** means to marry or to be a husband to. *Ruth 3:9; Ezek. 16:8.*

slave. A person in bondage. Slavery was widely practiced in ancient times. The chief source of slaves consisted of the people taken in war, but there was always considerable trade in slaves. In Israel, foreign slaves belonged to their owners for life unless sold to someone else. It was possible for a slave to buy his freedom if he could accumulate enough wealth to do so. Sometimes Israelite children were sold as slaves, and a man might be forced to sell himself in order to pay off debts. Israelites were supposed to release such slaves after six years, or a person might be redeemed by his relatives. *Ex. 21:2, 20-21; Deut. 16:12; 1 Kings 9:20-21; 1 Chron. 2:34; Matt. 8:9; Rom. 6:17; 1 Cor. 7:21-22; Col. 3:11; Philemon 15-16.*

slept with his fathers. In the books of the Kings and of the Chronicles, a formula at the end of the account of a king's reign, meaning " he died and was buried with his ancestors." *I Kings 2:10; 2 Kings 10:35; 2 Chron. 32:33;* also *Ps. 13:3.* (See *fell asleep.*)

sling. A weapon of O.T. times, made of a wide center portion of leather or cloth, with two strings attached. One of the strings was tied to the wrist; the other was held in the hand. A stone was placed in the sling and whirled around the head. Then the loose string was let go, releasing the stone. A group of men called **slingers** constituted a division of the army in some ancient nations. The rounded **slingstones** were carried in a bag on the shoulder. *Judg. 20:16; 1 Sam. 17:40; 2 Kings 3:25; 1 Chron. 12:2; 2 Chron. 26:14; Job 41:28.*

smelt. To separate copper or iron from the ore, charcoal fires were used in furnaces. The ore was placed directly on the fire, and the melted metal collected at the bottom of the furnace. *Job 28:2; Isa. 1:25.* (See *furnace* for list of words related to the production of metals.)

smith. A craftsman, a worker in metals, making such things as tools and weapons of bronze, copper, or iron, as well as jewelry, idols, and overlays of gold or silver. Even after the Israelites began to use iron implements, they were handicapped by not having any smiths to make or sharpen tools. See *1 Sam. 13:19-21; Judg. 17:4; 2 Kings 24:14; Neh. 3:31; Isa. 44:12; 46:6; Acts 19:24; 2 Tim. 4:14.* (See *furnace* for list of words related to production of metals.)

snare. A net or pit used in hunting. (See *trap* for description.) *Ps. 91:3; 124:7; Prov. 7:23; Isa. 24:18; Hos. 9:8; Amos 3:5.* See also *Ex. 34:12; Ps. 119:110; Luke 21:34; Rom. 11:9.*

Sodom and Gomorrah (sŏd'əm, gə môr'ə). Two cities of the time of Abraham, located probably near the southern end of the Salt Sea. They were destroyed, according to the legend in Genesis, for their great wickedness. *Gen. 18:16 to 19:29; Isa. 13:19; Jer. 23:14; Amos 4:11; Matt. 10:15; Luke 17:29; 2 Peter 2:6.*

sodomites in *1 Tim. 1:10* means homosexuals, and is derived from " Sodom."

sojourner. In the O.T., a person living among people who are not his own. Among the Israelites such people were to live freely, with similar rights and privileges, and even some participation in worship. They had no inheritance or land, however, and were therefore poor and often servants. For this reason there were special laws of consideration for sojourners, along with the poor and the widowed. *Gen. 23:4; Ex. 2:22; Lev. 19:10; 24:22; Num. 9:14; Deut. 10:19; Mal. 3:5; Eph. 2:19* (see *v. 12*).

soldier. In the O.T., a member of the Israelite armies from the time of Saul on, or a fighter from a foreign army. *1 Sam. 4:10; 1 Chron. 19:18; Jer. 41:3; Joel 2:7.* (See *army*.)
In the N.T., a member of the Roman occupying forces. *Matt. 8:9; Luke 23:11; Acts 21:32; 27:32.* (See *Rome* for words related to Roman Army.)

Solomon (sŏl'ə mən), meaning " peaceable." A son of David who succeeded him as the third king of Israel. Solomon established himself as a king like those of other nations, with a large court and harem, and extensive building programs that demanded forced labor. He taxed the people in order to support his luxurious court. He established international trade and built the house of God that

David had wanted to build. At the same time he allowed the worship of gods in Jerusalem for his foreign wives. *2 Sam. 12:24; 1 Kings, chs. 1 to 11* (for some of the details above see *1 Kings 2:12; 4:7, 22-28; 5:2-5, 13-18; 7:2, 6-8; 8:1; 9:26-28; 10:23-25, 26-28; 11:1, 5); Neh. 13:26; Jer. 52:20; Matt. 12:42; Luke 12:27; Acts 7:47.* (See Time Line.)

son of God. In the O.T., a heavenly being, perhaps an angel or a star. *Gen. 6:2; Job 1:6; 38:7; also Dan. 3:25.* Also used of the people of God, indicating that God had chosen them and that they were related to him in that obedience which is given by a son. *Deut. 14:1; 2 Sam. 7:14* (David as king); *Hos. 1:10; see also Rom. 8:19; Gal. 3:26.*

son of man. In the O.T., a man. *Ps. 8:4; 89:47; 144:3; Ezek. 2:1; see also Mark 3:28; Eph. 3:5.*
In later O.T. times (as we know from sources outside the Bible) "son of God" was frequently used for the chosen people of God. "Son of man" was increasingly used as a title for the coming king, or Messiah. The only example of this use in the O.T. is *Dan. 7:13-14.*
In the N.T., **Son of God,** in the second sense above, was what Jesus' followers called him. *Matt. 26:63; Mark 1:1; Luke 4:41; 9:35; John 1:34, 49; Rom. 1:4; Gal. 2:20.* The phrase **son of man** was used by Jesus of himself. *Matt. 8:20; 16:13; Mark 2:10; Luke 6:5; John 9:35.*

Son of David. In N.T. times, a title for the coming king, who, like David, would be a righteous ruler of the kingdom of Israel; same as Messiah.

Matt. 9:27; see also Mark 12:35.

Song of Solomon, The. O.T. book, a collection of love poems and marriage songs, edited by an unknown author probably in the fourth century B.C. It has been interpreted in a great variety of ways, ranging from the supposition that some of the songs were used in wedding ceremonies to the idea that it is an allegory of Christ and the church.

soothsayer. One who practiced the art of divination, predicting future events by signs. *2 Kings 21:6; Isa. 2:6; Jer. 27:9; Micah 5:12; Acts 16:16.* (See *magic* for a list of similar practices.)

sorcerer. One who practiced magic, or who divined, especially under the influence of potions. *Ex. 22:18; Deut. 18:10; 2 Kings 17:17; Isa. 19:3; Micah 5:12; Gal. 5:20.* (See *magic* for list of similar practices.)

soul. What today would be called the self; not a separate part of a person. *Deut. 6:5; 1 Sam. 18:1; Mark 12:30; Acts 2:43; 1 Peter 2:25.* (See *spirit.*)

sow. Sowing began with the early rains in the fall and continued through the winter and spring. Sometimes the ground was not plowed beforehand; rather, the plow followed the sower. Seeds were carried in a basket or bag on the left side and scattered with the right hand, not in furrows, but simply over the ground. *Lev. 19:19; Isa. 61:11; Jer. 2:2; Hos. 8:7; Matt. 13:3-9; 25:26; Luke 13:19; John 4:37; 1 Cor. 15:42-44; Gal. 6:7-8.* (See *wheat* for list of words related to farming.)

span. A unit of measurement of length, equal to the distance from little finger to thumb when the hand is spread, or about eight inches. Two spans made a cubit. *Ex. 28:16; 1 Sam. 17:4;* see also *Luke 12:25.* (See *cubit* for table of measurements of length.)

spear. In O.T. times, a weapon of war, a long pole of wood with a stone or metal point that was often barbed; for thrusting or throwing. The stone point had a projection that was driven into a split in the shaft. Metal points were longer, and socketed into the shaft of the spear. *Judg. 5:8; 1 Sam. 18:11; 26:7; 1 Chron. 12:8; 2 Chron. 14:8; Joel 3:10.*
The spear of the Roman soldier in N.T. times consisted of a three-foot metal pointed shaft attached to a wooden shaft of equal length. *John 19:34; Acts 23:23.*

spelt. A kind of wheat, probably of an inferior quality. *Ex. 9:32; Isa. 28:25.* (See *wheat* for other grains and for words related to farming.)

spices. Made from fragrant leaves, roots, and gums; used less for cooking (as they are today) than for cosmetics, perfumes, and medicines. Much of the caravan trade of ancient times consisted of spices. *Ex. 25:6; 1 Kings 10:2; 2 Chron. 2:4; 16:14; Ezek. 27:22; Mark 16:1; John 19:40.* (See, for uses, *anoint; incense; oil; ointment; perfume.* See, for kinds of spices, *aloes; cassia; coriander; dill; frankincense; galbanum; mint; myrrh; nard; onycha; rue; stacte.*)

spin. To make thread of wool or flax, the women used a distaff (stick) to hold the mass of fibers by putting it under the arm or in the ground. The ends of the fibers were twisted lightly by hand. Then they were fastened to the spindle, a food-long stick with a disk at one end, and twisted into thread by dropping the spindle so that it rotated. *Ex. 35:25; Prov. 31:19; Matt. 6:28.* (See *weave* for list of words related to the making of cloth.)

spirit. Originally, "wind" or "breath"; the self, similar to "soul." *Gen. 41:8; Ex. 35:21; 2 Sam. 13:39; Ezra 1:1; Ps. 51:10; Matt. 5:3; Mark 8:12; Rom. 8:10.* Also a being, as in *1 Sam. 16:14; 1 Kings 22:21.* In this sense in the Gospels and The Acts, chiefly evil or unclean spirits. *Matt. 12:43-45; Mark 1:27; Luke 6:18; Acts 8:7.* (See *demon; unclean spirit.*)
elemental spirits of the universe. The beings which some pagan beliefs held were in control of the elements of the natural world. *Gal. 4:3; Col. 2:8.*
Spirit of God or Spirit of the Lord. In the O.T., the activity of God or his power given to leaders and prophets. *Gen. 1:2; Judg. 3:10; 1 Sam. 10:6; 11:6; Job 33:4; Ps. 104:30; Isa. 32:15; 63:14; Micah 3:8.*
In the N.T., used similarly, *Matt. 3:16; 12:28; Luke 4:18; Acts 2:17,* but chiefly as the Holy Spirit.
spiritual. In the N.T., not "religious" as commonly used today, but "in the Holy Spirit." Sometimes in contrast, as: *Rom. 2:29* (in contrast with the literal); *Rom. 12:1-2* (in contrast with the world); *1 Cor. 2:14-15* (in contrast with the unspiritual); see

also *1 Cor. 3:1; 15:44; Eph. 1:3; Col. 3:16.* (See *Holy Spirit.*)

spit. To spit on someone was to express contempt for him. *Num. 12:14; Deut. 25:9; Job 17:6; Mark 14:65.* In the N.T. some of the healings performed by Jesus reflect the common idea of the time that saliva had curative powers. *Mark 7:33; 8:23; John 9:6.*

spoil. In the O.T., goods taken from conquered enemies. Under the terms of ancient warfare, taking spoil was the privilege of the victor. Sometimes it was divided into three portions: part to be devoted to the Lord or given to a sanctuary; part to be shared among all or allotted to the king; part to go to the fighters as their pay. *Num. 31:10-11; 1 Sam. 30:22-25; 2 Sam. 12:30; 1 Chron. 26:27; Isa. 9:3.* (See *booty; devote.*)

square of the city. In O.T. times, usually the open space inside a gate where goods were sold and the elders sat to hear legal cases. *Judg. 19:14-21; 2 Chron. 32:6; Ezra 10:9; Neh. 8:3; Job 29:7.*

stacte. A spice made from the resin of a desert shrub; used in making incense. *Ex. 30:34.*

stadia. In the N.T., plural of *stadium*, a Greek measurement of distance, equal to about two hundred yards today. *Rev. 14:20; 21:16;* see also footnotes, *Luke 24:13; John 6:19; 11:18.*

staff. A long pole carried for support and for defense by shepherds and travelers. *Ex. 12:11; Lev. 27:32; 2 Kings 18:21; Ps. 23:4; Isa. 10:5; Jer. 48:17; Mark 6:8.*
break the staff of bread refers to famine. *Lev. 26:26; Ps. 105:16; Ezek. 4:16;* also *Isa. 3:1.*

standard. In O.T. times, a symbol of a tribe or an army. *Num. 2:2; Isa. 31:9; Jer. 4:5-6.* (See *banner* for description.)

statute. In the O.T., a rule usually having to do with ritual, feasts, and the like; often with "commandments." *Ex. 27:21; Num. 9:14; 1 Sam. 30:25.* (See *law* for related words.)

steadfast love. In the O.T., the continuing goodness of God toward the people with whom he chose to be bound in a covenant relationship. *Deut. 7:9; 2 Sam. 15:20; Neh. 9:17; Ps. 6:4; 36:5; 136;* also *Hos. 6:6.* (See *grace.*)

Stephen. One of the men chosen to serve tables in the church at Jerusalem; later an evangelist, and the first martyr among the Christians. He was stoned to death as the result of an argument with Hellenist Jews. *Acts 6:5 to 8:2; 11:19; 22:20.*

steward. An official of a large household, such as that of a king, in charge of servants, meals, household supplies, and expenses. Similar to chamberlain. *Gen. 43:19; 1 Chron. 27:31; Luke 16:1; John 2:8; 1 Cor. 4:1-2; Eph. 3:2.* (See *chamberlain.*)

stiff-necked. Unleadable, referring

to the way an ox refuses direction in a yoke. *Ex. 32:9; 2 Chron. 36:13; Acts 7:51.*

Stoic (stō'ĭk). In N.T. times, one of the two main schools of philosophy of the Greek-Roman world, founded in the fourth century B.C. The founder taught in the *stoai* (porches) of the market place in Athens; thus his followers were called Stoics. The main teaching of the philosophy was that men could live reasonably, rising above their feelings and the conditions of their lives. *Acts 17:18.* (See *Epicurean.*)

stonecutter. *2 Kings 12:12; 1 Chron. 22:2.* (See *mason* for list of words related to brick and stone work; *quarry*, for methods.)

stoning. A method of execution required by O.T. laws for adultery and blasphemy, as well as for other offenses. The witnesses who testified against the offender led the stoning, which usually took place outside a town. *Ex. 21:29; Lev. 24:14; 1 Kings 12:18* (a case of mob violence); *21:8-14; John 8:59; Acts 7:58-59; 2 Cor. 11:25.*

store-cities. Places where government supplies, especially grain, were stored. *Ex. 1:11; 1 Kings 9:19; 2 Chron. 17:12.*

stronghold. A fortified place, such as a tower in a wall or a citadel within a city. *Judg. 9:46-55; 1 Sam. 22:4; 2 Sam. 5:7, 9; Ps. 9:9; 144:2; Amos 1:10.*

surety. In O.T. customs regarding loans, a person who, in the presence of witnesses, made himself responsible for the repayment of another's debt. He was a pledge in human form. *Gen. 43:9; Job 17:3; Prov. 6:1; Heb. 7:22.*

surname, *v.* To give an additional name to a person. *Isa. 45:4; Mark 3:16; Acts 1:23.* (See *name.*)

Susa (soo'sə). In O.T. times, a city in what is now the country of Iran, made one of the capitals of the Persian empire by Cyrus. Archaeologists have excavated the remains of the palace built there by another Persian emperor, Darius. Among the ruins there were found tables of the law codes of Hammurabi, a Babylonian emperor of the eighteenth century B.C. The laws have many resemblances to those in the O.T. *Ezra 4:9; Neh. 1:1; Esth. 1:2; Dan. 8:2.*

swaddling. A newborn baby was wrapped in a square cloth to prevent the child from moving his arms and legs. Two corners of the cloth were folded over the arms, a third corner was folded over the feet and legs, and the fourth was used as a covering for the head. Bands were wrapped around the outside. Swaddling cloths were used until the baby was six months old. *Job 38:9; Luke 2:7, 12.*

swear. To take an oath, often **swear by,** that is, to call someone to witness. *Gen. 21:23; Lev. 19:12; Deut. 26:15; 1 Sam. 24:21; 2 Chron. 6:22; Ps. 24:4; Matt. 5:33-37; Mark 14:71.* (See *curse; oath.*)

sword. A weapon of war used chiefly after the time of David. The sword had a two-edged blade made of bronze or iron, and a handle made of wood or bone. It was carried in a sheath attached to the girdle, usually at the left side. The phrase **men who drew the sword** refers to soldiers or armies. *Ex. 32:27; Judg. 3:16; 1 Sam. 25:13; 1 Chron, 21:27; Isa. 2:4.* Figuratively used to mean violence or war. *Ps. 63:10; Jer. 14:15; Ezek. 30:4; Matt. 10:34; Rom. 8:35.*

sycamore. A type of fig tree, bearing inferior fruit that was not edible at all unless pierced just before ripening, to allow insects to escape. *1 Kings 10:27; 1 Chron. 27:28; Luke 19:4.* (See *dresser of sycamore trees.*)

sycamine. Probably the same as sycamore; or a mulberry tree. *Luke 17:6.*

synagogue, meaning "assembly house." In the N.T., a community meeting place for Jews; used mainly for worship, but also for schools and other gatherings. Although not mentioned in the O.T., synagogues probably originated during the exile in Babylon as meetings of the people to hear the writings and to pray. By the time of Jesus, each community of Jews, anywhere in the Roman world, had its synagogue. The building was rectangular, and its doorways faced Jerusalem. Along the walls on the inside were benches. A board of elders supervised each synagogue, and there were other officers, such as the ruler. The services in a synagogue consisted of readings, a talk (or sermon), and prayers. The great annual feasts were still celebrated at the temple in Jeru-salem, the only place where sacrifices were made. *Matt. 12:9; Mark 5:36; Luke 4:15; John 16:2; Acts 9:2; 18:4.* (See *worship.*)

Syria. In the O.T., same as Aram, an area to the northeast of Canaan. **Syrians.** Inhabitants of several small states in the area, such as Damascus and Zobah. The Syrians fought with the Israelites during the time of David, and in later years until overcome by the Assyrians. *Judg. 10:6; 2 Sam. 10:6; 1 Kings 15:18; 2 Chron. 16:2; Isa. 7:8; Jer. 35:11.* (See Time Line; map Plate VI, D-3.)
In N.T. times, a province of the Roman Empire, including Cilicia, Phoenicia, Galilee, Samaria, Judea, the Decapolis, and other areas. *Matt. 4:24; Mark 7:26* ("Syrophoenician"); *Luke 2:2; Acts 15:41; 18:18; Gal. 1:21.* (See map Plate XV, G-3.)

T

tabernacle, meaning "dwelling" or "tent." A tent equipped as a sanctuary during the journey of the Israelites from Egypt to Canaan. It symbolized the presence of God with his people, as did the ark, which was kept in it. The description of the making of the tabernacle, *Ex., chs. 25 to 27; 36 to 40,* was written much later, after the destruction of Solomon's temple. Perhaps the actual tabernacle was less elaborate and more temporary than the description, which sounds much like the temple in Jerusalem. *Ex. 40:34; Num. 9:15; 1 Chron. 21:29.* (See *tent* [tent of meeting]. See *temple* for a general description.)

tabernacles, feast of, also called feast of ingathering or feast of booths. The last of the three major feasts of the year, a harvest festival during which families built and lived in booths, or tabernacles, for seven days in memory of the tent life of the Israelites during their journey from Egypt to Canaan. *2 Chron. 8:13; John 7:2.* (See *feast.*)

table. In O.T. times, used only by the wealthy or by royalty, or in a sanctuary as the table for the showbread. Most people used a skin or mat spread on the floor. *Gen. 43:34; Ex. 25:30; 1 Sam. 20:5; 1 Chron. 28:16.* Tables at a dinner or banquet in N.T. times were low, and usually small, so

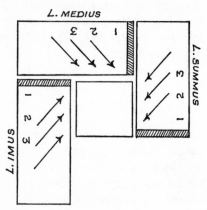

Diagram of Roman table and couches. *Mensa,* table. *L(ectus) summus,* highest couch. *L. medius,* middle couch. *L. imus,* lowest couch.

that three people reclining on a couch alongside shared a table. *Matt. 26:20; Luke 7:36-38; 16:20-21; John 13:28.* (See *place of honor.* See *house* for list of other household furnishings.)
tables of the money-changers were trays on low bases. *Matt. 21:12; John 2:15.*

tablet. A writing surface of unbaked clay or of stone, covered with a layer of plaster, or of wood with a thin covering of wax. *Isa. 8:1; 30:8; Jer. 17:1; Luke 1:63; 2 Cor. 3:3.* (See *write* for list of related words.)

talent. In the O.T., a standard weight used in payment before coins were used. It was equal to three thousand shekels, or approximately seventy-five pounds. Other nations used talents of differing weights. *2 Sam. 12:30; 1 Kings 20:39; 2 Kings 5:23; 2 Chron. 36:3.* (See *money; weigh.* See *shekel* for a table of other main weights.)
In the N.T., a unit of money, not a coin but money on account, as a check or draft; equal to about one thousand dollars today. *Matt. 18:24; 25:14-28.* (See *money,* in N.T. times.)

tambourine. In O.T. times, played usually by women for dancing and other festive occasions, shaken or beaten as are tambourines today. Same as timbrel. *Gen. 31:27; 2 Sam. 6:5; Job 21:12.* (See *timbrel.*)

tanner. Craftsman who prepared leather by using several kinds of plant juices and solutions made from bark. Because his occupation meant that he must handle dead animals, a tanner was not liked, and was usually located outside of town. *Ex. 25:5; Acts 9:43; 10:6.* (See *leather.*)

Tarshish (tär'shish). In the O.T., a city or country very distant from Canaan, perhaps Spain. The **ships of Tarshish** were any large, seagoing commercial ships. *1 Kings 10:22;*

2 Chron. 20:36; Ps. 72:10; Isa. 2:16; Jonah 1:3.

Tarsus (tär′səs). Capital of the Roman province of Cilicia in N.T. times, a port ten miles inland on the northeastern coast of the Mediterranean Sea. It was noted for its schools, for the weaving of linen cloth, and for tentmaking. *Acts 9:11, 30; 11:25; 21:39; 22:3.* (See map Plate XV, F-3.)

Tartan (tär′tăn). Title for a commander in the Assyrian army. *2 Kings 18:17.*

Rabsaris (răb′sə rĭs). Title of the chief officer of the household of the Assyrian kings. *2 Kings 18:17; Jer. 39:3.*

Rabshakeh (răb′shə kə). Title of the cupbearer of the Assyrian king. The Rabshakeh was an administrative officer. *2 Kings 18:17 to 19:8; Isa. 36:2 to 37:8.*

taskmaster. In O.T. times, one who assigned and supervised the work of forced labor; same as overseer. *Ex. 1:11; 3:7; 5:6-14; 2 Chron. 10:18; Isa. 60:17.*

tax. In O.T. times, chiefly tithes for the temple and the priests. *2 Chron. 24:6-11.* Solomon was the first king to take taxes from the people to support the royal court. They were paid in produce such as grain or wine. *1 Kings 4:7.* Later kings also collected taxes. *2 Kings 23:35.* The Persian empire, instead of exacting tribute from a state, levied taxes on the people. *Neh. 5:4.*

In N.T. times the Romans levied several kinds of taxes on the people of the provinces. Romans purchased the duty of collecting taxes and delegated their work to **tax collectors,** usually natives of the provinces. The tax collector paid to the Roman a sum larger than the amount of the tax he was authorized to collect. In order to get back his payment and to make a profit, he charged the people more than the actual tax. A **tax office** was a table or desk set up in the market place, or beside a highway if it was for collection of duties on transported goods. *Matt. 9:9-13; Mark 12:14; Luke 7:34; 18:10; 19:2.*

The **half-shekel tax** was paid to the temple by every adult male Jew once a year in N.T. times. It was collected in the towns or at the temple at the time of a feast. *Matt. 17:24.* (See *money-changer; shekel,* in N.T. times.)

Teacher. In the N.T., a title of respect given to Jesus; same as rabbi. *Matt. 8:19; Mark 9:17; Luke 20:28; John 1:38.*

teacher. Perhaps an officer in the early churches. *Acts 13:1; 1 Cor. 12:28; Eph. 4:11.* (See *church* for list of officers.)

Tekoa (tə kō′ə). In O.T. times, a fortified city south of Bethlehem about six miles, home of the prophet Amos. *2 Sam. 14:2; 2 Chron. 11:6; 20:20; Jer. 6:1; Amos 1:1.*
Also a personal name.

temple. According to ancient beliefs, a dwelling place for God or for gods. Temples, or sanctuaries, of the gods usually housed idols. *1 Sam. 31:10; 1 Chron. 10:10; Ezra 5:14; Jer. 43:13.* In O.T. times there were temples of some sort at several places, such as Shiloh and Bethel. (See *house of God* for description.) David planned to build a temple in Jerusalem, but it was Solomon who carried out the plans. *2 Sam. 7:1-13.* The building of this temple is described in *1 Kings, chs. 5 to 8.* In the O.T. it is also called the house of the Lord or the house of God. The temple built by Solomon was destroyed when the Chaldeans took Jerusalem. *2 Chron. 36:18-19.* Jews who returned from exile in Babylon built another temple. *Ezra 6:1-5, 15.* (See, for some officers of the temple in O.T. times, *high priest; keepers of the threshold; Korah; Levite; priest.*)

In N.T. times a new temple was being built by Herod. Work was started in 20 B.C. and completed around A.D. 64. *John 2:20.* It was destroyed by the Romans in A.D. 70. Today the site of the temple in Jerusalem is occupied by a Muslim shrine, the "Dome of the Rock." The site is believed to include the threshing floor that David bought as a place for the ark, on which Solomon's temple was later built.

The general plan of each of the three main temples (also the tabernacle) was the same. The temple building itself was surrounded by a courtyard, or several courts. The building had a porch, called the vestibule, and two inner rooms, the holy place, or nave, and the most holy place. In the court just outside the building were an altar for sacrifices, the sea, and the lavers. The holy place contained the altar of incense, the lampstand, and the table for the bread of the Presence. In Solomon's temple the most holy place con-

tained the ark and cherubim; in later temples this room was empty.

In N.T. times there were porticoes on the inner side of the courtyard walls. Classes were sometimes held in them, or people gathered informally to hear teachers. *John 10:23-24; Acts 3:11-12.* The money-changers placed their tables in the outer court. *Mark 11:15.* The treasury was located in the next inner court. *Mark 12:41.* (See, for additional information, *altar; ark; bread of the Presence; holy place; incense* [altar of incense]; *lampstand; laver; money-changer; sea; treasury; veil.*)

ten commandments. The ten words, the basic requirements of the covenant between God and his people. *Ex. 34:28; Deut. 4:13; 10:4.* The commandments as given in *Ex. 20:1-17* and *Deut. 5:6-21* are probably expanded statements of originally brief sayings. (See *law.*)

tent. Homes in early O.T. times. Made of goat's-hair cloth, probably black, elevated on poles and held by cords and pegs. The interior was divided into two rooms by a curtain hung from the poles. The room toward the back of the tent was for the women. *Gen. 18:1-10; Num. 11:10; Judg. 4:21; Isa. 33:20; Jer. 10:20.* In later times, when people lived in houses, the word "tent" still meant home. *1 Kings 12:16; Ps. 15:1; 91:10; Jer. 30:18; 2 Cor. 5:1.*

tent of meeting; or tent of the testimony. Other names for the tabernacle. *Ex. 27:21; Num. 17:7; Josh. 18:1; 1 Sam; 2:22; 1 Kings 8:4; Acts 7:44.*

tentmakers. Weavers of tent cloth. *Acts 18:3.*

teraphim (tĕr'ə fĭm). In O.T. times, small images used in divination or as household gods, images kept in a shrine in a home and worshiped by the family. *Gen. 31:19* (" household gods"; *Judg. 17:5; 2 Kings 23:24; Zech. 10:2.* (See *image.* See *gods* for list of related words.)

testimony. Evidence, especially of the actions of God. In the O.T., **ark of the testimony; tabernacle of the testimony; tent of the testimony,** all referring to the tables of the commandments (testimonies of God) kept in the ark. The word **testimonies** in the O.T. is often used with " statutes " and " commandments." *Ex. 25:21; Num. 1:50; 9:15; Deut. 6:17; Ps. 19:7; Mark 14:55; John 1:19; 8:14; Acts 4:33.*

tetrarch (tĕt'rärk). In N.T. times, a ruler over part of a Roman province. *Matt. 14:1* (" king " in *v. 9*); *Luke 3:1; 9:7; Acts 13:1.*

Thaddaeus (thă dē'əs). One of Jesus' twelve disciples. Believed to be the same as Judas the son of James in *Luke 6:16; John 14:22; Acts 1:13.* (See *disciple* for Bible references to lists of the twelve.)

theater. In Greek-style cities of N.T. times, an outdoor meeting place consisting of semicircular rows of seats constructed on a hillside above a flat place that served as a stage. Used for shows and for public meetings. *Acts 19:29, 31.* (See *Ephesus.*)

Thessalonians, The First and Second Letters to the (thĕs'ə lō'nĭ ənz). Two N.T. books, letters from Paul to the church at Thessalonica, which he had started. The first letter was written about A.D. 50, when Paul received a report about the church from Timothy, who had visited Thessalonica. The letter was intended to encourage the Thessalonians in their faith and to tell them about the expected return of Christ. The second letter is also about the expected return of Christ, which some Christians were misunderstanding. The date of this letter is uncertain.

Thessalonica (thĕs'ə lə nī'kə). In N.T. times, a city of the Roman province of Macedonia, in what is now Greece. It was an important commercial center, a seaport located on an overland highway from Rome to the east. *Acts 17:1, 11; Phil. 4:16; 1 Thess. 1:1; 2 Thess. 1:1; 2 Tim. 4:10.* (See map Plate XV, D-3.)

Thomas. One of the twelve disciples of Jesus. *Matt. 10:3; John 11:16; 20:24-29.* (See *disciple* for Bible references to lists of the twelve.)

threshing floor. A flat, open space, usually outside a town, with a floor of rock or pounded earth. The sheaves of grain were brought by cart and spread on the threshing floor. Then oxen trampled them or drew a **threshing sledge** over them. A sledge was made of wooden planks, with stones or pieces of metal embedded in the bottom. The grain was then ready for winnowing. *Ruth 3:2; 2 Sam. 24:21;*

Job 41:30; Isa. 27:12; Micah 4:12; also *1 Cor. 9:9.* (See *harvest* for list of words related to harvesting.)

throne. Solomon's throne, described in *2 Chron. 9:17-19,* was probably typical of ancient times. A king occupied his throne when declaring laws or making judgments. Thus it is a symbol of the power or rule of a king. (See *enthroned* for application of this symbolism to God.) *Ex. 11:5; 2 Sam. 3:10; 1 Chron. 28:5; Ps. 9:4; 11:4; Matt. 5:34; 25:31.* (See, for details, *at his right hand; cherub; footstool.*)

Tiberias (tī bǐr'ǐ əs). In N.T. times, a city on the Sea of Galilee. Herod had built the city, naming it for the emperor Tiberius. Jews avoided it because it was built over a cemetery. Also a name for the Sea of Galilee. *John 6:1, 23; 21:1.* (See map Plate XIV, D-3.)

Tiberius Caesar (tī bǐr'ǐ əs). In N.T. times, the second emperor of the Roman Empire, succeeding Augustus in A.D. 14. *Luke 3:1;* also *Matt. 22:20-21; John 19:12* ("Caesar"). (See *Caesar; Time Line.*)

Tiglath-pileser (tǐg'lăth pǐ lē'zər); or **Tilgath-pilneser.** King of the Assyrian empire 745 to 727 B.C. After conquering Babylon, he became king there also, under the name "Pul." He attacked the Northern Kingdom, Israel, exacted tribute from the king, and deported some of the population. The king of the Southern Kingdom, Judah, appealed to him for help against Israel and Damascus, and was forced to pay tribute to him also. *2 Kings 15:19* ("Pul"), *29; 16:7-10; 2 Chron. 28:20.* (See Time Line.)

timbrel. A musical instrument, same as tambourine. *Ex. 15:20; Judg. 11:34; Ps. 68:25; Isa. 30:32.* (See *tambourine.*)

Timothy. A fellow worker with Paul whom the apostle called his "child." He was often sent to churches when Paul himself could not go to them, and was in charge of the church at Ephesus for a time. *Acts 16:1-3; Rom. 16:21; 1 Cor. 4:17; 1 Thess. 3:2; 1 Tim. 1:2.*

Timothy, The First and Second Letters of Paul to. Two N.T. books, letters to Timothy when he was in charge of the church at Ephesus; intended to help and encourage him in his duties. A very old tradition holds that Paul wrote these letters, but the ideas and the style do not seem to be Paul's. Perhaps a later writer refashioned some letter or fragments of letters that had been written by Paul. If Paul wrote the letters to Timothy, scholars believe he must have done so sometime after his imprisonment in Rome, assuming that he was acquitted and released.

tithe. A tenth of the produce of fields, orchards, vineyards, and flocks, which was considered as belonging to God (in other nations, to the king, *1 Sam. 8:15, 17*), and was given as offerings. It was used in part for the support of the priests, in part for sacrifices, and in part for charity. The tithing described in *Matt. 23:23* represents very meticulous keeping of the law. *Lev. 27:30-33; 2 Chron. 31:5-6;*

Neh. 13:5; Mal. 3:8; Luke 18:12.

Titus (tī'təs). A Gentile Christian who worked with Paul, and was at one time in charge of the churches in Crete. *2 Cor. 2:13; 8:23; Gal. 2:1, 3; Titus 1:4.*

Titus, The Letter of Paul to. N.T. book, a personal letter to Titus, who was then in Crete. It is similar to the letters to Timothy, and the same questions about its authorship are raised. (See *Timothy, The First and Second Letters of Paul to.*)

tomb. In O.T. times, from about 900 B.C., a chamber carved out of a hillside or a natural cave. Steps led down to a court and the entrance. Inside was a large room with shelves cut out of rock on the walls. Bodies were not put in coffins; sometimes large jars were used. It was the custom to bury a few personal or household belongings with the dead, although not with the Egyptian idea that they would be needed in the life after death. *Gen. 50:5; 2 Kings 9:28; Isa. 22:16.* The poor were buried in a common cemetery. *2 Kings 23:6; Jer. 26:23.*
In N.T. times, tombs were similar, but larger and somewhat more elaborate. Some were sealed with upright round stones rolled before the entrance in a groove. Because contact with the dead led to uncleanness, tombs were whitewashed to warn people to stay away. *Matt. 8:28; 23:27; Mark 15:46; 16:2-8; John 11:38; 20:11.* See also *Matt. 27:7.* (See *sepulchre.* See *death* for list of other customs.)

tongues. Languages, as in *Acts 2:4.*

Elsewhere in the N.T., **speaking in tongues** or **tongues,** an ecstatic experience in which a person made sounds that were not intelligible; considered to mean that a person was possessed by the Holy Spirit. The apostle Paul apparently felt that some control was needed over this phenomenon among early Christians. See *1 Cor. 12:10; 14:1-33;* also *Acts 10:46; 19:6.*

tore his robes [garments]. N.T. equivalent of O.T. " rent his clothes," but chiefly a reaction to blasphemy. *Matt. 26:65; Mark 14:63; Acts 14:14.* (See *rent his clothes.*)

tower. In O.T. times, part of a city wall, citadel, or fortress. It was a place for watchmen as part of the defense system. Sometimes the tower was the last place of safety for the people of a city when it was under attack. Or a similar tower might be built in O.T. times in the open country. Vineyards and fields often had brick or stone towers for watchmen to live in during harvest time. *Judg. 9:51; 2 Kings 17:9; 18:8; 2 Chron. 14:7; 26:10; 27:4; Ps. 61:3; Isa. 5:2; Mark 12:1.*

trade. In the O.T., usually international commerce by sea or by overland caravan. In *Ezek. 27:12-36* there is a description of Tyre, a great trading center of ancient times, and a list of nations and their products. *Gen. 37:28; 1 Kings 10:15, 28-29.* (See *merchant.*)

tradition. In the Gospels, commentaries on the written law, making applications of it to particular circumstances. The traditions that had grown during later O.T. times were considered by the Pharisees to be equal in importance to the law. *Matt. 15:1-6; Mark 7:1-8.*

transgress. To go against the will of God, to rebel; **transgression,** same as sin. *1 Sam. 15:24; 2 Kings 18:12; Ps. 32:1; Isa. 53:8; Matt. 15:2; Luke 22:37; Rom. 4:15.* (See *sin.*)

trap. Birds were snared in triggered nets. To catch animals, hunters used nooses, nets, or lightly covered pits. *Josh. 23:13; Job 18:9-10; Ps. 142:3; Isa. 42:22; Rom. 11:9.* (See *net; snare.*)

tread. In addition to the usual meaning, to press with the feet, as grapes and olives, to extract the juice; or to mix clay or mortar. Oxen were used to tread grain in threshing. *Job 24:11; Isa. 41:25; Jer. 25:30; Micah 6:15; Nahum 3:14; 1 Tim. 5:18.*

treasury. In the O.T., rooms for storage of valuables; or the contents of the rooms. *1 Kings 7:51; 1 Chron. 26:24* (of the temple); *2 Kings 20:12-15; 2 Chron. 25:24* (of the king). In the N.T., trumpet-shaped collection boxes located in the inner court of the temple. *Mark 12:41; John 8:20.*

tree, under every green. In O.T. times the nations around Israel believed that trees were sacred, or inhabited by spirits. Canaanite worship centers, " high places," were often located in groves of trees, or trees were planted as Asherim. *Deut. 16:21; 2 Chron. 28:4; Isa. 57:5; Jer. 2:20; 17:2; Ezek. 6:13.* (See *Asherah.* See *gods* for list of related words.)

trespass. Same as sin. *Ezra 10:10; Matt. 6:14-15; Rom. 5:18; 2 Cor. 5:19; Eph. 2:5.* (See *sin.*)

tribe. Especially in the O.T., descendants of a common ancestor. The Israelites in early times were grouped in units of families, clans made up of several families, and the larger tribes made up of a number of clans. Such organization was typical of seminomadic people such as the Israelites were before they settled in Canaan. According to the tradition, the people of Israel were made up of the twelve tribes descended from the sons of Jacob. To each of these tribes, except the Levites, a portion of the land of Canaan was allotted. As the Israelites began to live in towns and become a nation, probably others besides members of one tribe lived in the territory traditionally assigned to it. However, family connections were always important. Even in N.T. times, people were identified by the tribes to which their families belonged. *Gen. 49:28; Num., ch. 1* (a census listing the tribes); *Josh. 18:11-20* (example of allotment of land to tribes); *2 Sam. 5:1; Ps. 122:4; Matt. 19:28; Luke 2:36.* (For the twelve tribes, see *Asher; Benjamin; Dan; Ephraim* and *Manasseh,* the sons of Joseph; *Gad; Issachar; Judah; Naphtali; Reuben; Simeon; Zebulun.*) Menbers of the tribes were called " sons of ———— " or -ites. The names were also used to mean their territories. (See *Israel;* also *census; enrollment; genealogy; register.* See, for customs related to tribal loyalties, *avenger; marriage* [the custom concerning widows]; *ransom; redeem.*)

tribunal. In the N.T., the judgment seat in the praetorium from which the Roman governor heard cases as a judge. *Acts 18:12; 25:6.*

tribune. In N.T. times, the officer in charge of a cohort in the Roman Army. *Acts 21:31-33; 23:17; 24:22;* also *John 18:12* ("captain"). (See *Rome* for words related to army.)

tribute. Forced payment in goods or money made by a vassal state to

also used to announce certain feasts or occasions for assembling. The trumpets used in the temple were made of metal, and were straight, not curved. They were used in pairs or larger numbers for special services. *Judg. 3:27; 1 Sam. 13:3; 2 Sam. 15:10; 2 Chron. 5:12; 29:28; Ps. 81:3; 98:6; Joel 2:1.* (See *horn.*)

tunic. Same as coat. It was a straight undergarment, sometimes like a short-sleeved shirt. *Job 30:18; Matt. 10:10;*

King Jehu presenting tribute to Shalmaneser, king of Assyria, from a carving on the Black Obelisk

its conquerors or overlords. *Num. 31:28; Judg. 3:15-18; 2 Sam. 8:6; 2 Chron. 28:21; Hos. 10:6; Matt. 17:25.*

Troas (trō'ăs). In N.T. times, a city in the Roman province of Asia on the east shore of the Aegean Sea (not the Troy of Greek history and literature, which was to the north). *Acts 16:8; 20:5-6; 2 Cor. 2:12; 2 Tim. 4:13.* (See map Plate XV, E-3.)

trumpet. In early O.T. times, the horn of an animal, used in warfare to muster fighters, to signal for attack, or to announce the end of battle;

John 19:23. (See *coat.*)

turban. A linen cap worn by a priest. *Ex. 28:4; Lev. 16:4; Ezek. 44:18; Zech. 3:5.*

turtledove. A pigeon, used in sacrifices. *Lev. 5:7; 12:6; Num. 6:10; Luke 2:24.*

Twin Brothers. Castor and Pollux, twin gods in Greek and Roman mythology, especially known as guardians of sailors. *Acts 28:11.*

Tychicus (tĭk'ə kəs). A Christian

151

from Asia who worked with Paul. *Acts 20:4; Eph. 6:21; Col. 4:7; 2 Tim. 4:12; Titus 3:12.*

Tyre (tīr); usually **Tyre and Sidon** in the N.T. A seaport and commercial center on the east coast of the Mediterranean Sea (in general history known as a Phoenician city). In O.T. times it was a city-state with its own king. From Tyre, ships went all over the Mediterranean world to trade and to establish colonies. One of the chief products of Tyre was a dye known as Tyrian purple, made from shellfish. *Josh. 19:29; 2 Sam. 5:11; 1 Kings 5:1; Isa. 23:1; Ezek., ch. 27* (description of Tyre as a trading center); *Matt. 11:21; Mark 7:24; Acts 21:3-7.* (See *Phoenicia; Sidon;* map Plates V, C-3; XIV, C-2.)

U

uncircumcised. In Judges and 1 and 2 Samuel, the Philistines. Generally, in the O.T. and the N.T., non-Israelites. *Judg. 14:3; 2 Sam. 1:20; Jer. 9:25-26; Acts 11:3; Rom. 4:9; 1 Cor. 7:19.* (See *circumcise.*)

unclean. In O.T. times, certain things were declared unclean, and contact with them meant that a person must cleanse himself. Any bodily discharge was unclean, also childbirth, the dead, lepers, and certain animals that were not to be eaten. *Lev. 10:10; Isa. 6:5; Hos. 9:3; Matt. 23:27; Acts 10:9-16, 27-28.* (See *clean; defile; purification; wash.*)

unclean spirit. In N.T. times, a being or demon believed to be the cause of illness or insanity. *Matt. 10:1; Luke 4:33; Acts 8:7.* (See *spirit.*)

unleavened bread. Bread made without yeast, used in certain kinds of offerings, such as the bread of the Presence, and during the feast of Passover. The process of leavening was considered a form of corruption. Unleavened bread symbolized purity. *Ex. 12:39; Lev. 2:11; Deut. 16:3; 1 Cor. 5:7-8.*

feast of unleavened bread, also called Passover. A celebration commemorating the rescue of the Israelites from Egypt. After a supper in remembrance of the last night in Egypt, the seven days of the feast were observed by eating only unleavened bread. Perhaps originally the feast of unleavened bread was a separate celebration later combined with the Passover. *Deut. 16:16; 2 Chron. 30:13; Mark 14:1; Luke 22:1.* (See *feast.*)

upper room. A small room on the roof of a house, usually a guest room. *2 Kings 4:10; Mark 14:15; Acts 1:12-13; 9:37.* (See *house; roof.*)

Ur (ûr). Ancient city on the lower Euphrates River. It was the birthplace of Abraham. Before his time, Ur had been the capital of a people known in general history as the Sumerians. At the time of Abraham, Ur was part of the first Babylonian empire. When the Bible accounts were written, the area was part of the empire of the Chaldeans; thus it is called Ur of the Chaldeans. *Gen. 11:28, 31; 15:7; Neh. 9:7.* (See map Plate II, F-3.)

Urim and Thummim (ōŏr'ĭm, thŭm'-

152

ĭm). In O.T. times before Solomon, objects of uncertain nature used to determine the will of God for actions concerning the people as a whole. They were probably either stones like the lots, or sticks of different length. They were kept in the breastpiece above the priest's ephod. The word "Urim" begins with the first letter of the Hebrew alphabet, and the word "Thummim" begins with the last. *Lev. 8:8; Num. 27:21; 1 Sam. 14:41-42; 28:6; Ezra 2:63.* (See *cast lots; inquire of God.*)

Uzziah (ə zī'ə). King of the Southern Kingdom, Judah, in the eighth century B.C. who strengthened the defenses and the agriculture of the kingdom. He died around 742 B.C. *2 Chron., ch. 26; 2 Kings 15:1-7* (under the name Azariah). The work of three prophets is dated according to Uzziah's reign. *Isa. 6:1; Hos. 1:1; Amos 1:1.* (See *king;* Time Line.) Others.

V

vanity. Nothingness or unsubstantiality; used especially in the O.T. book of Ecclesiastes. *Ps. 89:47; Eccl. 1:2-11; Isa. 49:4.* See also *Ex. 20:7; Acts 14:15.*

vassal. A nation or a king who becomes subject to a foreign ruler; usually forced to pay tribute. *2 Kings 17:3; Lam. 1:1.*

veil. Stolelike head covering worn usually by women. A bride covered her face with a veil from the time she left her father's house until she was alone with the groom. Otherwise,

women did not cover their faces. *Gen. 24:65; Ex. 34:33; Isa. 3:23; 1 Cor. 11:5-6; 2 Cor. 3:13.*
Also the curtain between the two inner rooms of the tabernacle or the temple. *Ex. 26:31-33; Lev. 16:12; Luke 23:45* ("curtain"). (See *holy place; most holy place.*)

vestments. Special garments worn by a priest when officiating at services. *2 Kings 10:22; Ezra 3:10.* (See, for some of the vestments of the priests of Israel, *breastpiece; breeches; ephod; robe; turban.*)

village. In the O.T., an unwalled town often near a city and dependent on it for markets and for shelter in time of war. "Town" refers to either a city or a village. *Lev. 25:31; Josh. 15:32; 1 Sam. 6:18; Neh. 12:29.*

vinedresser. Workman who cut off the weak and nonbearing branches of grapevines to improve the fruit. *2 Kings 25:12; John 15:1; also Isa. 5:6.* (See *pruning hook.*)

vinegar. In the N.T., probably a sour wine used by the Roman soldiers. *Mark 15:36; Luke 23:36; John 19:29-30.*

vineyard. A description of the planting and care of a vineyard is given in *Isa. 5:1-6.* See also *Lev. 19:10; Deut. 28:39; 1 Kings 21:1; Neh. 9:25; Matt. 20:1-16; Mark 12:1-9.* (See, for words related to the growing and the use of grapes, *booth; grape; pruning hook; tower; tread; vinedresser; wine.*)

vision. Dreamlike experience in

which God made something known, usually to a prophet. *Gen. 15:1; Isa. 1:1; Jer. 38:21; Ezek. 1:1; Acts 9:10; 11:5.*

vow. A promise made to God, often as a bargain. *Gen. 28:20-22; 2 Sam. 15:7-8.* Devoted things were vowed. *Num. 21:2.* The Nazirite took a special kind of vow. *Num. 6:21; Acts 18:18.*

votive gift or **votive offering** was made as part of a vow. *Deut. 12:17; 2 Kings 12:18; 2 Chron. 15:18.* (See *offering.*)

W

wagon. Same as cart. *Gen. 45:19; 46:5; Num. 7:2-3; Ezek. 23:24.* (See *cart.*)

waistcloth. A short, skirtlike garment worn wrapped around the waist. Probably used before the coat, which developed from it. *Job 12:18; Jer. 13:1-11.* (See *coat* for list of other clothing.)

wall. City walls were built for defense against enemy attack. The lower part was made of hewn stone, the upper part of brick. Often there were two walls, and the space between them was used for storerooms, or was roofed over so that houses could be built on the double wall. *Lev. 25:31; Josh. 2:15; 2 Sam. 11:20-21; 2 Chron. 8:5; 25:23; Ezra 4:12; Acts 9:25.* (See *fortified city; gate; rampart; siege; tower; watchman.*)

war. (For customs relating to war in O.T. times see the following: Types of warfare: *ambush; besiege; champion; raid; siege.* Types of fighters: *army* [list of types of troops]; *muster.* Methods of defense: *bulwark; citadel; city; fortified city; fortress; garrison; gate; rampart; siege; stronghold; tower; wall; watchman.* Conquest: *booty; devote; slave; spoil; tribute; vassal.* Also: *armor* [list of pieces of armor]; *weapon* [list of kinds of weapons].)

wash. Washing was emphasized for cleanliness, as part of making sacrifices, and as purification from uncleanness. Washing the feet of guests was a part of hospitality. *Gen. 18:3-4; Lev. 11:39-40; 2 Chron. 4:6; Matt. 6:17; Mark 7:3-4; John 13:5.*

watch. In O.T. times the night was divided into three watches: from sunset to midnight; from midnight to cockcrow, *Judg. 7:19;* and from cockcrow to sunrise, *Ex. 14:24; 1 Sam. 11:11.*
In N.T. times the Romans divided the twelve hours of the night into four watches. *Mark 6:48; Luke 12:38.*

watchman. Might be stationed in the fields or vineyards at harvest time, living in a temporary booth or a watchtower. Cities had watchmen on the walls or the towers. *1 Sam. 14:16; 2 Sam. 18:24; 2 Kings 9:17; Job 27:18; Jer. 6:17; 51:12.*

water. (For words relating to methods of collecting and storing water, see *cistern; conduit; fountain; jar; pool; well.* See also *city* and *siege* for explanation of the importance of water supplies to people in a city.)

water jar. Large, narrow pottery container for drawing water from the community well or cistern, and for storage at home. The work of drawing water was customarily done by women. *Gen. 24:15; Mark 14:13; John 4:28.*

Way. In the book of The Acts, a name for the church. *Acts 9:2; 19:9; 22:4; 24:14, 22.* (See *Christians* for other names for church members.)

weapon. Various weapons are mentioned in *2 Chron. 26:14-15; Ezek. 39:9.* (See *armor* [list of pieces of armor]; *arrow; axe; bow; javelin; sling; spear; sword;* also *siege.*)

weave. In early O.T. times, cloth was woven at home by the women. Heavy cloth of goat's hair was made for tents; garments were made of wool. The usual practice was to weave a garment in one piece rather than to weave a length of cloth from which to cut a garment. A **weaver's beam** was the heavy top beam of the loom, to which the warp threads were at-

tached and weighted with stones at the other end. The **weaver's shuttle** was used to pass the woof threads through the warp by hand. In later times, some cities were centers of commercial weaving and dying. *Ex. 28:39; Judg. 16:13-14; 2 Sam. 21:19; Job 7:6; Isa. 19:9* (Egyptian weavers); *38:12.* (See, for other words related to the making of cloth, *dyed; flax; fuller; linen; loom; spin.*)

wedding. *Matt. 22:8-12; Mark 2:19.* (See *marriage.*)

weeks, feast of. O.T.; called Pentecost in the N.T. An annual harvest festival held seven weeks after the barley harvest, at the end of the wheat harvest. *Ex. 34:22; Num. 28:26; Deut. 16:10, 16; 2 Chron. 8:13.* (See *feast.*)

weigh. In O.T. times, goods were weighed on balances or scales using standard weights of stone or metal. Payment was made with a standard weight of metal in lumps, rings, or bars; thus, money was also weighed. *Gen. 24:22; 2 Sam. 12:30; 2 Kings 12:11; 2 Chron. 3:9; Isa. 46:6; Jer. 32:10; Ezek. 5:1.* (See *money* for fur-

Weight found at Lachish; and weights in the form of a lion and a duck, which were Nineveh.

ther information; *shekel* for table of weights. See also *balances; scales.*)

well. Shaft or pit dug to reach underground water, or an enclosure for a spring. Some wells were reached by a flight of steps down to the water level; others had a leather bucket and rope for lifting water. In *Gen. 24:10-20; 26:17-22; 29:1-10* are three stories about wells in nomadic times, when they were often a cause of strife between tribes. *Num. 21:16; 2 Sam. 17:18-19; 23:15-16; Jer. 6:7; John 4:6-15.* (See *water* for list of related words.)

wheat. The main food crop, used chiefly for making flour and meal for bread; also eaten roasted (called parched grain, *Ruth 2:14; 1 Sam. 25:18*). *Ex. 29:2; Deut. 8:8; Judg. 6:11; 1 Chron. 21:20; Isa. 28:25; Amos 8:5; Matt. 3:12; Luke 22:31.* (See, for other grain crops, *barley; spelt.* See, for methods of farming, *harvest* [list of words related to harvesting processes]; *plow; rain, the early and the later; sow.*)

widow. In the Hebrew family pattern, a widow inherited nothing from her husband. If she was childless, she might remain in her husband's family if one of her brothers-in-law would marry her, or she might return to her father's house and remarry. But a widow with children might have no one to provide for her. For this reason the O.T. contains laws of consideration for widows, and they were a special concern of the early church. *Gen. 38:11; Deut. 24:19; 26:12; Ps. 146:9; Isa. 1:17; Jer. 22:3; Mark 12:42;* *Acts 6:1; 1 Tim. 5:3-16.* (See *marriage; distribution.*)

wilderness. A desert area. In O.T. stories of the Israelites' journey from Egypt to Canaan, areas of the Sinai Peninsula, such as the wilderness of Zin. In the N.T. (except when referring to the Israelites' journey from Egypt to Canaan), part of Judea, highlands northwest of the Dead Sea. *Ex. 15:22; Num. 33:8, 11, 15, 36; Judg. 1:16; Isa. 27:10; Matt. 3:1; 4:1; John 6:31; Acts 7:36.* (See map Plate III.)

window. An opening in a wall of a building, usually high up if on a street; sometimes covered with a lattice. *Judg. 5:28; 1 Sam. 19:12; 1 Kings 7:4-5; Isa. 24:18; Jer. 22:14; Acts 20:9.*

winds, four. An expression for the four corners, or ends, of the earth. *Jer. 49:36; Ezek. 37:9; Zech. 2:6; Matt. 24:31.* (See *earth.*)

wine. Made from grapes put into a wine press consisting of two vats. In the first vat, the grapes were pressed by foot by treaders. The juice flowed into the second vat placed on a slightly lower level, where it was allowed to ferment and then was put into jars or bottles. Wine was used in offerings and as medicine, but mainly as a food. *Gen. 14:18; Num. 15:10; Deut. 16:13; Judg. 19:19; Isa. 5:2; 16:10; Jer. 23:9; Matt. 21:33; Mark 15:23; Luke 10:34; 22:17-18; John 2:1-11; Acts 2:13.* (See *vineyard* for words related to the growing of grapes; *bread* for list of other foods.)

wineskin. (See *skin of water.*)

winnow. To separate the heads of grain from the straw, the threshed grain was thrown into the air with a **winnowing fork.** This was usually done in the late afternoon on the threshing floor, so that the wind coming up at that time would carry the chaff away while the grain fell to the ground. *Ruth 3:2; Isa. 41:16; Jer. 15:7; Matt. 25:24; Luke 3:17.* (See *harvest* for list of words related to harvesting.)

wise men. Magicians or sorcerers. *Gen. 41:8; Ex. 7:11; Isa. 19:12; Jer. 50:35.* In the Persian empire and following that time, a class of priests in eastern religions. *Matt. 2:1;* also *Acts 13:6.* (See *magic* for list of practices.)
The **wise man,** and **wisdom,** meaning the knowledge of right living, are the subjects of the O.T. books of The Proverbs and Ecclesiastes. With Job, they are called the wisdom books, and represent a kind of teaching popular in late O.T. times.

witness. Evidence, in the form of a person or thing, to an agreement. *Gen. 31:48; Josh. 22:26-27; Judg. 11:10; Ruth 4:9-11.* (See *heap.*)
When the elders of a city were judging a case that involved a possible death sentence, two witnesses were required. If the person was condemned, the witnesses led the stoning. *Ex. 20:16; Deut. 19:15-19; 1 Kings 21:9-13* (story of two false witnesses); *Mark 14:56-57; Acts 7:58.*
In The Acts and the letters, one who testified to Christ, sometimes in the face of danger. *Acts 1:8; 5:32; 22:20; 1 Tim. 6:12; Heb. 12:1.*

wizard. One who divined by communicating with the dead; same as necromancer. *Deut. 18:11; 1 Sam. 28:3; 2 Kings 21:6; Isa. 8:19.* (See *magic* for list of similar practices.)

word of the Lord. A message: the means of God's revealing himself to men, especially through the prophets. *Gen. 15:4; Deut. 5:4-5; 2 Sam. 24:11; Ps. 33:4, 6; Isa. 1:10; Jer. 1:2;* and opening phrases of other books of prophets. (See *says the Lord.*)
In the Gospels, **the word** or **word of God.** *Mark 2:2; 4:14-20, 33; Luke 3:2; 5:1; 11:28.*
To people in ancient times words were powerful. A curse was not idle words, but words with power to carry out the thing expressed. In this sense the world came into being through God's word. *Gen. 1:3; John 1:1.* In the Gospel of John, this power of God is Jesus Christ, *1:14.*
In The Acts and the letters, **the word** is the gospel of Jesus Christ. *Acts 8:4; 19:20; 1 Cor. 1:18; Eph. 5:26; Col. 4:3.*

works. Similar to "signs and wonders"; often **mighty works** or **wonderful works.** *Judg. 13:19; Ps. 96:3; 107:8; John 5:20; Acts 2:22.* (See *sign.*)

world. For the people of the Bible, the world, that is, the known world, consisted of the area around the Mediterranean Sea, east to India and southward into Africa. To Israelites of O.T. times, the coastlands and isles of the Mediterranean Sea were vague and distant lands. *1 Sam. 2:8; Ps. 9:8; Isa. 23:17; Nahum 1:5.* (See, for O.T. ideas of the universe, *earth.*)

To people of N.T. times, the world was more or less equivalent to the Roman Empire. *Mark 14:9; 16:15; Luke 2:1.* (See *Rome.*)

In the N.T., because the kingdom of God had come into the world in Jesus Christ, the word " world " often carries a note of opposition to the kingdom, or of incompleteness where it is not acknowledged. *Matt. 13:38; John 1:10; 3:16-17; 15:18-19; 1 Cor. 2:12; 2 Cor. 5:19; Col. 2:20; 1 John 2:15-17.*

wormwood. A bitter-tasting plant, poisonous in large quantities. *Jer. 9:15; Lam. 3:19; Amos 5:7.*

worship. To serve God or the gods, especially in certain acts or ceremonies. *1 Sam. 1:3; 2 Sam. 12:20; Ps. 22:27; Isa. 46:6; Matt. 4:10; Mark 5:6; Acts 17:23; Rom. 12:1.*

In O.T. times, worship consisted chiefly of making offerings and sacrifices, not always attended by a gathering of people. Prayers were also used. Hymns and psalms were sung by the choirs at temple services, and musical instruments were used. *1 Chron. 15:16; The Psalms.* After the exile, the custom of gathering in the synagogues grew. At these services there was reading of the scriptures, teaching, and prayer.

In the early churches, worship took its form from the synagogue service, not from the temple services. Members of the churches met on the first day of the week in commemoration of the resurrection of Christ. Not much is known about the form of meetings for worship, but it included reading and preaching, prayer and hymns, the breaking of bread, and

sometimes speaking in tongues. For details see *Acts 20:7; 1 Cor. 11:20-29; 14:26; Eph. 5:19; Col. 4:16.*

write; writer. Writing was invented and in use long before the time of Abraham. However, few people in the ancient world learned to write.

Part of a letter found at Lachish, dating from around 600 B.C. Written on a fragment of pottery.

They depended on professional writers to prepare letters, legal documents, court records, and the like for them. *Josh. 18:8; Isa. 8:1; Jer. 30:2; Ezek. 9:2; Luke 1:63; Rom. 16:22; Col. 4:18.* (See, for words related to writing, *book; ink; letter; papyrus; pen; potsherd; scribe,* in O.T. times; *seal; signet; tablet.*)

Y

yard. A term from modern methods of measurement used to mean two cubits in measurements of N.T. times. *John 21:8.* (See *cubit* for table of measurements of length.)

year. In O.T. times, twelve lunar months, with an extra month added, not at regular intervals (as days are added to leap years in the present calendar), but when it seemed necessary. In early O.T. times, the year began with the fall plowing. Probably in later times the year began in the spring. *Ex. 23:16; 2 Sam. 11:1; 1 Kings 14:25; Ps. 90:4, 10.* (See *month; new moon.* See, for seasons of the year, *harvest; rain, the early and the later.*)

yoke. A wooden bar with loops of rope or rods; used to harness two oxen to a cart or a plow. *Num. 19:2; 1 Kings 19:19; Job 1:3; Jer. 27:2; Matt. 11:29; Luke 14:19; Phil. 4:3.*
Often a figure of speech for oppression. *2 Chron. 10:4; Jer. 27:8; Hos. 10:11; Gal. 5:1.*

Z

Zealot (zĕl'ət). In N.T. times, a member of a patriotic group that advocated violent means of ending Roman rule over the Jews. *Luke 6:15; Acts 1:13.* The Assassins in *Acts 21:38* were probably similar to the Zealots.

Zebulun (zĕb'yə lən). One of the twelve sons of Jacob; the tribe descended from him; and their territory west of the Sea of Galilee. *Gen. 30:20; Num. 2:7; Judg. 12:12; 1 Chron. 12:40; Matt. 4:13.* (See map Plate IV, C-3.)

Zechariah (zĕk'ə rī'ə). A prophet associated with Haggai, about 520 B.C., in the rebuilding of the temple in Jerusalem after the exiles returned from Babylon. *Ezra 5:1; Zech. 1:1.* Others (a common name in O.T. times).
In the N.T., the father of John the Baptist. *Luke 1:5-25, 57-79; 3:2.*
In *Matt. 23:35* and *Luke 11:51,* the son of a priest in the Southern Kingdom, Judah, in the ninth century B.C., whom the king had ordered stoned to death in the temple. *2 Chron. 24:20-22.* In Matthew this Zechariah is identified with the O.T. prophet, probably because some copyist added a note that he thought would make the matter clearer.

Zechariah, The Book of. O.T. book consisting of visions of the prophet Zechariah about a restored Jerusalem, *chs. 1 to 8.* Probably *chs. 9 to 14* are two anonymous books from later prophets.

Zedekiah (zĕd'ə kī'ə). The last king of the Southern Kingdom, Judah. He was a puppet king put on the throne by Nebuchadnezzar, king of Babylon. His revolt led to the siege and capture of Jerusalem in 587 B.C. The prophet Jeremiah taught during his reign. *2 Kings 24:17 to 25:7; Jer. 1:3; 27:1; 52:3-11.* (See *Judah; king;* Time Line.) Others.

Zephaniah (zĕf'ə nī'ə). A prophet in the Southern Kingdom, Judah, in the seventh century B.C. (See Time Line.) Others.

Zephaniah, The Book of. O.T. book of teachings of the prophet Zephaniah. He warned that the day of the Lord would be a time of judgment for the people of God.

Zeus (zōōs). The chief god of Greek mythology in N.T. times. *Acts 14:12-13.*

Ziklag (zĭk'lăg). O.T. city in the territory of Judah, north of Beersheba. In the time of Saul, a Philistine city in which David made his headquarters for a time. *1 Sam. 27:6; 30:1, 14, 26; 2 Sam. 1:1; 1 Chron. 12:1.* (See map Plate IV, B-6.)

Zion (zī'ən); or **Mount Zion,** meaning "fortress." In the time of David, a hilltop fortress in Jerusalem under the Jebusites. After Jerusalem was captured, Zion was renamed the city of David and the ark was placed there. *2 Sam. 5:7; 1 Kings 8:1; Ps. 76:2.* (See map Plate XVI — city of David.)
Also the temple in Jerusalem. *Isa. 8:18.* Or Jerusalem itself. *Ps. 69:35; Jer. 31:6.*
daughter of Zion; or **Zion.** The people of God. *Ps. 126:1; Isa. 52:2; Micah 4:10; Matt. 21:5.*

Zoar (zō'ər). O.T. city east of the Dead Sea in the territory of the Moabites. In the time of Abraham, a city-state, now probably under the waters of the southeastern Dead Sea. *Gen. 13:10; 14:2; 19:30; Deut. 34:3; Isa. 15:5.*

BIBLIOGRAPHY

Albright, W. F., *The Archaeology of Palestine*, Rev. Ed. (Pelican Book, Penguin Books, Inc., 1960).

Bouquet, A. C., *Daily Life in New Testament Times* (Charles Scribner's Sons, 1953).

Burrows, Millar, *What Mean These Stones?* (American Schools of Oriental Research, 1941).

Dale, Edgar, and Eicholz, Gerhard, *Children's Knowledge of Words*, an interim report, Sept., 1954, to June, 1960 (Bureau of Educational Research, Ohio State University).

Davis, John D., revised and rewritten by Gehman, Henry Snyder, *The Westminster Dictionary of the Bible* (The Westminster Press, 1944).

de Vaux, Roland, *Ancient Israel: Its Life and Institutions* (McGraw-Hill Book Company, Inc., 1961).

du Buit, M., *Biblical Archaeology* (Hawthorn Books, Inc., Publishers, 1960).

Finegan, Jack, *Light from the Ancient Past* (Princeton University Press, 1946).

Glueck, Nelson, *The Other Side of the Jordan* (American Schools of Oriental Research, 1945).

—— *The River Jordan* (The Westminster Press, 1940).

—— *Rivers in the Desert* (Grove Press [London], 1960).

Heaton, Eric W., *Everyday Life in Old Testament Times* (Charles Scribner's Sons, 1956).

Illustrated World of the Bible Library, Vol. 1, " The Law "; Vol. 3, " The Latter Prophets " (McGraw-Hill Book Company, Inc., 1958).

The Interpreter's Bible (Abingdon Press, 1952).

The Interpreter's Dictionary of the Bible (Abingdon Press, 1962).

Miller, Madeleine S., and Lane, J., *Harper's Bible Dictionary* (Harper & Row, Publishers, Inc., 1952).

Nelson's Complete Concordance of the Revised Standard Version Bible (Thomas Nelson & Sons, 1957).

Pritchard, J. B., *Archeology and the Old Testament* (Princeton University Press, 1958).

Richardson, Alan, *Theological Word Book of the Bible* (The Macmillan Company, 1955).

Terrien, Samuel, *Lands of the Bible* (Simon and Schuster, Inc., 1957).

Thorndike, E. L., and Barnhart, Clarence L., *Thorndike-Barnhart Advanced Junior Dictionary* (Scott Foresman & Company, 1962).

The Westminster Study Edition of the Holy Bible (The Westminster Press, 1948).

Wright, George Ernest, and Filson, Floyd Vivian, eds., *The Westminster Historical Atlas to the Bible*, Rev. Ed. (The Westminster Press, 1956).

WESTMINSTER HISTORICAL MAPS
OF BIBLE LANDS

EDITED BY

G. ERNEST WRIGHT

Associate Professor of Old Testament
McCormick Theological Seminary

AND

FLOYD V. FILSON

Professor of New Testament Literature and History
McCormick Theological Seminary

TABLE OF MAPS

MAP INDEX

PLATE I

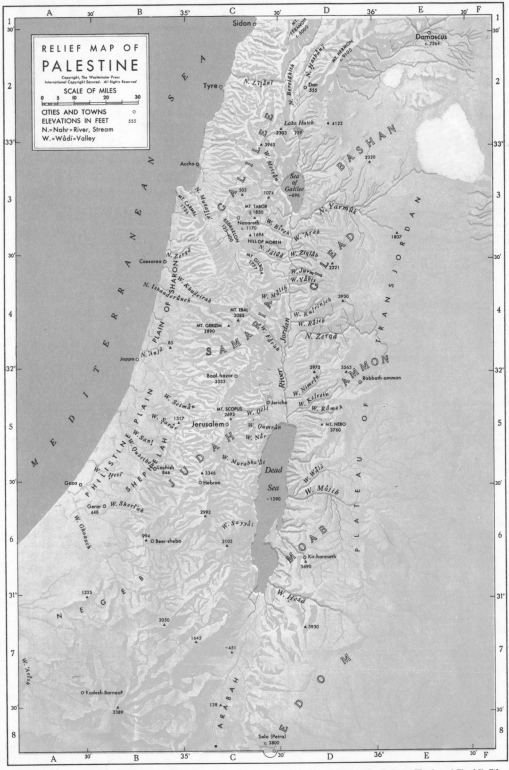

RELIEF MAP OF
PALESTINE
Copyright, The Westminster Press
International Copyright Secured. All Rights Reserved
SCALE OF MILES
0   5   10   20   30
CITIES AND TOWNS   o
ELEVATIONS IN FEET   555
N.=Nahr=River, Stream
W.=Wâdi=Valley

MEDITERRANEAN SEA

Sidon

Damascus
c. 2264

Tyre

N. Lîţâni

N. Bereighith

N. Ḥaşbâni

MT. HERMON c. 9100

Dan
555

Lake Huleh
2303   229

BASHAN

Accho

2320

3963

GALILEE

MT. CARMEL
1736

N. Mu'atta

502   1074

Sea of Galilee
−696

MT. TABOR
± 1850

N. Yarmûk

1807

Caesarea

N. Zerqâ

Nazareth
c. 1170

ESDRAELON
125-400

1694

HILL OF MOREH

N. Jâlûd

W. Bireh

W. 'Arab

2221

GILEAD

MT. GILBOA
1725

W. Ziqlâb

W. Jurm

W. Yâbis

N. Iskanderûneh

PLAIN OF SHARON

W. Khudeirah

W. Mâlih

3930

W. Kufrinjeh

MT. EBAL
3085

W. Râjeb

MT. GERIZIM
2890

SAMARIA

W. Fâriah

N. Zerqa

85

N. 'Auja

Joppa

Jordan River

2972

3563

AMMON

Baal-hazor
3333

W. Nimrîn

Rabbath-ammon

W. Selmân

W. Ķelrein

MT. SCOPUS
2693

W. Şarâr

1317

Jericho

W. Qelt

W. Râmeh

Jerusalem

W. Qumrân

MT. NEBO
3760

W. Nâr

W. Sant

PHILISTINE PLAIN

SHEPHELAH

W. Ouhelbeh

W. Murabba'ât

W. Ḥesî

W. Wâla

Lachish
846

JUDAH

3346

Dead Sea
−1290

W. Môjib

Gaza

Hebron

PLATEAU OF MOAB

Gerar
448

W. Sherî'ah

2992

W. Sa'yâl

994

Beer-sheba

2103

Kir-hareseth
3690

NEGEB

W. Ghazzeh

1225

W. Ḥesâ

2050

3930

1645

−451

W. 'Arîsh

Kadesh-Barnea

128

ARABAH

3389

EDOM

Sela (Petra)
c. 3800

Cartography By G. A. Barrois and Hal & Jean Arbo

Edited By G. Ernest Wright and Floyd V. Filson

PLATE II

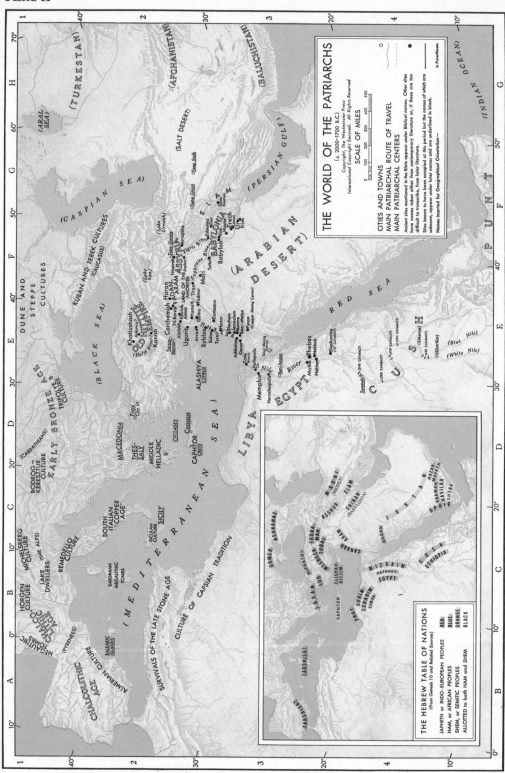

THE WORLD OF THE PATRIARCHS
(c. 2000–1700 B.C.)

Copyright, The Westminster Press
International Copyright Secured. All Rights Reserved

SCALE OF MILES

CITIES AND TOWNS

MAIN PATRIARCHAL ROUTE OF TRAVEL

MAIN PATRIARCHAL CENTERS

Ancient sites mentioned in the Bible appear under Biblical names. Other sites have names taken either from contemporary literature or, if these are too difficult to transcribe, from later literature.

Sites known to have been occupied at this period but the names of which are unknown, appear under later names and are underlined in black.

Names inserted for Geographical Orientation—

In Parentheses

THE HEBREW TABLE OF NATIONS
(from Genesis 10 and Related Sources)

JAPHETH, or INDO-EUROPEAN PEOPLES — RED
HAM, or AFRICAN PEOPLES — BLUE
SHEM, or SEMITIC PEOPLES — ORANGE
ALLOTTED to both HAM and SHEM — BLACK

Edited By G. Ernest Wright and Floyd V. Filson

Cartography By Hal & Jean Arbo

PLATE III

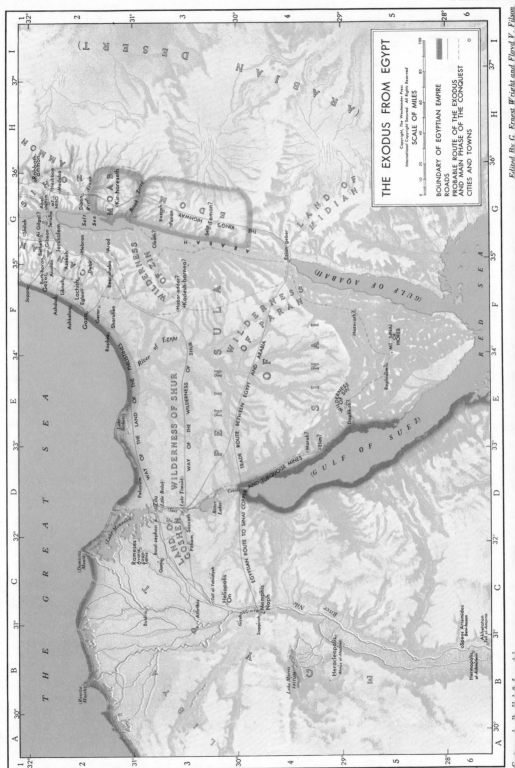

THE EXODUS FROM EGYPT

SCALE OF MILES

0   10   20   40   60   80   100

BOUNDARY OF EGYPTIAN EMPIRE

ROADS

PROBABLE ROUTE OF THE EXODUS
AND MAIN PHASE OF THE CONQUEST

○ CITIES AND TOWNS

Edited By G. Ernest Wright and Floyd V. Filson

PLATE IV

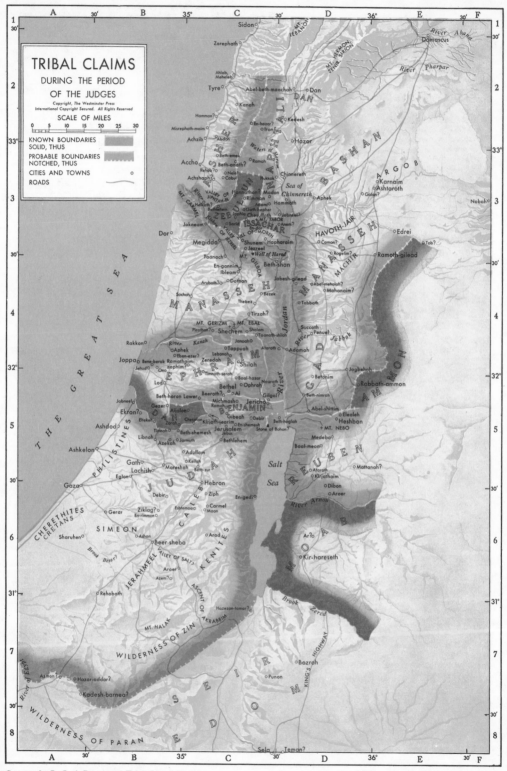

TRIBAL CLAIMS
DURING THE PERIOD
OF THE JUDGES

Copyright, The Westminster Press
International Copyright Secured. All Rights Reserved

SCALE OF MILES

0   5   10   15   20   25   30

KNOWN BOUNDARIES
SOLID, THUS
PROBABLE BOUNDARIES
NOTCHED, THUS
CITIES AND TOWNS   o
ROADS

Cartography By G. A. Barrois and Hal & Jean Arbo

Edited By G. Ernest Wright and Floyd V. Filson

Plate V

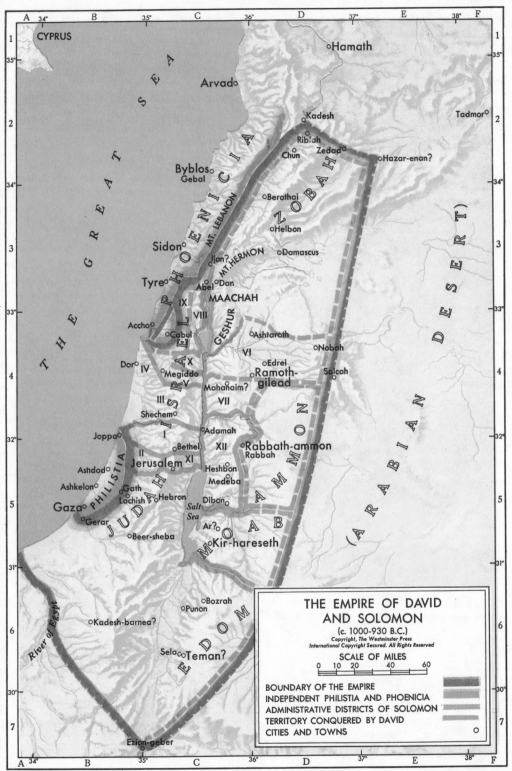

CYPRUS

Hamath

Arvad

THE GREAT SEA

Kadesh
Tadmor
Riblah
Zedad
Chun
Hazar-enan?

Byblos
Gebal

ZOBAH

Berothai

Helbon

Sidon
Damascus

Jion?
MT. HERMON
MT. LEBANON
Tyre
Abel Dan

IX
MAACHAH

VIII
Accho
GESHUR
Ashtaroth

Cabul
Nobah

X
VI
Dor
IV
Edrei
Salcah

Megiddo
V
Ramoth-
gilead

III
Mahanaim?
VII

Shechem

ISRAEL

PHOENICIA

AMMON

Joppa
Adamah

I

II
Bethel
XII
Rabbath-ammon

Jerusalem XI
Rabbah

Ashdod
Heshbon

PHILISTIA
Gath
Medeba

Ashkelon
Lachish
Hebron

Gaza
Dibon

Gerar
Salt
Sea

Beer-sheba
Ar?

JUDAH
MOAB

Kir-hareseth

(ARABIAN DESERT)

River of Egypt

Bozrah
Punon

Kadesh-barnea?

EDOM

Sela
Teman?

**THE EMPIRE OF DAVID
AND SOLOMON**

(c. 1000–930 B.C.)
Copyright, The Westminster Press
International Copyright Secured. All Rights Reserved

SCALE OF MILES
0   10   20   40   60

BOUNDARY OF THE EMPIRE
INDEPENDENT PHILISTIA AND PHOENICIA
ADMINISTRATIVE DISTRICTS OF SOLOMON
TERRITORY CONQUERED BY DAVID
CITIES AND TOWNS   ○

Ezion-geber

Cartography By Hal & Jean Arbo

Edited By G. Ernest Wright and Floyd V. Filson

PLATE VI

A B C D E F
34° 35° 36° 37° 38°

CYPRUS

THE GREAT SEA

Hamath

Arvad

Tadmor

Kadesh
Riblah
Chun
Zedad
Hazar-enan?

Byblos
Gebal

Berothai

Helbon

Sidon

MT. LEBANON
MT. AMANA
MT. HERMON

Damascus

Tyre
Ijon?
Abel
Dan

PHOENICIA

ARAM (SYRIA)

(ARABIAN DESERT)

Accho
Cabul

Ashtaroth

Nobah

Dor
Megiddo
Tishbeh?
Mahanaim?
Edrei
Ramoth-gilead
Salcah

Samaria

ISRAEL

AMMON

Joppa

Bethel
Jericho
Rabbath-ammon

Ashdod
Jerusalem
Heshbon
Medeba

Ashkelon
Gath
Lachish
Hebron

Gaza
Salt
Sea
Dibon

Gerar
Ar?
Kir-hareseth

PHILISTIA
JUDAH
MOAB

Beer-sheba

River of Egypt

Bozrah
Punon

Kadesh-barnea?

EDOM

Sela
Teman?

Ezion-geber

THE KINGDOMS OF ISRAEL AND JUDAH IN ELIJAH'S TIME

(c. 860 B.C.)

Copyright, The Westminster Press
International Copyright Secured. All Rights Reserved

SCALE OF MILES

0 10 20 40 60

KINGDOM OF ISRAEL
KINGDOM OF JUDAH
KINGDOM OF AMMON
KINGDOM OF ARAM (SYRIA)
PHILISTINE AND PHOENICIAN TERRITORY
CITIES AND TOWNS   ○

Cartography By Hal & Jean Arbo

Edited By G. Ernest Wright and Floyd V. Filson

PLATE VII

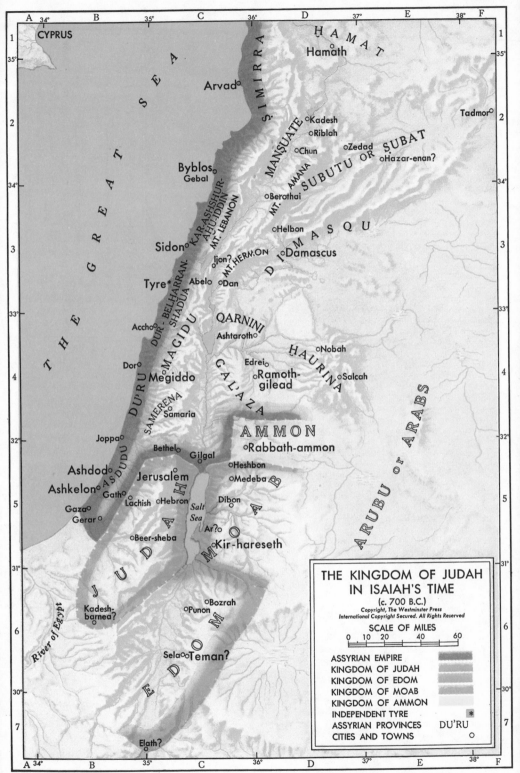

THE KINGDOM OF JUDAH
IN ISAIAH'S TIME
(c. 700 B.C.)
Copyright, The Westminster Press
International Copyright Secured. All Rights Reserved

SCALE OF MILES
0 10 20   40   60

ASSYRIAN EMPIRE
KINGDOM OF JUDAH
KINGDOM OF EDOM
KINGDOM OF MOAB
KINGDOM OF AMMON
INDEPENDENT TYRE   *
ASSYRIAN PROVINCES   DU'RU
CITIES AND TOWNS   o

Cartography By Hal & Jean Arbo   Edited By G. Ernest Wright and Floyd V. Filson

PLATE VIII

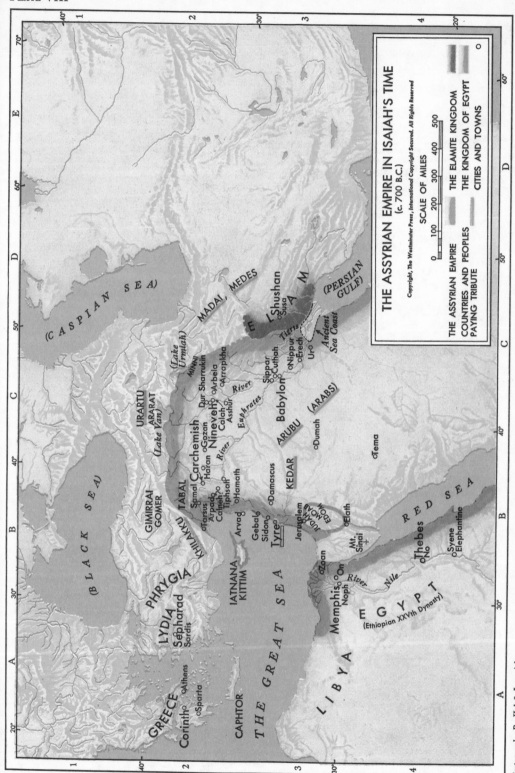

THE ASSYRIAN EMPIRE IN ISAIAH'S TIME
(c. 700 B.C.)

Copyright, The Westminster Press, International Copyright Secured. All Rights Reserved

SCALE OF MILES

0   100   200   300   400   500

THE ASSYRIAN EMPIRE
COUNTRIES AND PEOPLES
PAYING TRIBUTE
THE ELAMITE KINGDOM
THE KINGDOM OF EGYPT
CITIES AND TOWNS

Cartography By Hal & Jean Arbo

PLATE IX

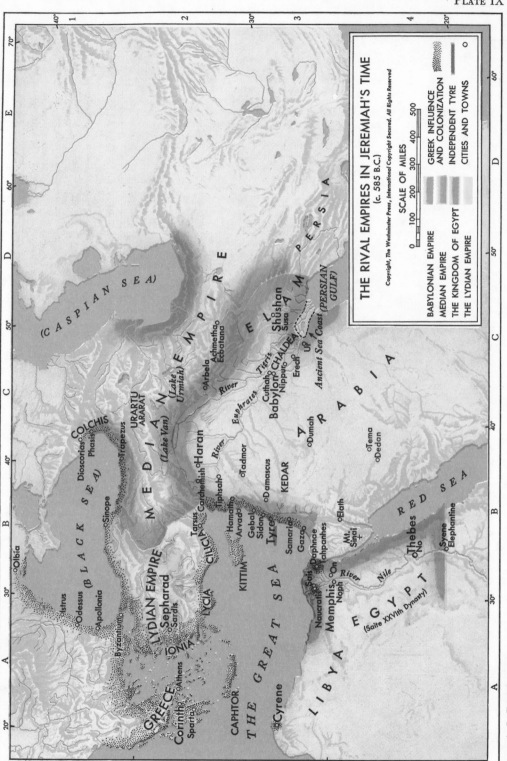

THE RIVAL EMPIRES IN JEREMIAH'S TIME
(c. 585 B.C.)

SCALE OF MILES

0   100   200   300   400   500

BABYLONIAN EMPIRE

MEDIAN EMPIRE

THE KINGDOM OF EGYPT

THE LYDIAN EMPIRE

GREEK INFLUENCE
AND COLONIZATION

INDEPENDENT TYRE

CITIES AND TOWNS   o

Edited By G. Ernest Wright and Floyd V. Filson

Cartography By Hal & Jean Arbo

40°   1

70°

2   -30°

3   4   -20°

E   60°   D   50°   C   40°   B   30°   A   20°

(CASPIAN SEA)

PERSIA

E L A M

Shushan
Susa   o

Ancient Sea Coast (PERSIAN GULF)

Ur   o

MEDIAN EMPIRE

Achmetha
Ecbatana   o

Arbela   o

Tigris

River   Euphrates   River

CHALDEA

Babylon   o   Cuthah
Nippuro   Erech   o

URARTU
ARARAT

(Lake Van)

(Lake Urmiah)

COLCHIS

Dioscorias   o
Phasis   o

Trapezus   o

Sinope   o

Haran   o

Carchemish   o
Tiphsah   o

Tadmor   o

A R A B I A

Dumah   o

Tema   o
Dedan   o

BLACK   SEA)

Olbia   o

Istrus   o
Odessus   o
Apollonia   o

Byzantium   o

LYDIAN EMPIRE
Sepharad

Sardis   o

IONIA

Tarsus   o

CILICIA

LYCIA

KITTIM

Hamath   o
Arvad   o

Gebal   o
Sidon   o

Tyre

Samaria   o
Gaza   o

Damascus   o

KEDAR

Elath   o

RED SEA

GREECE

Corinth   o   Athens   o
Sparta   o

CAPHTOR

THE   GREAT   SEA

Sais   Daphnae
Tahpanhes   o

Naucratis   o
Memphis   o   On   o
Noph   o

Nile   River

E G Y P T
(Saite XXVIth Dynasty)

L I B Y A

Cyrene   o

Mt.
Sinai   +

Thebes   o
No

Syene   o
Elephantine   o

40°   1   2   3   4   30°

PLATE X

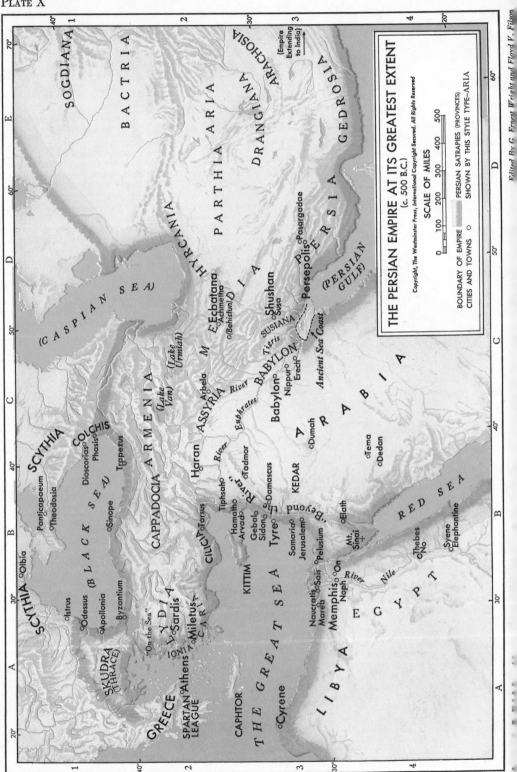

THE PERSIAN EMPIRE AT ITS GREATEST EXTENT

(c. 500 B.C.)

SCALE OF MILES

0   100   200   300   400   500

BOUNDARY OF EMPIRE

PERSIAN SATRAPIES (PROVINCES)
SHOWN BY THIS STYLE TYPE–ARIA

CITIES AND TOWNS o

Edited By G. Ernest Wright and Floyd V. Filson

SOGDIANA

BACTRIA

PARTHIA   ARIA

DRANGIANA

ARACHOSIA

(Empire
Extending
to India)

GEDROSIA

PERSIA

Pasargadae

Persepolis

Pul   Pasargadae

(PERSIAN
GULF)

HYRCANIA

M E D I A

Ecbatana
Achmetha

(Behistun)

Shushan
Susa

SUSIANA

Ancient Sea Coast

(C A S P I A N   S E A)

ARMENIA

(Lake
Urmiah)

(Lake
Van)

Arbela

ASSYRIA

Tigris

BABYLON

Babylon   Erech

Nippur

River

Euphrates

A R A B I A

Dumah

SCYTHIA

COLCHIS

Dioscorias   Phasis

Trapezus

Sinope

CAPPADOCIA

Haran

River

Tiphsah

Tarsus

CILICIA

Hamath

Arvad

Gebal
Sidon

Tyre

"Beyond   the   River"

Tadmor

Damascus

KEDAR

Tema

Dedan

RED   SEA

Panticapaeum

Theodosia

(B L A C K   S E A)

Byzantium

Apollonia

Odessus

Istrus

Olbia

SCYTHIA

LYDIA

Sardis

"On the Sea"

IONIA

Miletus

CARIA

SKUDRA
(THRACE)

GREECE

SPARTAN
LEAGUE   Athens

CAPHTOR

Cyrene

T H E   G R E A T   S E A

KITTIM

Samaria

Jerusalem

Pelusium

Mt.
Sinai

Elath

Naucratis
Mareb   Sais

Memphis   On
Noph

River   Nile

Thebes
No

Syene
Elephantine

E G Y P T

L I B Y A

40°   50°   60°   70°

40°   50°   60°

30°

20°

30°

40°

PLATE XI

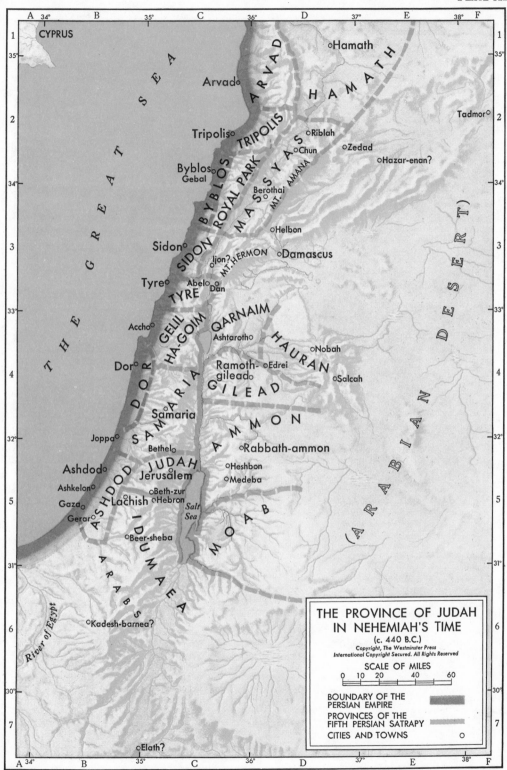

THE PROVINCE OF JUDAH
IN NEHEMIAH'S TIME
(c. 440 B.C.)
Copyright, The Westminster Press
International Copyright Secured. All Rights Reserved

SCALE OF MILES
0   10   20   40   60

BOUNDARY OF THE
PERSIAN EMPIRE
PROVINCES OF THE
FIFTH PERSIAN SATRAPY
CITIES AND TOWNS   o

Cartography By Hal & Jean Arbo

Edited By G. Ernest Wright and Floyd V. Filson

PLATE XII

PALESTINE
IN THE
MACCABEAN PERIOD
(168-63 B.C.)

Copyright, The Westminster Press
International Copyright Secured. All Rights Reserved

SCALE OF MILES

0 5 10 20 30

BOUNDARY LINE SHOWS MAXIMUM
EXTENT OF MACCABEAN KINGDOM
UNDER ALEXANDER JANNAEUS
(103-76 B.C.)

KINGDOM OF
ALEXANDER JANNAEUS

FREE CITY

CITIES AND TOWNS

Cartography By G. A. Barrois and Hal & Jean Arbo   Edited By G. Ernest Wright and Floyd V. Filson

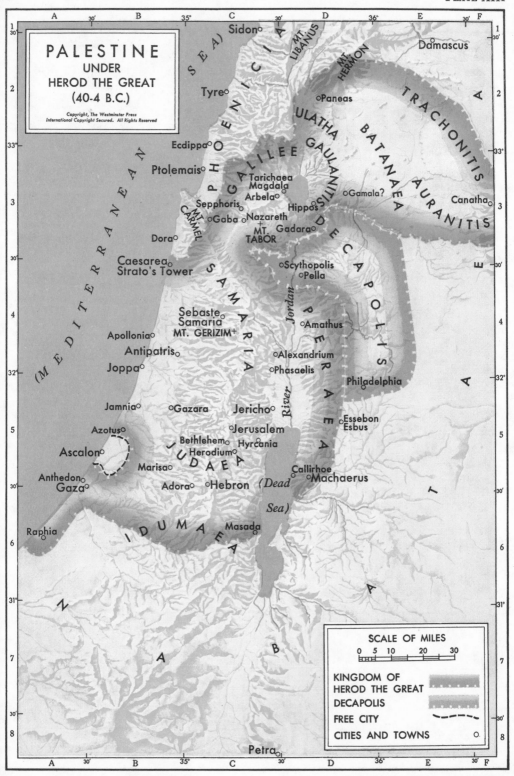

PLATE XIII

PALESTINE
UNDER
HEROD THE GREAT
(40-4 B.C.)

Copyright, The Westminster Press
International Copyright Secured. All Rights Reserved

SEA)

Sidon

PHOENICIA

MT. LIBANUS

Damascus

MT. HERMON

Tyre

Paneas

TRACHONITIS

ULATHA

Ecdippa

Ptolemais

GALILEE

GAULANITIS

BATANAEA

AURANITIS

Tarichaea
Magdala
Arbela

Sepphoris
Gaba
Nazareth

Hippos

Gamala?

Canatha

MT. CARMEL

MT. TABOR

Gadara

DECAPOLIS

Dora

Scythopolis
Pella

Caesarea
Strato's Tower

MEDITERRANEAN

Sebaste
Samaria
MT. GERIZIM

SAMARIA

Amathus

Apollonia

PEREA

Antipatris

Alexandrium
Phasaelis

Joppa

Philadelphia

Jordan River

Jamnia

Gazara

Jericho

Essebon
Esbus

Azotus

Jerusalem

Ascalon

Bethlehem
Herodium

Hyrcania

JUDAEA

Callirhoe
Machaerus

Marisa

Anthedon
Gaza

Adora

Hebron

(Dead

Sea)

Raphia

IDUMAEA

Masada

NABATA

ARABIA

Petra

SCALE OF MILES
0 5 10   20   30

KINGDOM OF
HEROD THE GREAT

DECAPOLIS

FREE CITY

CITIES AND TOWNS

Cartography By G. A. Barrois and Hal & Jean Arbo

Edited By G. Ernest Wright and Floyd V. Filson

PLATE XIV

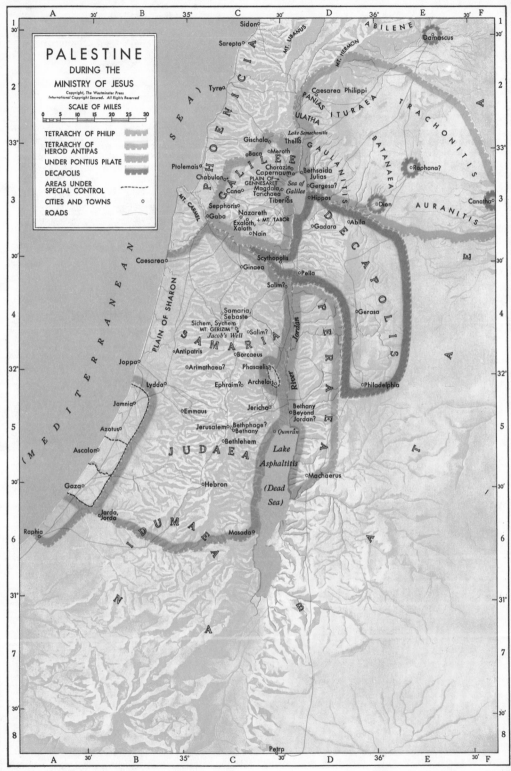

PALESTINE
DURING THE
MINISTRY OF JESUS

Copyright, The Westminster Press
International Copyright Secured. All Rights Reserved

SCALE OF MILES

0   5   10   15   20   25   30

TETRARCHY OF PHILIP
TETRARCHY OF
HEROD ANTIPAS
UNDER PONTIUS PILATE
DECAPOLIS
AREAS UNDER
SPECIAL CONTROL
CITIES AND TOWNS   o
ROADS

Cartography By G. A. Barrois and Hal & Jean Arbo

Edited By G. Ernest Wright and Floyd V. Filson

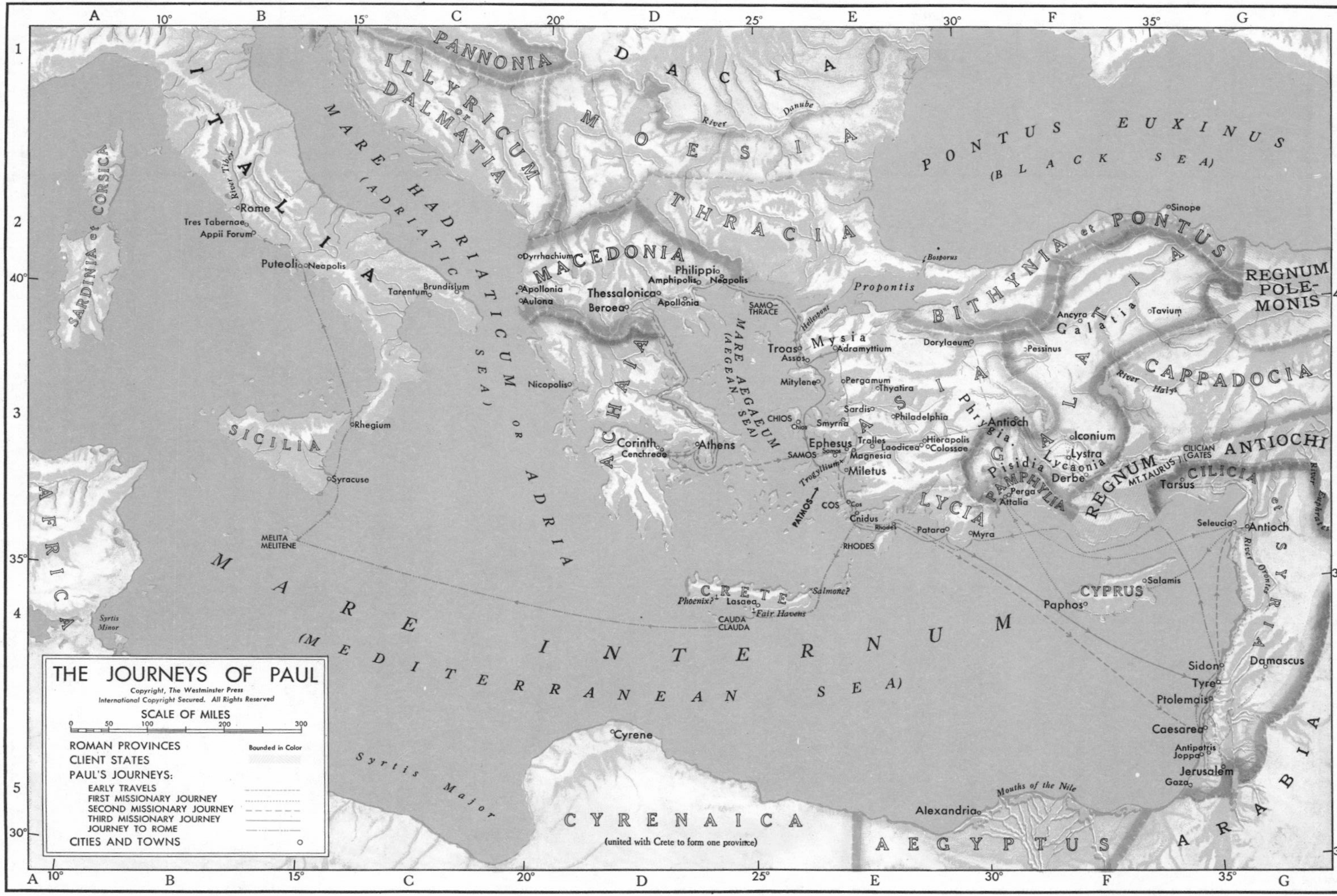

PLATE XV

THE JOURNEYS OF PAUL

SCALE OF MILES

0   50   100   200   300

Bounded in Color

ROMAN PROVINCES
CLIENT STATES
PAUL'S JOURNEYS:
EARLY TRAVELS
FIRST MISSIONARY JOURNEY
SECOND MISSIONARY JOURNEY
THIRD MISSIONARY JOURNEY
JOURNEY TO ROME
CITIES AND TOWNS

Edited By G. Ernest Wright and Floyd V. Filson

Cartography By Hal & Jean Arbo

PLATE XVI

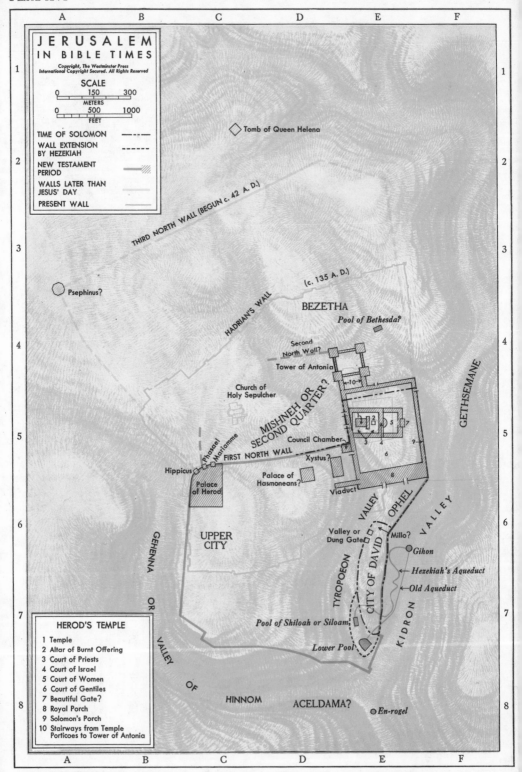

JERUSALEM
IN BIBLE TIMES

Copyright, The Westminster Press
International Copyright Secured. All Rights Reserved

SCALE

0   150   300
METERS

0   500   1000
FEET

TIME OF SOLOMON
WALL EXTENSION
BY HEZEKIAH
NEW TESTAMENT
PERIOD
WALLS LATER THAN
JESUS' DAY
PRESENT WALL

HEROD'S TEMPLE

1 Temple
2 Altar of Burnt Offering
3 Court of Priests
4 Court of Israel
5 Court of Women
6 Court of Gentiles
7 Beautiful Gate?
8 Royal Porch
9 Solomon's Porch
10 Stairways from Temple
   Porticoes to Tower of Antonia

Tomb of Queen Helena

THIRD NORTH WALL (BEGUN c. 42 A.D.)

HADRIAN'S WALL

(c. 135 A.D.)

BEZETHA

Pool of Bethesda?

Psephinus?

Second
North Wall?

Tower of Antonia

Church of
Holy Sepulcher

MISHNEH OR
SECOND QUARTER?

GETHSEMANE

Phasael
Mariamne
Hippicus
FIRST NORTH WALL

Council Chamber

Xystus?

Palace of
Hasmoneans?

Viaduct

Palace
of Herod

UPPER
CITY

GEHENNA OR VALLEY OF

Valley or
Dung Gate

VALLEY
OPHEL

Millo?

Gihon

Hezekiah's Aqueduct

Old Aqueduct

TYROPOEON

CITY OF DAVID

KIDRON VALLEY

Pool of Shiloah or Siloam

Lower Pool

HINNOM

ACELDAMA?

En-rogel

Cartography By Hal & Jean Arbo

Edited By G. Ernest Wright and Floyd V. Filson